Ableism in Academia

Ableism in Academia

Theorising experiences of disabilities and chronic illnesses in higher education

Edited by Nicole Brown and Jennifer Leigh

First published in 2020 by
UCL Press
University College London
Gower Street
London WC1E 6BT

Available to download free: www.uclpress.co.uk

Text © Contributors, 2020
Collection © Editors, 2020
Figures © as noted under each one.

Nicole Brown and Jennifer Leigh have asserted their rights under the Copyright, Designs and Patents Act 1988 to be identified as the editors of this work.

A CIP catalogue record for this book is available from The British Library.

This book is published under a Creative Commons 4.0 International licence (CC BY 4.0). This licence allows you to share, copy, distribute and transmit the work; to adapt the work and to make commercial use of the work providing attribution is made to the authors (but not in any way that suggests that they endorse you or your use of the work). Attribution should include the following information:

Brown, N. and Leigh, J. (eds) 2020. *Ableism in Academia: Theorising experiences of disabilities and chronic illnesses in higher education.* London: UCL Press. DOI: https://doi.org/10.14324/111.9781787354975

Further details about Creative Commons licences are available at http://creativecommons.org/licenses/

Any third-party material in this book is published under the book's Creative Commons licence unless indicated otherwise in the credit line to the material. If you would like to reuse any third-party material not covered by the book's Creative Commons licence, you will need to obtain permission directly from the copyright holder.

ISBN: 978-1-78735-499-9 (Hbk.)
ISBN: 978-1-78735-498-2 (Pbk.)
ISBN: 978-1-78735-497-5 (PDF)
ISBN: 978-1-78735-500-2 (epub)
ISBN: 978-1-78735-501-9 (mobi)
DOI: https://doi.org/10.14324/111.9781787354975

*To everyone who is directly or indirectly affected by ableism in academia.
And to those who need to learn about it.*
NB

*To my wonderful, beautiful and miraculous family. All of you.
I could not have done any of this without you.*
JL

Contents

List of figures and tables — viii
List of contributors — ix
Preface — xiv
Nicole Brown and Jennifer Leigh

Introduction: Theorising ableism in academia — 1
Nicole Brown

1. The significance of crashing past gatekeepers of knowledge: Towards full participation of disabled scholars in ableist academic structures — 11
   Claudia Gillberg

2. I am not disabled: Difference, ethics, critique and refusal of neoliberal academic selves — 31
   Francesca Peruzzo

3. Disclosure in academia: A sensitive issue — 51
   Nicole Brown

4. Fibromyalgia and me — 74
   Divya Jindal-Snape

5. A practical response to ableism in leadership in UK higher education — 76
   Nicola Martin

6. Autoimmune actions in the ableist academy — 103
   Alice Andrews

7. 'But you don't look disabled': Non-visible disabilities, disclosure and being an 'insider' in disability research and 'other' in the disability movement and academia 124
Elisabeth Griffiths

8. Invisible disability, unacknowledged diversity 143
Carla Finesilver, Jennifer Leigh and Nicole Brown

9. Imposter 161
Jennifer A. Rode

10. Internalised ableism: Of the political and the personal 164
Jennifer Leigh and Nicole Brown

11. From the personal to the political: Ableism, activism and academia 182
Kirstein Rummery

12. The violence of technicism: Ableism as humiliation and degrading treatment 202
Fiona Kumari Campbell

13. A little bit extra 225
El Spaeth

Concluding thoughts: Moving forward 226
Nicole Brown and Jennifer Leigh

Afterword 237
Jennifer Leigh and Nicole Brown

Index 239

List of figures and tables

Figure 3.1:	Screenshot of an email sent to Nicole Brown.	54
Figure 5.1:	Four charts depicting the percentages of staff known to have a disability. Source: HESA 2018.	79
Figure 12.1:	Technicians of certification. Source: Campbell 2001.	216
Table 5.1:	Academic staff, managers, directors and senior officials by age, disability, ethnicity and gender, 2016/17. Source: HESA 2016/17.	80

List of contributors

Nicole Brown is a Lecturer in Education and Academic Head of Learning and Teaching at the UCL Institute of Education and Director of Social Research & Practice and Education Ltd. Nicole gained her PhD in Sociology at the University of Kent for her research into the construction of academic identity under the influence of fibromyalgia. She has edited *Lived Experiences of Ableism in Academia: Strategies for Inclusion in Higher Education* for Policy Press, co-authored *Embodied Inquiry: Research Methods* for Bloomsbury and is currently authoring *How to Make the Most of Your Research Journal* for Policy Press. Nicole's research interests relate to physical and material representations and metaphors, the generation of knowledge and, more generally, research methods and approaches to explore identity and body work, as well as to advance learning and teaching within higher education. She tweets as @ncjbrown, @FibroIdentity and @AbleismAcademia.

Jennifer Leigh is a Senior Lecturer at the Centre for the Study of Higher Education, University of Kent. Jennifer joined the Centre for the Study of Higher Education full-time in 2013. She initially trained as a chemist and a somatic movement therapist before completing her doctorate in education, and is a founder member of WISC (an international network for Women in Supramolecular Chemistry). She is a Senior Fellow of the Higher Education Academy, teaches on postgraduate programmes in higher education and works closely with the Graduate School at Kent. She is the editor of *Conversations on Embodiment across Higher Education* (2018) for Routledge, co-authored *Embodied Inquiry: Research Methods* for Bloomsbury, and her next book for Bristol University Press will explore the boundaries of qualitative research with art, education and therapy. Her research interests include embodiment, phenomenological and creative research methods, academic practice, academic development and ableism, as well as aspects of teaching and learning in higher education. She tweets as @drschniff and @SupraChem.

Alice Andrews is a Lecturer in Visual Cultures at Goldsmiths University. Alice's current research examines an embodied relationship to illness as it is informed by (bio)technology, biopolitical control and narrative fictions of the self in art and science. The focus of this research is the figure of autoimmunity – both as illness and as this term supplements the deconstructive oeuvre of Jacques Derrida – and the implications of this thought for an ethics of risk within contemporary discourses of life. This research crosses the disciplinary boundaries of art (feminism, systems, animals), science (biology, technology, systems theory and sociology), literature (science fiction and autobiography) and political ethics (biopolitics, futurity and the terroristic).

Fiona Kumari Campbell FRSA is Professor of Disability and Ableism Studies in the University of Dundee's School of Education and Social Work. She is an Adjunct Professor in Disability Studies, Faculty of Medicine, University of Kelaniya, Sri Lanka, and a disabled BAME person. She writes about Global South theory, disability studies, ableism, disability in Sri Lanka and dis/technology and is a world leader in scholarship around studies in ableism. Following the publication of *Contours of Ableism: The Production of Disability and Abledness* (2009) she is working on two books: *#Ableism: An Interdisciplinary Introduction to Studies in Ableism*; and *Textures of Ableism: Disability*.

Carla Finesilver is a Lecturer in Mathematics Education at King's College London. She works mainly in the areas of mathematics education and inclusion, with a particular focus on making education more accessible and inclusive for disabled and disadvantaged learners. Her research has included using multimodal qualitative methods to study the creative and diverse representational strategies and reasoning of those who have struggled with school mathematics taught in 'standard' or 'traditional' ways. She lectures and supervises research on various postgraduate programmes.

Claudia Gillberg is a researcher at the Swedish National Centre for Lifelong Learning (ENCELL), Jönköping University. Claudia has higher education teaching experience at all levels and has managed teacher education programmes and developed new modules focusing on collaborative learning in the field of professional development. In recent years she has increasingly focused on issues of access and parity of participation for ill and disabled children and adults. She has been vocal about the necessity for feminist methods of inquiry in healthcare, especially for chronically ill patients. Despite her own severe disability, she has remained affiliated with ENCELL, and is a Fellow at the Centre for Welfare Reform in the UK.

Elisabeth Griffiths is an Associate Professor at Northumbria School of Law, Northumbria University. Elisabeth is a solicitor (now non-practising) and specialises in employment law and discrimination law. She has worked in academia for over twenty years, teaching undergraduate and postgraduate students. Elisabeth's research interests are in equality, diversity, discrimination law and disability legal studies. She is using her research in disability legal studies as part of her professional doctorate in law, which is on the lived experience of disability and the law and its impact on student identity in transition to graduate employment.

Divya Jindal-Snape is Professor of Education, Inclusion and Life Transitions at the University of Dundee. Divya gained her undergraduate and master's qualifications in India. She taught in an all-through school and worked as a Lecturer in Education for a few years before moving to Japan to do a PhD at the University of Tsukuba. After living in Japan for nearly five and a half years, enjoying research and teaching, she moved to Dundee. Her research interests lie in the field of inclusion, and educational and life transitions. A significant proportion of her work has been with children and young people with additional support needs, especially visual impairment, autism, learning difficulties, emotional and behavioural needs, and complex life-limiting conditions. Her research has led to the creation of educational resources to enhance inclusion and facilitate transitions through drama (inspired by Augusto Boal's Theatre of the Oppressed), stories, games and other creative art forms.

Nicola Martin is a Professor in the Law and Social Sciences School at London South Bank University. Nicola is a National Teaching Fellow, a Fellow of the RSA and a Visiting Fellow at the University of Cambridge and Sheffield Hallam University. Nicola is a disabled leader from a critical disability studies background. As well as working in academia and research, Nicola has led professional services departments, which focus on the equalities agenda, in three UK universities. She played a leading part in the development of the National Association of Disability Practitioners (NADP) and is an editor of the *Journal of Inclusive Practice in Further and Higher Education*.

Francesca Peruzzo has completed her doctoral studies at the UCL Institute of Education in the Department of Education, Practice and Society. Francesca also holds two degrees in sociology of education and disability studies. She is Associate Teaching Fellow of the Higher Education Academy and a former disabled student assistant. Francesca's interests lie in approaches to disability policies and inclusive practices in higher education. Her doctoral research merges a sociological perspective and Foucauldian tools to challenge ableism in Italian higher education, investigating the production of disability discourses, practices and subjectivities in the Italian university, and their implications for inclusive policies and practices and equity in opportunities in academic contexts.

Jennifer A. Rode is a Senior Lecturer at UCL's Knowledge Lab. Jennifer's research lies in the areas of human–computer interaction and ubiquitous computing. Her work examines the values of users and designers, and how those values influence the user-centred design process. She looks reflexively at the design process to see how our implicit biases and practices shape the artefacts we design, especially as we reconcile the values of designers and users. Jennifer uses a multi-disciplinary theoretical approach that draws from anthropology, gender studies, science and technology studies, design research, social informatics and ubiquitous computing.

Kirstein Rummery is a Professor in Sociology, Social Policy and Criminology at the University of Stirling. Kirstein is a founder member of the Women's Equality Party and a disabled feminist and activist. She is currently undertaking research into the costs and benefits of self-directed support for disabled people and carers, and the experiences of people with dementia engaging with their neighbourhoods. She recently completed a comparative study on international long-term and childcare policies and their effects on gender equality, *What Works in Gender Equality*, which will be published in 2020. She is a mother, a carer and owned by two cats and a dog.

El Spaeth is an Academic Development and Digital Advisor at the University of Glasgow. El lectures and advises in academic and digital development, which primarily involves working with new lecturers to develop their teaching practice. She holds a PhD in clinical psychology and music and is passionate about combining expertise in the areas of mental health and pedagogy to promote inclusive learning and teaching environments.

Preface

Nicole Brown and Jennifer Leigh

In September 2017, Nicole came across an announcement for a symposium in the United States that would explore academic ableism and the notion that disability in higher education is conceptualised as a problem in need of a solution, rather than a different way of working. Unfortunately, unless you were in the lecture room at that particular university at the time, there was no way to be involved in the symposium, nor was it possible to access any materials from it. The irony of this academic ableism was not lost on us; and the idea for a different kind of academic ableism event in the UK was born. The aim would be to have an event that would be fully accessible at all levels and that would produce concrete outcomes, of which an edited book would be one. This event would not be yet another symposium or conference that left delegates feeling that nothing had changed or been achieved once it ended.

The 'Ableism in Academia' conference that resulted from this idea was held at the UCL Institute of Education in March 2018. Initially the conference was going to be for 40 delegates, but these tickets were sold out within the first 24 hours. Consequently, the number of tickets was increased to 80, and these sold out within the subsequent few days with more than 100 people on a waiting list. As there were so many who wanted to attend and could not, we organised livestream viewing opportunities at the University of Kent, the University of Manchester and Birkbeck, University of London. Additionally, anyone was able to view the livestream or catch up with the recording via the UCL TV YouTube channel: https://www.youtube.com/watch?v=6ZScXkO40Pk. At the time of writing, in March 2020, the YouTube video has had more than 1,000 views and the @AbleismAcademia Twitter handle has more than

1,000 followers (it only follows 37 accounts). The 2018 conference hashtag #AIA2018 generated 978 tweets from January before the conference to three days after the conference.

The event was not only popular but also topical. In the course of the #MeToo movement it emerged more strongly than ever before how certain voices in society had become marginalised. With the conference we offered individuals a safe space to explore and theorise what it feels like to be 'othered' and 'different' in an environment that is usually seen as privileged, yet where many feel they cannot openly disclose their needs (see Brown and Leigh 2018). Most delegates and speakers had been personally affected by ableist attitudes within academia and had felt that something needed to be done to change these. The conference was organised in two parts, with lightning talks in the morning and a workshop in the afternoon seeking to answer five key questions:

1. How does your disability/disadvantage affect you in the workplace and what practical effects does it have on your ability to perform your role?
2. What does your employer do to help you, and what more could they do?
3. What forum(s) is/are there at your institution for discussing matters related to ableism?
4. What forums are there in higher education to deal with these matters (from trade unions to Higher Education Funding Council for England)?
5. What could/should be done to encourage members of academia to disclose their concerns/disabilities?

The thought processes and preparation that had gone into the organisation of the conference were unique and unprecedented. The main conference room was spacious enough to allow for manoeuvring several types of wheelchairs and mobility aids; we ensured access to disabled toilets via a RADAR key; we had organised a quiet room equipped with a sofa, blankets, cushions, eyepatches, socks and the like; we distributed blankets and cushions in the conference room to make delegates more comfortable; we had British Sign Language interpreters and one deaf-blind interpreter in the room, and we had enlisted a captioning service for the entire day; we provided height-adjustable chairs; the conference programme was available in large print; we offered snacks from 'free-from' ranges with the packaging openly laid out so delegates were able to read the labels to consider their personal dietary requirements; we had hot food delivered as per delegates' advance orders that would also cater for dietary requirements, such as sugar-free, gluten-free, vegan and all potential combinations thereof; and food was handed out to delegates so that nobody would need to navigate a lunchtime buffet queue. Our conference was well received and we ensured accessibility as much as we could, but we are under no illusion: it was not perfect (see Brown et al. 2018). However, this conference was an opportunity for many academics to engage in relevant debates and discussions from the comforts of their own homes: a factor that was particularly commended by the Twitter community.

This book comes out of the unique experience from March 2018. And yet this collection is not a collection of conference proceedings. Some contributors to this book were involved with the conference, including our keynote Fiona Kumari Campbell, but others were not. It was always our aim not only to present lived experiences, but also to provide scholarly debates and theorisation to add much-needed gravitas to individuals' ongoing narratives. Therein lies the strength of this collection.

References

'Ableism in Academia' conference held at the UCL Institute of Education, 23 March 2018, conference recording. Online. https://www.youtube.com/watch?v=6ZScXkO40Pk&t=9792s (accessed 1 June 2020).

Brown, Nicole and Leigh, Jennifer. 'Ableism in Academia: Where are the Disabled and Ill Academics?' *Disability and Society* 33/6 (2018): 985–9. Online. https://doi.org/10.1080/09687599.2018.1455627 (accessed 19 May 2020).

Brown, Nicole, Thompson, Paul and Leigh, Jennifer S. 'Making Academia More Accessible', *Journal of Perspectives in Applied Academic Practice* 6/2 (2018): 82–90. Online. https://doi.org/10.14297/jpaap.v6i2.348 (accessed 19 May 2020).

Introduction: Theorising ableism in academia

Nicole Brown

In the contemporary context of social rights and activist movements such as those associated with combatting sexual harassment, gun and knife crime or climate change, we can observe a typical pattern of public responses. These movements offer voices to those who are marginalised, and indeed provide the confidence needed for many people to stand up for specific issues. This, in turn, increases awareness and understanding of and for the marginalised. However, the stronger specific movements become, the more likely it is that the general public will experience a sense of saturation, leading individuals from marginalised groups to be sidelined once more. Collections like this one are necessary to bring into the public consciousness the matters of those who are marginalised and who negotiate difficult contexts.

Traditionally, academia has been seen as an ivory tower, as elitist and privileged. However, publications in the first decade of the twenty-first century have highlighted some of the realities of contemporary academics. Such publications have focused on the narratives of women of colour in academia (Gabriel and Tate 2017) and the depiction of neoliberal academia from a feminist perspective (Taylor and Lahad 2018), emphasising how navigating academia is a personal and political endeavour requiring intense emotion work. To further debates in and around academia, this collection focuses on experiences relating to disabilities, chronic illnesses and neurodiversity within higher education. Drawing on theoretical frameworks usually associated with sociology, anthropology and disability studies, for example, the contributors in this collection theorise their personal experiences and contextualise these within the wider societal, social, cultural and academic discourses. The contributions in this collection therefore provide an insightful snapshot of what it means to be 'othered' in contemporary neoliberal academia.

Context of contemporary higher education

Over the last three decades the UK higher education sector has seen drastic changes: it has become marketised and bureaucratised (Hussey and Smith 2002; Tilak 2008; Gewirtz and Cribb 2013). Government cuts to direct funding and the introduction of new funding systems have devolved financial responsibility to higher education institutions (Thompson and Bekhradnia 2010; Department for Business Innovation and Skills 2011). This means that institutions are under increasing pressure to attract students who are effectively the financers of their own studies, and higher education institutions compete directly for students. The process of universities turning into corporate businesses is stimulated further by globalisation and internationalisation (Law and Hoey 2018). As emerging Asian and South American economies look towards English-speaking countries to provide education for their students, competition within the UK higher education sector becomes fiercer, particularly as international students bring in more money than students from the UK. The result of such cost-benefit approaches is consumerist behaviour on the part of students and their parents and a tertiary sector that is about meeting students' expectations, bettering value for money, improving employment opportunities, enhancing employability skills and achieving specific outcomes (Hussey and Smith 2002; Department for Business Innovation and Skills 2016; Robinson and Hilli 2016). These external factors related to neoliberalism within higher education, and the resultant changes to academic career paths, budgetary developments and student intakes impact academics' roles and identity (Marr and Forsyth 2011; Henkel 2000). And yet working in academia continues to be romanticised (Lovin 2018) and is still seen as a career worth striving for (Bauman 2001) as it evokes the image of like-minded individuals sharing knowledge and expertise in collegial collaboration for the betterment of society and the common good (Lewis 2008; Tilak 2008). Academia represents privilege, autonomy and flexibility, although having freedom and autonomy does not mean academics can do what they want (Bauman 2001). They are continuously required to carry out high-quality research, acquire relevant research funding and produce reputable research publications (Abouserie 1996; Watermeyer

2015). This is in addition to teaching commitments and consistent engagement with the public to ensure long-term research impact. The universities' subjection to consumerism is further compounded by government initiatives that link student fees to institutional achievements such as research outputs or teaching excellence. Measures to ensure that targets are met and that courses retain credibility include the introduction of benchmarks, frameworks and criteria. These policies and initiatives resulting from the demand for accountability lead to managerialism and bureaucratisation within higher education (Winter 2009; Waitere et al. 2011). Paradoxically, universities are under pressure to perform and demonstrate high levels of achievement, but at the same time concede to massification of higher education (Harris 2005). The pursuit of excellence is crucial if an institution is to gain higher status and a better reputation across the higher education market, which in turn attracts more students, more staff and more funding. Excellence therefore leads to prestige, a relational value against which institutions measure themselves (Blackmore 2016). For individuals, working in a prestigious institution is a motivation to increase their productivity and the quality of their own work as a way of contributing to the institution's collective prestige (Blackmore 2016). The premise for such a rigid regime of productivity, effectiveness and excellence geared towards tangible outcomes and outputs in order to support the prestige economy (Blackmore 2016) of a university is a standard, normative, fully able and abled being. In brief, ableism in academia is endemic.

Studies in ableism

The difficulty with conceptualisations is employing a definition that is generic and encompassing enough to include as many perspectives and theoretical lenses as possible, yet specific and precise enough to allow theorisations to be contained. Ableism is no different. As a term, ableism evolved in the 1960s and 1970s from social rights movements within the disability communities in the UK and the US (Albrecht 2006). Ableism then described the prejudices and discrimination the disability community was faced with. In this original iteration, ableism was a specific form of -ism relating to and experienced by those whose bodies or whose 'physical, mental, neuronal, cognitive or behavioural abilities' (Wolbring 2012, 78) were not standard, normative, typical, but somehow different. The development of the concept is closely linked to the cultural lens within disability studies and so ableism is described as

> a network of beliefs, processes and practices that produces a particular kind of self and body (the corporeal standard) that is projected as the perfect, species-typical and therefore essential and fully human. Disability then is cast as a diminished state of being human. (Campbell 2001, 44)

As explorations of lived experiences increased within disability studies but also beyond, there came the recognition that ableism affects more than visible forms of disability. Over time therefore the term evolved to signify an 'umbrella ism for other isms' (Wolbring 2008, 253). Consequently, in public discourses ableism has become synonymous with experiences of racism, sexism and ageism, but also of invisible disabilities and chronic illnesses, the 'non-normative other'. Scholarly explorations have warned about the dangers in separating studies in ableism from disability studies and the risks individuals take by researching ableism without knowing the breadth and depth of the disability studies canon (Campbell 2009). At the same time, however, personal experiences cannot be dismissed. While ableism has been defined (see e.g. Campbell 2009; Wolbring 2012; Dolmage 2017) and an outline for how to study ableism has also been developed (Goodley 2014), little work has yet been undertaken in relation to the higher education context. This collection calls into question the many binaries we encounter: academics' multiple identities, which are often at odds with one another; the role of internalised norms, which we all strive for; the scientific research we undertake, which is opposed to the validity of personal experiences and personal positioning. And in the middle of all this sits the concept of the perfect academic. It is therefore the context of higher education with its emphasis on performativity, efficiency, productivity and personal reflectiveness that requires our attention. This is where individual experiences often jar with the focus of the disability studies canon. Disability studies emphasise social and societal barriers and challenges, reject the (bio)medical model of a body at fault and seek to embrace disability as an asset and as a different way of working. Within academia, where perfectionism, productivity and excellence are internalised, individuals may not necessarily be able to subscribe to this philosophy. This is why the concept of ableism and studies in ableism provide a helpful theoretical framework and an effective lens to theorise and make sense of personal experiences.

Ableism in academia: Disabilities and chronic illnesses in higher education

Rather than embracing difference as a reflection of wider society, academic ecosystems seek to normalise and homogenise ways of working and of being a scholar. Academics with chronic illness, disabilities or neurodiversity are practically unseen and starkly under-represented in comparison to students with disabilities or disabled people in the general public (Brown and Leigh 2018). More recently, interest in ableism in academia has grown with publications such as *Academic Ableism* (Dolmage 2017), *Negotiating Disability: Disclosure in Higher Education* (Kerschbaum et al. 2017) and *Mad at School: Rhetorics of Mental Disability and Academic Life* (Price 2011). However, to date no attempt has been made to theorise ableism in academia. This book provides the interdisciplinary outlook on ableism that is missing. Drawing on research data and personal experiences, members of academia theorise and conceptualise what it means to be and to work outside the stereotypical norm. The focus of the book and its outlook on ableism are not grounded within approaches commonly associated with disability studies. The theoretical conceptualisation of ableism is set within the context of the variety of knowledge production in academia. As such, contributors define disability, ableism, chronic illness and neurodiversity on their own terms rather than following the prescription of a specific interpretative model. Through engagement with scholarly debates and theorisations of the body and embodiment, and emotion and identity work, and drawing on theories from sociology, disability studies, education studies and the like, this book foregrounds how individuals make sense of their experiences of ableism in academia. It is this particular approach to theorising disability and chronic illnesses that explains why some conceptualisations and outlooks are more prominent than others. Throughout the book, many contributors have used Goffman's *Presentation of Self in Everyday Life* (Goffman 1990/1959) and *Stigma: Notes on the Management of Spoiled Identity* (Goffman 1990/1963) to make sense of their experiences, while others refer heavily to feminist and poststructuralist philosophy. Three contributors used poetic inquiry to theorise and make sense of their experiences of ableism in academia, which resulted in a poetic form of expression. As a scholarly endeavour and a specific form of arts-based research, poetic inquiry is a qualitative research approach that helps to provide new insights and learning; to describe, explore, discover, problem-solve; to forge micro-macro connections; to engage holistically; to be evocative and provocative; to raise awareness and empathy; to unsettle stereotypes, challenge dominant ideologies, and include marginalized voices and perspectives; and to open up avenues for public scholarship, usefulness and social justice. (Leavy 2015, 21–7)

Using poetry as/in/for inquiry connects the private with the public, the specific with the general, the personal and intimate with the cultural and social to 'lay naked the taken-for-granted assumptions and social structures' (Faulkner 2020, 7). As this book seeks to provide insight into the wide range of issues and concerns of those who may not fit the expected norms of the stereotypical academic, so its form was opened to poetic inquiry.

As a result, this book offered contributors the all-important space and opportunity to explore and theorise personal experiences. More specifically, the aim of the collection is to provide an open engagement with ableism issues that is not confined by or restricted to disciplinary conventions or categories. Therefore, researchers and students will find the book interesting, as it offers a topic that has yet to be covered in this specific way of theorisation and personal experiences. Higher education researchers may be used to interdisciplinary approaches, but disability, chronic illness and neurodiversity are not commonly explored in these ways. For disability studies researchers, the approach of combining disability, chronic illness and neurodiversity will be novel, as from a disability studies point of view the three are seen as different experiences. From an ableism studies point of view, however, they are clearly related. Researchers from sociological studies will find this collection particularly fruitful and interesting, as the societal ramifications are laid bare. For staff and students in the tertiary sector this book provides theory and conceptualisation, theorisation and also personal interpretations of ableism in academia. Academic and non-academic staff members, as well as students, will benefit from the combination of theory and experiences. The debates around ableism, equality, disabilities and inclusion are meeting the current trend within academia, and this book offers a wide range of readings.

The opening chapter by Claudia Gillberg is concerned with knowledge production and ways of working in academia, while also addressing prejudices and expectations of disabled bodies. In her chapter, Gillberg argues that disabled people are often seen as non-academic or intellectually weaker and therefore, for her, education and participation in academia are an issue of social justice. Her suggested way forward is to break down existing norms and conventions and for academia to reflect differences in knowledge production accordingly. In her chapter, Francesca Peruzzo also explores ableism from personal experiences, but from the position of a non-disabled academic researching disabilities. Drawing on Foucault, Peruzzo questions and challenges the expectation that only the disabled should be engaged in ableism studies. Thereby, Peruzzo hints at the normative body within disability scholarship needing to be an otherwise non-normative body. The chapter by Nicole Brown reports on an empirical study with academics with fibromyalgia. The author focuses on how disclosing a condition in academia is a sensitive issue, requiring individuals to grapple personally and privately as well as publicly with appearing weak. Disclosure in this sense exposes individuals as vulnerable and therefore sensitivity is required in responding to disabled or chronically ill colleagues. Divya Jindal-Snape's poem 'Fibromyalgia and me' is a moving expression of the narrative I's self-doubts linked with the experience of having a contested, invisible illness. In her poem the author acknowledges the significant role the illness experience plays, but at the same time emphasises that there is more to an academic self than an illness.

The subsequent chapter by Nicola Martin reports on findings from a research project and so provides evidence-based insights into the lived experience of disabled academics. Using the findings from her research Martin offers a solid basis for future steps, making clear recommendations on how to develop more inclusive practices within academia. In her contribution Alice Andrews explores Derrida's concept of autoimmunity and McRuer's crip theory to theorise what it feels like when one's body is attacking itself, thus one's self. In her discussion of ableism Andrews specifically discusses the contemporary context of the neoliberal academy in the United Kingdom. In doing so, Andrews considers, questions and critiques the position of the standard normative self and the pressures of advocating specifically for those who do not fit the mould. Elisabeth Griffiths explores the tensions she has experienced as an academic interested in disability rights and disability research, while at the same time looking well and passing as non-disabled. Starting from a very personal experience of disclosing a disability and of dealing with the consequences of that disclosure, Griffiths reflects on how specific forms of knowledge production and particular ways of working are normalised and disability is not considered appropriately. Ultimately, she asks for a wider acceptance of differences.

The theme of being different is also explored in the chapter by Carla Finesilver, Jennifer Leigh and Nicole Brown. The focus of their chapter lies with the expectations that disabilities and illnesses take specific forms and kinds. Often such conditions are interpreted as binary, consistent and visible, when in reality the lived experience of disability and chronic illness tends to be one of fluctuating invisible symptoms. The personal narratives in this chapter highlight the tensions in trying to meet expectations while at the same time needing to negotiate the specificities of one's body. Jennifer Rode's contribution is the poem 'Imposter', a powerful stream of consciousness from the point of view of someone whose 'different' body and mind impact their academic work, while simultaneously causing self-doubt. The work by Jennifer Leigh and Nicole Brown demonstrates that disabilities, illnesses and neurodiversity are not only an external and public matter, but also a personal concern. They argue that ways of working in academia are often internalised to such an extent that individuals feel committed and obligated to fit within the existing norms, and thereby touch upon how the structural and political aspects of academia impact upon the personal and private.

Kirstein Rummery's exploration of the personal and political is the author's journey between social activism, political campaigning and an academic career. Writing from the perspective of a person who has acquired lived experience of disability over the course of several years, Rummery explains the barriers to political engagement as a person with disability, and the tensions in the public image of a campaigner and activist afforded by her institutional membership. Drawing on her extensive professional expertise regarding the studies in ableism, Fiona Kumari Campbell's chapter discusses the ramifications of disability and accessibility policies and reasonable adjustments. Campbell highlights how ableism equals social exclusion. She urges us to rethink our current approaches to inclusion to ensure that well-meant practices do not humiliate individuals. This chapter is followed by El Spaeth's 'A little bit extra', in which Spaeth thematises reasonable adjustments. The poem represents a raw account of how chronically ill or disabled individuals are misunderstood and othered in academia.

Nicole Brown and Jennifer Leigh use the conclusion to bring together key themes of the individual chapters and to outline what it meant and means to bring this collection to fruition. The final section in this collection is dedicated to recommendations for practices within higher education institutions to further the case the contributors make in ensuring the disabled and chronically ill are included in the academy of the future.

References

Abouserie, Reda. 'Stress, Coping Strategies and Job Satisfaction in University Academic Staff', *Educational Psychology* 16/1 (1996): 49–56. Online. https://doi.org/10.1080/0144341960160104 (accessed 19 May 2020).

Albrecht, Gary L., ed. *Encyclopedia of Disability*. Thousand Oaks, CA: Sage, 2006. Online. http://dx.doi.org/10.4135/9781412950510 (accessed 19 May 2020).

Bauman, Zygmunt. *Community: Seeking Safety in an Insecure World*. Cambridge: Polity Press and Malden, MA: Blackwell, 2001.

Blackmore, Paul. *Prestige in Academic Life: Excellence and Exclusion*. Abingdon and New York: Routledge, 2016.

Brown, Nicole and Leigh, Jennifer. 'Ableism in Academia: Where are the Disabled and Ill Academics?' *Disability and Society* 33/6 (2018): 985–9. Online. https://doi.org/10.1080/09687599.2018.1455627 (accessed 19 May 2020).

Campbell, Fiona Kumari. 'Inciting Legal Fictions: "Disability's" Date with Ontology and the Ableist Body of the Law', *Griffith Law Review* 10/1 (2001): 42–62.

Campbell, Fiona Kumari. *Contours of Ableism: The Production of Disability and Abledness*. Basingstoke and New York: Palgrave Macmillan, 2009.

Department for Business Innovation and Skills. *Students at the Heart of the System*. London: Department for Business Innovation and Skills, 2011. Online. https://www.gov.uk/government/uploads/system/uploads/attachment_data/file/31384/11-944-higher-education-students-at-heart-of-system.pdf (accessed 7 September 2016).

Department for Business Innovation and Skills. *Success as a Knowledge Economy: Teaching Excellence, Social Mobility and Student Choice*. London: Department for Business Innovation and Skills, 2016. Online. https://www.gov.uk/government/uploads/system/uploads/attachment_data/file/523396/bis-16-265-success-as-a-knowledge-economy.pdf (accessed 7 September 2016).

Dolmage, Jay Timothy. *Academic Ableism: Disability and Higher Education*. Ann Arbor: University of Michigan Press, 2017. Online. https://doi.org/10.3998/mpub.9708722 (accessed 19 May 2020).

Faulkner, Sandra L. *Poetic Inquiry: Craft, Method and Practice*, 2nd ed. New York: Routledge, 2020.

Gabriel, Deborah and Tate, Shirley Anne. *Inside the Ivory Tower: Narratives of Women of Colour Surviving and Thriving in British Academia*. London: Trentham Books, 2017.

Gewirtz, Sharon and Cribb, Alan. 'Representing 30 Years of Higher Education Change: UK Universities and the *Times Higher*', *Journal of Educational Administration and History* 45/1 (2013): 58–83. Online. https://doi.org/10.1080/00220620.2013.730505 (accessed 19 May 2020).

Goffman, Erving. *The Presentation of Self in Everyday Life*. London: Penguin Books, 1990, originally 1959.

Goffman, Erving. *Stigma: Notes on the Management of Spoiled Identity*. London: Penguin Books, 1990, originally 1963.

Goodley, D. *Dis/ability Studies: Theorising Disablism and Ableism*. London: Routledge, 2014.

Harris, Suzy. 'Rethinking Academic Identities in Neo-liberal Times', *Teaching in Higher Education* 10/4 (2005): 421–33. Online. https://doi.org/10.1080/13562510500238986 (accessed 19 May 2020).

Henkel, Mary. *Academic Identities and Policy Change in Higher Education*. Higher Education Policy Series 46. London and Philadelphia: Jessica Kingsley, 2000.

Hussey, Trevor and Smith, Patrick. 'The Trouble with Learning Outcomes', *Active Learning in Higher Education*, 3/3 (2002): 220–33. Online. https://doi.org/10.1177/1469787402003003003 (accessed 19 May 2020).

Kerschbaum, Stephanie L., Eisenman, Laura T. and Jones, James M., eds. *Negotiating Disability: Disclosure and Higher Education*. Ann Arbor: University of Michigan Press, 2017. Online. https://doi.org/10.3998/mpub.9426902 (accessed 19 May 2020).

Law, David and Hoey, Michael, eds. *Perspectives on the Internationalisation of Higher Education*. Abingdon and New York: Routledge, 2018.

Leavy, Patricia. *Method Meets Art: Arts-Based Research Practice*, 2nd ed. New York: Guilford Press, 2015.

Lewis, Magda. 'Public Good or Private Value: A Critique of the Commodification of Knowledge in Higher Education – A Canadian Perspective'. In *Structure and Agency in the Neoliberal University*, edited by Joyce E. Canaan and Wesley Shumar, 65–86. (Routledge Research in Education 15.) Abingdon and New York: Routledge, 2008. Online. https://doi.org/10.4324/9780203927687 (accessed 19 May 2020).

Lovin, C. Laura. 'Feelings of Change: Alternative Feminist Professional Trajectories'. In *Feeling Academic in the Neoliberal University: Feminist Flights, Fights and Failures*, edited by Yvette Taylor and Kinneret Lahad, 137–62. (Palgrave Studies in Gender and Education). Cham, Switzerland: Palgrave Macmillan, 2018. Online. https://doi.org/10.1007/978-3-319-64224-6_7 (accessed 19 May 2020).

Marr, Liz and Forsyth, Rachel. *Identity Crisis: Working in Higher Education in the 21st Century*. Stoke on Trent: Trentham Books, 2011.

Price, Margaret. *Mad at School: Rhetorics of Mental Disability and Academic Life*. Ann Arbor: University of Michigan Press, 2011. Online. https://doi.org/10.3998/mpub.1612837 (accessed 27 May 2020).

Robinson, Wendy and Hilli, Angelique. 'The English "Teaching Excellence Framework" and Professionalising Teaching and Learning in Research-Intensive Universities: An Exploration of Opportunities, Challenges, Rewards and Values from a Recent Empirical Study', *Foro de Educación* 14/21 (2016): 151–65. Online. https://doi.org/10.14516/fde.2016.014.021.008 (accessed 19 May 2020).

Taylor, Yvette and Lahad, Kinneret, eds. *Feeling Academic in the Neoliberal University: Feminist Flights, Fights and Failures*. Palgrave Studies in Gender and Education. Cham: Palgrave Macmillan, 2018. Online. https://doi.org/10.1007/978-3-319-64224-6 (accessed 19 May 2020).

Thompson, John and Bekhradnia, Bahram. *The Independent Review of Higher Education Funding: An Analysis*. London: Higher Education Policy Institute, 2010. Online. https://www.hepi.ac.uk/2010/10/15/the-independent-review-of-higher-education-funding-an-analysis/ (accessed 19 May 2020).

Tilak, Jandhyala B.G. 'Higher Education: A Public Good or a Commodity for Trade?' *Prospects* 38/4 (2008): 449–66. Online. https://doi.org/10.1007/s11125-009-9093-2 (accessed 19 May 2020).

Waitere, Hine Jane, Wright, Jeannie, Tremaine, Marianne, Brown, Seth and Pausé, Cat Jeffrey. 'Choosing Whether to Resist or Reinforce the New Managerialism: The Impact of Performance-based Research Funding on Academic Identity', *Higher Education Research and Development* 30/2 (2011): 205–17. Online. https://doi.org/10.1080/07294360.2010.509760 (accessed 19 May 2020).

Watermeyer, Richard. 'Lost in the "Third Space": The Impact of Public Engagement in Higher Education on Academic Identity, Research Practice and Career Progression', *European Journal of Higher Education* 5/3 (2015): 331–47. Online. https://doi.org/10.1080/21568235.2015.1044546 (accessed 19 May 2020).

Winter, Richard. 'Academic Manager or Managed Academic? Academic Identity Schisms in Higher Education', *Journal of Higher Education Policy and Management* 31/2 (2009): 121–31. Online. https://doi.org/10.1080/13600800902825835 (accessed 19 May 2020).

Wolbring, Gregor. 'The Politics of Ableism', *Development* 51/2 (2008): 252–8. Online. https://doi.org/10.1057/dev.2008.17 (accessed 19 May 2020).

Wolbring, Gregor. 'Expanding Ableism: Taking Down the Ghettoization of Impact of Disability Studies Scholars', *Societies* 2/3 (2012): 75–83. Online. https://doi.org/10.3390/soc2030075 (accessed 19 May 2020).

1
The significance of crashing past gatekeepers of knowledge: Towards full participation of disabled scholars in ableist academic structures

Claudia Gillberg

Academic knowledge, historically speaking, is intrinsically elitist and exclusive and has served to uphold a hierarchical power system in which the professions enjoy supreme status and privileges such as remuneration exceeding that of other members of society (Abbott 2001; Witz 2004). Initially, the professions were informed by the opinions and ideas of a handful of people who were passionate about their work and were often driven by intellectual curiosity, but there was a dark side to this: a sharp divide between the public and private sphere leading to a gendered divide in knowledge, with sometimes disastrous consequences for women's possibilities to influence policy let alone the politically confined spaces to which they were restricted. While Ann Oakley's research provides a new picture of some women's astounding agency and high-ranking roles in public life (Oakley 2018), the role that class, race and disability (the lack of) played concerning women who had opportunities was conspicuously lacking.

Mainstream, unlike academic, knowledge in this article is defined as recognised knowledge that a critical mass of academics and the wider population can agree on. It is also knowledge people think they know to be true, where there is no or limited controversy in public. Examples of such known and broadly recognised truths are that fresh air is good for you, and the work environment benefits from physically present employees.

Academia, in this chapter and context, is the seat of learning at which a formally recognised and institutionalised body of knowledge lying at the heart of a profession is debated, determined, taught, examined and perpetuated and/or sometimes re-evaluated. For instance, medical knowledge is taught at medical school, social work is taught to future social workers, engineering is taught to future engineers and the law is taught to law students. Subject matter constitutes an agreed-upon set of basic, non-negotiable skills that each member of a profession must possess. These are the bare minimum. Then there are more specialised skills, usually still part of what is required in order to be deemed fit to become a member of a certain profession, and highly specialised skills that are outside the mandatory coursework but will lead to expert roles and positions for some.

It can be argued that access to and participation in higher education is a social justice issue, with the case for broadening and widening access to higher education having been made and driven by differing ideologies and agendas for several decades (Morley and Walsh 1995; Delanty 2001; Percy, Zimpher and Brukardt 2006; Shah, Bennett and Southgate 2015; Alphin, Lavine and Chan 2017; Gillberg 2018a). The Open University, for example, has played a special role in the UK with its vision of lifelong learning as a tenet of a democratic, participatory society, expressed through courses and modules open to all people, but recent years have seen changes for the worse for disabled and chronically ill students, especially following the UK government's higher education reforms of 2012 (see http://www.open.ac.uk/about/main/strategy-and-policies/mission, https://theretiringacademic.wordpress.com/2018/04/13/closure-at-the-open-university). The introduction of tuition fees increased costs considerably for Open University students and, combined with the introduction of time limits for the funding of degree courses, made the completion of a degree for those suffering from a chronic illness, whose health may fluctuate, more difficult.

In debates on higher education an oft-forgotten aspect is that members of faculty or temporary academic staff might also be disabled and have difficulty conforming to norms dictating physical presence in the workplace (Lloyd 2015; Brown and Leigh 2018; Brown, Thompson and Leigh 2018; Johnston, MacNeill and Smyth 2018). Disabled academics have extensive lived experience of disability and, even if their field of expertise is far removed from disability studies, will at some point feel prompted, encouraged or even forced to contribute with knowledge engendered by that experience, relating to disability and academia (Wendell 1997; Honeyman 2016). This may make an impression but their contribution as disabled academics, while also representing disabled people, might slowly change some people's perception of their disabled colleagues, if the latter choose to come out as disabled – a difficult choice to make, given the negative impact it may have on their future career opportunities, presenting a potential conflict between personal ambition and the societal good. This touches on Kafer's (2013) ideas about the political/relational model of disability rather than fully subscribing to either the medical or social models of disability, both of which, she argues, are problematic relating to the disability/impairment divide. Kafer's proposition makes sense in relation to Fraser's concept of recognition and representation and discussions about political spaces of justice (Fraser 2008; Fraser et al. 2004; Fraser and Honneth 2003).

'Coming out' and the complex issue of representation for disabled academics is a double-edged sword involving an intricate web of negotiations, rarely with the promise of a positive career outcome. If they focus solely on their core work, they may face trouble involving other issues, e.g. having to explain lengthy absences from work, or continued sick leave, with no possibility of demanding that reasonable adjustments be made *if* they previously decided not to disclose. This needs to be understood as a personal and political decision in a highly politicised context, not only in academia but also in disability activism and the academic professions. Whatever disabled academics decide about embodying disability in academia, the issue will arise of the extra workload required for anyone with a disability to participate on the same terms as able-bodied colleagues. This unremunerated additional labour is an unfair burden for disabled academics, made more difficult by the fact that *all* academics are often expected to shoulder excessive workloads, especially early career researchers lacking permanent employment (Lloyd 2015).

Why would change in academia be required at all? As previously suggested, a social justice issue arises when there is a power imbalance impeding people's possibilities to participate on their own terms in contexts that affect them. For clarity, in this article the term 'professions' relates to those closely linked to academic disciplines, e.g. medicine. Professional bodies are traditional upholders of societal order and norms, the medical and legal professions being the archetypes of traditional professions that used to be deeply respected. While this respect may have diminished, there is no denying that medical doctors and lawyers still have a firm grip on sometimes rather intimate aspects of people's lives. For example, women with conditions such as endometriosis can wait many years for a correct diagnosis on the strength of which they may then gain access to quality healthcare. During the years in which they are ill without a diagnosis, they risk being misunderstood, stigmatised and maligned, and losing their jobs and family support. The absence of a legitimate diagnosis can mean loss of status, loss of identity and loss of life, be that through suicide or premature death (Gillberg 2018a, 2018b; Gillberg and Jones 2019).

In a chapter called 'Feminism' (Gillberg 2014), I addressed 'gate-crashing past established knowledge'. Key to this debate is the role that activism has played and can play regarding transformative change of the status quo. What are the possibilities and obstacles towards participatory knowledge production that rejects hierarchical ideas of knowledge having an intrinsic or inherent value depending on who and in what context it evolved? Drawing on Fraser's (2008) concept of recognition, it is worth considering her experience of activism. She harboured hopes of grassroots activism benefitting from her critical thoughts on how to advance feminist issues and assumed that writing for two audiences was possible, maybe even mutually beneficial, but soon discovered that her efforts were in vain.

Feminist scholars are not known for their propensity to help disabled scholars, something Shelley Tremain and Susan Wendell have described in what are recognised as mainstream feminist theories that tend to reassert the status quo – that is, disability as a failing body and frailty that is deficient and undesirable. Feminist and disability activism have not enjoyed a frictionless relationship in the past few decades, or perhaps ever (Morris 1993; Wendell 1989; 1997; Ryan 2014; Syfret 2015; Goyal 2016; Liebowitz 2019; Gillberg 2018a; 2018b; Tremain 2017). As Goodley and Moore have discussed, disability activism and academia are characterised by uneasiness (Goodley and Moore 2000). The question is whether this uneasiness presents an opportunity to channel new knowledge into academia and if such knowledge might be conducive to an academic discipline's development while offering new insights into what academia is and can be.

Knowledge and the formation of the professions

One of the most ancient and respected professions is medicine, which is also notable for having potentially the greatest impact on a person's wellbeing, especially if the person is female. Regardless of how empathetic a medical doctor may have been towards a female patient presenting with symptoms of severe pain, the recognised knowledge in the past was that women were frail and given to hysteria, an attitude that continues to this day (Gillberg and Jones 2019). Medical education as an academic discipline was complicit in legitimising this attitude by producing the knowledge that subjugated women: this was political, ensuring that women were kept out of the public sphere. The current Medically Unexplained Symptoms diagnosis is a flawed twenty-first century construct that has evolved from the same misogynistic prejudice that has permeated medical education and research for centuries (Gillberg and Jones 2019; Redinger et al. 2018).

Women from the period c. 1880 to 1920 deserve a special mention here, since figureheads such as Jane Addams (1860–1935) brought activism into academia and arguably contributed to the formation of the academic disciplines of sociology, social work, feminist philosophy, education and several others (Oakley 2018). Oakley discusses predominantly sociology and social work in the context of her research into that historical epoch (Fischer, Nackenoff and Chmielewski 2009; Gillberg 2012; Oakley 2018). There were also men who genuinely wished to be of service to society and were driven by compassionate insights into human suffering and visions of a fairer societal system (Dewey 1927, 1938), but delineation in the name of professionalisation has always been at the heart of knowledge production in academia. Academic disciplines are competing in the marketised higher education system, where the fight for limited funding is fierce.

Theoretical texts on knowledge and knowledge production in academia are plentiful (Bourdieu and Passeron 1990; Morley and Walsh 1995; Schuller and Watson 2009; Honeyman 2016), yet historically speaking a scarcity of theories on disabled academics' possibilities for contributing to the mainstream body of established knowledge is notable (Tremain 2019). Social media has opened alternative channels of communication for disabled academics to convey information, research questions and grassroots activism , and some have taken the opportunity that Twitter, for example, offers to initiate debate on controversial questions or issues that are not on any agenda in the academic sphere (e.g. Chronically Academic 2020).

Multiple meanings of participation

Some academic disciplines have concerned themselves with the concept of social citizenship, arguing that citizenship is more than being a recognised part of a sovereign state with clearly defined borders. Full social citizenship concerns the type of participation with which this chapter is concerned (Addams 1905; Dewey 1927; Duffy and Perez

2014; Sépulchre 2018). Political scientists may not like citizenship being used in contexts outside their political expertise but as Ruth Lister (2003) has also pointed out, citizenship comprises more than passports and the right to vote. This is the argument that some on the fringes of the suffragette movement offered when they started looking at issues other than the vote, so attempts to broaden the understanding of the materiality of citizenship are not new (Oakley 2018).

To be able to voice concerns within a social citizenship context is to engage actively in a country and in local communities. Utilising contacts and networks in which citizens' concerns are heard and potentially acted on is an expression of participation as a citizen. What is the opposite, the antonym of participation? It is the inaction of others. It is the refusal to react. This shifts the focus onto structures and systemic failings of individuals who do not participate to the best of their ability and knowledge, but it does not blame them for not managing to be included or for failing to adhere to preconceived notions of what should work for them. Meaningful analyses of such failings could involve the prerequisites for social citizenship by deconstructing it into its multifaceted activities.

By using participation as a theoretical concept and practical means with which to assess an individual's or group's involvement in certain contexts concerning the individual and group, participation allows a focus on what works and what does not. Participation as a concept is different from others, such as inclusion, in that it does not necessarily require an invitation or permission to participate, while barriers to participation lie elsewhere and can be addressed (Reid and Gillberg 2014), at least in part, by the social model of disability. Participation, while far from perfect, corresponds to Addams's vision of a pluralistic society that demands accountability and knowledge. It also corresponds with Fraser's social justice theory of the concept of recognition, because genuine participation must entail recognition of one's agency and knowledge.

Activism and reciprocal learning

Activism is defined here to mean concerted efforts to change the status quo based on jointly identified barriers that render parity of participation and full social citizenship difficult or impossible. Activism can mean many different things in practice, but it should not be conflated with actionism, the latter being ill defined, often a spuriously decided-upon measure to reach a short-term goal with little or no long-term effect, potentially causing more harm rather than creating wider understanding and acceptance (McRuer 2006; Gillies 2014; Disabled People Against Cuts 2018; Mann 2018).

Social activism is of prime importance in enabling the understanding of theories or methodologies involving participation and knowledge processes in a world where women's concerns, especially disabled women's concerns, are not the norm. Feminist pragmatism arose from a determination to comprehend the conditions of life experienced by women and, if necessary, to alter them for the better based on principles of participation, reciprocal learning and ethics, expressed by the inclusion of multiple perspectives of lived experience and collaborative decision-taking (Gillberg 2012).

Research-based activism was one of Addams's philosophical tenets (Gillberg 2009, 2012). Addams was a philosopher whose work united feminist perspectives with a determination to engender social change via co-operative action (Hamington 2018). Activism without a thoroughly researched knowledge base would not do for several reasons, including the ontological and epistemological. Addams realised that without established truths and conscious efforts to put realities on the map, there could be no social justice, irrespective of the enthusiastic activist efforts of her peers. Fraser's concept of recognition here translates as 'x is both recognised and affirmed, attributing a positive evaluation to x' (Fraser 2008). Kafer's (2013) political/relational model aligns with Fraser's critical concept of recognition, where the mutuality aspect is essential. In terms of change – that is, gatecrashing past keepers of mainstream knowledge – collective agency is at the heart of Addams's philosophy and it is the methodological prerequisite of reciprocal learning (Addams 1905, 2017). This is a critical validity criterion for knowledge production.

Ann Oakley (2018) provides a thorough and meticulous account of feminist activism and academic knowledge building in the period 1880–1920 that still holds currency in today's complex and confusing climate. Feminist pragmatism in its contemporary form addresses a multitude of social justice issues already making the case for broadening mainstream knowledge (Gillberg 2012; Hamington and Bardwell-Jones 2012). However, it is questionable how inclined academic feminists, irrespective of discipline, are to engage in activism. Does today's activism for social change require academic knowledge and collaboration with academic disciplines at all? Or are Addams's theories of social change obsolete? Also, do activists listen to academics, can there be any collaboration in Addams's spirit?

Reciprocal learning is a validity criterion for some methodologies; for instance, Reid and Gillberg (2014) argue that for there to be reciprocity, the transactional or reciprocal learning must be genuine, validated by each participant's involvement in collective action and decision-making processes. This requires the researcher(s) to be open to scrutiny and critique and to learn from their participants' concerns rather than to reject them. In other words, feminist participatory action researchers commit to creating parity of participation for the co-production of knowledge. Reciprocity, according to Addams, or transactional learning, according to Dewey, is an expression of democratic participation in a society that takes its citizens seriously. It becomes unacceptable in such a knowledge paradigm to produce knowledge for certain groups of people based on spurious assumptions about them. There is a discussion among researchers pertaining to the extent to which they need to be disabled themselves to understand their field of research in the area of disability studies, but this is a discussion that exceeds the parameters of this chapter and deserves to be thoroughly considered elsewhere.

Challenging ableism in academia

Academia houses many disciplines that are at odds with each other (Becher and Trowler 2001), mainly because they operate in different paradigms while also competing for funding. Universities' civic duty has often been replaced by corporate power philosophies or managerialism, erecting walls of pseudo-efficiency between those studying subject matter and their teachers (Percy, Zimpher and Brukardt 2006). This said, the normative framework of the ever-available able-bodied academic driven by ambition, and in a climate of university rankings, leaves little room for those who do not conform with this ableist framework (Morley and Walsh 1995; McRuer 2006; Brown and Leigh 2018). Insofar as a university is a centre for knowledge culture and making contributions upholding the social order, it is not just a knowledge producer but a transmitter of culture, and as such a central actor in society (Kadoda 2018). As Delanty says, 'the main social change that we need to note is that because of different rates of change the university has been most affected by the changes in the mode of knowledge and changes in the social order' (Delanty 2001, 57).

The difficulties with ableist knowledge and practices occur at all levels and are only perceived as such by those affected by the ableist knowledge paradigm in which academic disciplines exist and keep producing, perpetuating and endorsing ableism, mostly unwittingly. Oakley's most recent work (2018), brilliant as it is, is full of a history steeped in ableism: formidable, admirable activists producing knowledge that would not have been produced without them, because men would never have noticed the issues that blighted women's lives; strong, healthy bodies travelling around the world, putting their lives on the line, intellectually and physically, for social and political change. There was no room for the frail bodies, deformities or 'weakness' present in those suffering from disability and/or severe chronic illness. To enforce this point, Oakley (2018) mentions several feminist thinkers and activists who openly argued for eugenics, which represented the spirit of the time; I would argue such thinking prevails to this day.

As Gillberg and Pettersson argue (2019), ableism is deeply rooted in a historical understanding of the necessity to disregard unfit bodies. Based on such a historical understanding of ableism, Gillberg and Pettersson raise questions regarding legal, cultural and political recognition of disability rights in practice, while Brown and Leigh (2018) problematise scarce disclosure among disabled academics. Fraser's theory of social justice (2008) posits that recognition is about cultural and social status, i.e. groups that are denied recognition will systematically be oppressed and stigmatised by their own culture. In other words, recognition is about how certain groups are portrayed by others and what room for manoeuvre the groups themselves are given to vocalise their concerns. Fraser (2008) is adamant that social justice requires recognition and redistribution. The latter is not discussed in further detail in this chapter but pertains to reallocation of resources to historically and politically under-privileged groups.

Ableism inside academia is nothing less than a lack or absence of recognition. This is a structural problem that cannot be reasonably resolved at the individual level, though it is at the individual level that the implications and consequences of ableism are felt most keenly, and already precarious work conditions easily become untenable (Campbell 2009; Goodley 2014). Another consequence is that knowledge production inevitably suffers due to the multiple injustices imposed on disabled academics by ableist structures, such as numerous additional hours of unpaid labour to access facilities through making special arrangements, i.e. accessibility issues that require renegotiating ad infinitum.

Physical strength has traditionally been described as a moral and indeed intellectual virtue. Feeble-mindedness, by contrast, inhabits ailing bodies. So it is not a leap of the imagination to assume the reverse:

disabled bodies do not house sharp intellects. Whatever emanates from a disabled body must therefore comprise at best fringe or 'special' knowledge, an addition or footnote (Gillberg and Pettersson 2019). Ableism in academia may well express itself through fragmentation and over-specialisation, i.e. special education (Delanty 2001). This can be useful in some respects but there is a risk that such specialisation may lead to further marginalisation. Anyone who has mentioned 'crip theory' (or anything relating to disability) in a research seminar that was not explicitly about a 'special' topic (McRuer 2006) will remember the vacant non-stares, the polite murmurs or dismissal ('that is not what is being discussed').

Recognition through participatory frameworks

The question is, how can disabled academics negotiate the ableism in knowledge production and the institutional injustices they experience? The impeding of their professional development and their unique knowledge production often has nothing to do with disability. How can their lived experience of being disabled, but by no means inferior, academics lead to full recognition and respect for their work? I propose that one way of dealing with a lack of recognition is through engagement in knowledge production contexts (not limited to research projects but encompassing all activities within the organisational setting of academia). Good examples abound, and these will be presented here.

There are fundamental questions pertaining to knowledge and power because knowledge has been created, controlled and made available by hierarchical educational and political systems (Reid and Gillberg 2014). When engaging in participatory research, which some argue should be viewed as a new knowledge paradigm, an epistemological issue is what lies at the centre and margins of knowledge production, and for whom is knowledge generated, by whom and to what end? Examples of participatory frameworks will be described. These frameworks comprise both qualitative and quantitative methods; in other words, participatory frameworks do not subscribe to the qualitative/quantitative divide. Participatory frameworks are not limited to a handful of social sciences but may also apply in the natural sciences. The following are examples of such frameworks, all of which have a strong ambition to recognition and sustainable knowledge building that is meaningful.

In feminist participatory action research (FPAR; whereas the PAR framework is of a more generic nature, FPAR is about particularities stemming from lived experiences of women's, *all* women's, lives), the research is done with those involved as research participants, in stark contrast to some medical research that takes place without any meaningful participation of the patient population (Reid and Gillberg 2014; Gillberg and Jones 2019). In FPAR, as well as in other feminist and decolonising approaches to knowledge production, the web of power dynamics is referred to as oppression, marginalisation, discrimination, otherness, disempowerment and subordination. Irrespective of terminology, it is FPAR's ongoing effort to question, challenge and understand the complexities of power and to recognise the multitude of ways in which it can be expressed. FPAR's ontological and epistemological stance includes challenging the authority of the researcher and shifting traditional power relations, which can be seen as controversial and is accordingly met with resistance from mainstream researchers, who define scientific rigour solely as the ability to verify or falsify research results through enforcing distance between and ascribing differential statuses to the researcher and researched. Due to its critique of power, FPAR challenges dominant attitudes to research, disciplinary silos and taken-for-granted assumptions that render invisible the diverse experiences of marginalised groups (Reid and Gillberg 2014).

Another example of moving towards recognised academic knowledge is provided by the Centre for Action Research in Professional Practice (CARPP), in the school of management at the University of Bath, UK – particularly pertinent in this chapter as academia and the professions were mentioned as mutually enforcing power structures, but also jointly producing valuable knowledge. CARPP was created to develop the theory and practice of action research and it explicitly sought to reform academia by enabling postgraduate research that would meet the established quality criteria and then exceed these, leading to radical development of ideas and practice. A core purpose was to bring an attitude of inquiry and learning to key issues of our time – justice and sustainability. CARPP was part of an international network of people and institutions developing and legitimising action research in its many forms. Members saw this as 'political work about which knowledge(s) count especially countering the privileging of intellectual knowledge' (Marshall 2014, 91).

In yet another methodological example of how to challenge privileged knowledge, there is citizen participation in relation to action research, and, as Jaitli puts it, in all these approaches and methodologies, there is emphasis on the knowledge of the citizens and the recognition of individual and collective action to address issues of unequal powers which influence access and control over development processes. The most effective use of these participatory methodologies and approaches is evident when they are used as important means for change and not as ends in themselves. (Jaitli 2014, 96)

The validity criteria for participatory action research, here to be understood as a methodology, are outlined as follows:

- Catalytic validity – any rigorous action research project is expected to produce meaningful ways in which to implement and further develop jointly produced knowledge. There is always a risk that restricted funding and limited project timescales will produce flimsy results that are quickly forgotten. Participatory research, however, must be sustainable, continuing free from the original project. Therefore, new steps must be worded in an action plan; networks will need establishing and allies must be found (Gillberg 2012).
- Democratic validity – is the research problem of valid concern in terms of pertinence to the community or groups it claims to represent? Here a parallel can be drawn to an early feminist pragmatist, Mary Parker Follett (1868–1933), whose proposal for a radical form of democracy was based in local neighbourhoods. Follett's philosophy and practice were that 'the process of democracy is one that can only be engaged through concrete experience' (Whipps 2012).
- Ethical validity – are stakeholders harmed by the research? Yoak and Brydon-Miller (2014, 306) maintain that 'ethical systems are intended to clarify and advance our understanding of moral relationships and the value-based decisions we make'. In an action research context, this translates into the ability on the researcher's part to reflect self-critically on their bias, prejudice and preconceived notions. There is no such thing as unbiased research as that would entail knowledge being produced in a cultural, historical and political vacuum. Through such self-critical examination, the framing of the research problem emerges in collaboration with those directly affected by the proposed research, allowing for multi-perspective input as an intrinsic part of the project. This

largely removes the power hierarchy between researcher and researched while empowering the researched to be active in their own lives. Not all participatory research can grant such a degree of involvement but in FPAR and community-based research, the ethical aspect is non-negotiable (Campbell and Groundwater-Smith 2007).

- Outcome validity means the same here as in other research paradigms, but an outcome must also be validated by all research participants and the researcher's ability to agree on meaningful actions towards change for the common good. Such an action will be the outcome of other actions taken during the research process, undergoing the typical cycle of naming the problem, jointly deciding what action to take, critical evaluation, reflection and the next action towards problem solving. An outcome validity should always include clearly formulated statements by all participants concerning their learning process, a form of meta-learning for each participant that may not have anything directly to do with the project. An ideal outcome validity entails researchers who genuinely learnt from their research participants. This is what Addams referred to as reciprocity, an intrinsic part of being a fully participating citizen (Gillberg 2012).
- Process validity is a form of ongoing critical and self-critical evaluation of the knowledge production process. The aim is not to reach compromise but the relational/political engagement that Kafer (2013) posits in her feminist crip theory. In other words, process validity must be as strictly observed as outcome validity.

These validity criteria translate into material consequences for all parties involved in the research. The knowledge produced in such a paradigm (critical social theory, feminist pragmatism, action research, etc.) will differ from the knowledge produced in a positivist or interpretative paradigm, where the distance between the researcher and the researched remains wide and hierarchical power structures are upheld, thereby withholding recognition for the concerns and struggles of marginalised groups and further cementing the systemic ableism with which not only academic disciplines but also professions, and to some extent activist movements, are infused.

Feminist, queer crip meets feminist pragmatism, meets future

Feminist pragmatists posit that there is no need to choose between polarised positions when it comes to the creation of new knowledge. Minnich, for instance, holds that knowledge is at once subjective and objective: subjective because it is 'marked by the processes of its construction by specifically located subjects; objective in that the constructive process is constrained by a reality that is recalcitrant to inattentive or whimsical structurings' (Minnich 2005, 257). Those operating in a positivist paradigm need not fear that this means a relativist, 'anything goes' approach to knowledge. On the contrary (as mentioned earlier), Addams and her contemporaries were adamant that their activism towards social change be fact-based. They needed to provide rigorous statistics to convey the reality of multiple injustices such as uninhabitable housing, starving children and women's health, where they noted that immigrant women's quality of life was worse than that of the resident population. Oakley describes some of these women's work, including the foundation of the Children's Bureau in 1912 (the first US federal agency led by a woman), established by Florence Kelley, Lillian Wald, Julia Lathrop and Grace Meigs, the latter a doctor who conducted a major study on maternal mortality rates for the bureau (Oakley 2018, 229). There is a valid reason for remembering such women and their work, as many of them were both social activists and academics, providing a link to Kafer's (2013) queer crip future, or imagined future, when she argues that disability is devoid of feminist crip theory analysis. Kafer identifies this as a methodological problem that can be addressed by inserting such analysis in existing contexts, but in the gaps and spaces where disability is omitted.

Earlier in this text, the absence of disability, of physical frailty, was mentioned in relation to Oakley's sociological account of the period 1880–1920, but it can be assumed that it was embodied by some of the people for whom the early feminist pragmatists did so much knowledge building and activist political work. This work can only be described as political and relational, again a parallel to Kafer's envisaged future scenarios. The root problem, as identified by contemporary feminist pragmatists (Minnich 2005; Anderson 2007), is that beings are divided into ontologically, ethically, politically and epistemologically significant 'kinds', but then one 'kind' is defined to be the norm and the inclusive term and ideal for all. That is a dominance-serving definitional move, which leads directly to faulty generalisations that are perpetuated ad nauseam.

Finally, recognition?

When members from historically powerful academic disciplines denigrate knowledge production from other fields, for example rejecting knowledge due to its being anecdotal and of no significance or validity, it is often done based on hegemonic thinking uncritical of how various types of knowledge production have upheld professional boundaries specific to academic disciplines and recognition by regulatory bodies. The scientific method has been maintained as the gold standard for valid knowledge; all else is dismissed as anecdotal and unworthy of consideration or examination, let alone inclusion into the legitimate body of knowledge of one's own profession. Ableism is deeply rooted in historical and political ignorance of the material realities of disabled people's lives and there is no incentive to examine such ignorance as there are no repercussions. In addition, it serves to uphold historically and politically dominant knowledge systems, perpetuating systems of domination, something that Minnich (2005) identifies as the root problem regarding creating a fairer society in which recognition as envisaged by Fraser (2008) genuinely becomes conceivable.

The organisational framework of academia is not conducive to knowledge production in the spirit of solidarity and collaboration. The excellence framework is devoid of incentives for knowledge based in social realities for the simple reason that it is not produced fast enough to be published in the highest-ranking journals and for a university to maintain its position on prestigious ranking lists, which is exactly what the upholding of knowledge systems means. What I suggest and what the earlier examples describe is that through collaborative projects adhering to a certain standard – i.e. by observing the validity criteria – disabled academics can inhabit spaces in which transformative knowledge production becomes not only possible but a new norm. In order for these new spaces to increase and reach wider circles, knowledge collaboration with grassroot activists can be in many fields, which would be ideal, but the problem remains that the bases for transformation are narrowly defined, as Fraser discovered in the 1980s when she tried to work and write for two different audiences, a circle she found difficult to square.

As far as valid knowledge is concerned – at least, knowledge that the establishment will consider – activism must be fact-based. Again, this mirrors the insight of nineteenth-century feminist pragmatists who rejected unfounded actionism. It would be conducive to change if grassroots knowledge could reach mandatory reading lists and course modules in their respective disciplines. What is required is movement of people into areas of social transformation as envisaged by proponents of action research for the past few decades, or even going back to the early feminist pragmatists of the 1800s, who made a strong case for transcending the private/public sphere divide through thoughtful action-taking paired with academic knowledge.

Intersectional analyses are vital in coming to grips with multiple injustices while working towards creating a fairer society inclusive of disabled people. Such analyses must be effective in that they are clearly defined. It cannot be 'a bit of this, a bit of that' just to pay lip service to 'inclusivity' but must be a methodologically sound undertaking to enable radical objectivity.

Discussion

Gatecrashing connotes a methodological revolution in the sense that not only do we need knowledge built on disability as the norm, but we must also be able as a society to say *why* this is so. Unless we succeed in confidently discussing our knowledge-producing tools (i.e. the methods by which we arrive at our results), and critically examine the criteria based on which we consider knowledge to be reliable and valid, change at the systemic level will remain elusive.

Even in academia, methodology is often conflated with method and, even worse, data collection, which is not only reductive but incorrect. It results in tedious non-dialogue where a medical researcher can claim epistemic superiority over a disabled philosopher when the latter raises issues about the ontology and epistemology of lived experience, while the former insists on being in the right in denying the materiality of the latter's lived experience as a disabled academic. In other words, the different knowledge paradigms are not always conducive to a basic intellectual commonality that would facilitate such a methodological revolution, rendering gatecrashing a necessity. Gatecrashing represents a vision of the right to demand parity of participation in social life, transcending its narrower meaning in a strictly defined political science context and instead encompassing activism (Fraser 2008). This must happen to disrupt the misframing – whether unwitting or not – of disabled academics' realities, a meta-injustice that can have serious repercussions for the possibility to produce and co-produce knowledge in those potentially transformative spaces.

References

Abbott, Andrew. *Chaos of Disciplines*. Chicago: University of Chicago Press, 2001.
Addams, Jane. *Democracy and Social Ethics*. (The Citizen's Library). New York: Macmillan, 1905, originally 1902.
Addams, Jane. *On Education*. Abingdon and New York: Routledge, 2017, originally 1985. Online. https://doi.org/10.4324/9781315125541 (accessed 21 May 2020).
Alphin Jr, Henry C., Lavine, Jennie and Chan, Roy Y. *Disability and Equity in Higher Education Accessibility*. Advances in Educational Marketing Series. Hershey, PA: IGI Global, 2017. Online. https://doi.org/10.4018/978-1-5225-2665-0 (accessed 21 May 2020).
Anderson, Elizabeth. 'Feminist Epistemology and Philosophy of Science'. In *The Stanford Encyclopaedia of Philosophy*, winter 2007 edition, edited by Edward N. Zalta. Stanford, CA: Metaphysics Research Lab, Stanford University. Online. https://plato.stanford.edu/archives/win2007/entries/feminism-epistemology (accessed 21 May 2020).
Becher, Tony and Trowler, Paul. *Academic Tribes and Territories: Intellectual Enquiry and the Culture of Disciplines*. Buckingham: Open University Press, 2001.
Bourdieu, Pierre and Passeron, Jean-Claude. *Reproduction in Education, Society and Culture*. 2nd ed. London: Sage, 1990.
Brown, Nicole and Leigh, Jennifer. 'Ableism in Academia: Where are the Disabled and Ill Academics?' *Disability and Society* 33/6 (2018): 985–9. Online. https://doi.org/10.1080/09687599.2018.1455627 (accessed 19 May 2020).
Brown, Nicole, Thompson, Paul and Leigh, Jennifer S. 'Making Academia More Accessible', *Journal of Perspectives in Applied Academic Practice* 6/2 (2018): 82–90. Online. https://doi.org/10.14297/jpaap.v6i2.348 (accessed 21 May 2020).
Campbell, Anne and Groundwater-Smith, Susan, eds. *An Ethical Approach to Practitioner Research*. Abingdon and New York: Routledge, 2007.
Campbell, Fiona Kumari. *Contours of Ableism: The Production of Disability and Abledness*. Basingstoke and New York: Palgrave Macmillan, 2009.
Chronically Academic. Blog. 2020. Online. https://chronicallyacademic.blogspot.com/ (accessed 21 May 2020).
Delanty, Gerard. *Challenging Knowledge: The University in the Knowledge Society*. Buckingham: Open University Press, 2001.
Dewey, John. *The Public and its Problems*. Athens, OH: Swallow Press, 1927.
Dewey, John. *Experience and Education*. New York: Macmillan, 1938.
Disabled People Against Cuts. 'The History of Disability Activism: Looking Back at how Disabled People have Fought for Change'. 3 July 2018. Online. https://www.voicemag.uk/feature/4160/the-history-of-disability-activism (accessed 22 January 2019).
Duffy, Simon and Perez, Wendy. 'Citizenship for All: An Accessible Guide' [set of PowerPoint slides]. Sheffield: Centre for Welfare Reform, 2014. Online. https://www.centreforwelfarereform.org/uploads/attachment/419/citizenship-for-all-an-accessible-guide.pdf (accessed 21 May 2020).
Fischer, Marilyn, Nackenoff, Carol and Chmielewski, Wendy. *Jane Addams and the Practice of Democracy*. Urbana and Chicago: University of Illinois Press, 2009.
Fraser, Nancy. *Scales of Justice: Reimagining Political Space in a Globalising World*. Cambridge: Polity Press, 2008.
Fraser, Nancy, Dahl, Hanne Marlene, Stoltz, Pauline and Willig, Rasmus. 'Recognition, Redistribution and Representation in Capitalist Global Society: An Interview with Nancy Fraser', *Acta Sociologica* 47/4 (2004): 374–82. Online. https://doi.org/10.1177/0001699304048671 (accessed 21 May 2020).
Fraser, Nancy and Honneth, Axel. *Redistribution or Recognition? A Political-Philosophical Exchange*. London: Verso, 2003.

Gillberg, Claudia. *Transformativa Kunskapsprocessor för Verksamhetsutveckling*. Växjö, Sweden: Växjö University Press, 2009.

Gillberg, Claudia. 'A Methodological Interpretation of Feminist Pragmatism'. In *Contemporary Feminist Pragmatism*, edited by Maurice Hamington and Celia Bardwell-Jones, 217–37. New York: Routledge, 2012.

Gillberg, Claudia. 'Feminism'. In *The Sage Encyclopedia of Action Research*, edited by David Coghlan and Mary Brydon-Miller London: Sage, 2014.

Gillberg, Claudia. 'Working in Knowledge-intensive Organisations when it is Impossible to be Physically Present: Female Employees who Suffer from Chronic Illnesses'. In *Human Resource Management: A Nordic Perspective*, edited by Helene Ahl, Ingela Bergmo-Prvulovic and Karin Kilhammar, 177–89. New York: Routledge, 2018a.

Gillberg, Claudia. 'Feminism and Healthcare: Toward a Feminist Pragmatist Model of Healthcare Provision'. In *Handbook of Research Methods in Health Social Sciences*, edited by P. Liamputtong. Singapore: Springer, 2018b. Online. https://doi.org/10.1007/978-981-10-2779-6_64-1 (accessed 21 May 2020).

Gillberg, Claudia and Jones, Geoffrey. 'Feminism and Healthcare: Toward a Feminist Pragmatist Model of Healthcare Provision'. In *Handbook of Research Methods in Health Social Sciences*, edited by P. Liamputtong. Singapore: Springer, 2019. Online. https://doi.org/10.1007/978-981-10-2779-6_64-2 (accessed 21 May 2020).

Gillberg, Claudia and Pettersson, Andreas (2019). 'Between duty and right: Disabled schoolchildren and teachers' ableist manifestations in Sweden'. *Disability & Society* 34/9-10 (2019): 1668–73. Online. https://doi.org/10.1080/09687599.2019.1630592

Gillies, Donald. 'Knowledge Activism: Bridging the Research/Policy Divide', *Critical Studies in Education* 55/3 (2014): 272–88. Online. https://doi.org/10.1080/17508487.2014.919942 (accessed 21 May 2020).

Goodley, Dan. *Dis/ability Studies: Theorising Disablism and Ableism*. Abingdon and New York: Routledge, 2014.

Goodley, Dan and Moore, Michele. 'Doing Disability Research: Activist Lives and the Academy', *Disability and Society* 15/6 (2000): 861–82. Online. https://doi.org/10.1080/713662013 (accessed 21 May 2020).

Goyal, Nidhi. 'Why Does the Women's Rights Movement Marginalise Women with Disabilities?' *Guardian*, 7 September 2016. Online. https://www.theguardian.com/global-development/2016/sep/07/why-does-womens-rights-movement-marginalise-women-with-disabilities-nidhi-goyal (accessed 3 April 2019).

Hamington, Maurice. 'Jane Addams'. In *Stanford Encyclopedia of Philosophy*, edited by Edward N. Zalta. Stanford, CA: Metaphysics Research Lab, Stanford University, summer 2018 edition. Online. https://plato.stanford.edu/archives/sum2018/entries/addams-jane/ (accessed 22 May 2020).

Hamington, Maurice and Bardwell-Jones, Celia. *Contemporary Feminist Pragmatism*. New York: Routledge, 2012.

Honeyman, Susan. *Child Pain, Migraine, and Invisible Disability*. Abingdon and New York: Routledge, 2016.

Jaitli, Namrata. 'Citizen Participation'. In *The Sage Encyclopedia of Action Research*, edited by David Coghlan and Mary Brydon-Miller, 94–6. Thousand Oaks, CA: Sage, 2014. Online. http://dx.doi.org/10.4135/9781446294406.n49 (accessed 21 May 2020).

Johnson, Kelley and Porter, Sue. 'Disabled People's Organisations'. In *The Sage Encyclopedia of Action Research*, edited by David Coghlan and Mary Brydon-Miller, 270–3. Thousand Oaks, CA: Sage, 2014. Online. http://dx.doi.org/10.4135/9781446294406.n114 (accessed 21 May 2020).

Johnston, Bill, MacNeill, Sheila and Smyth, Keith. (2018). *Conceptualising the Digital University: The Intersection of Policy, Pedagogy and Practice*. Digital Education and Learning. Cham, Switzerland: Palgrave Macmillan. Online. https://doi.org/10.1007/978-3-319-99160-3 (accessed 21 May 2020).

Kadoda, Gada. 'Decolonising African Universities through Transformation into Endogenous Knowledge Producers'. In *Proceedings of 8th International Conference on Appropriate Technology*, Porto-Novo, Benin, 22–5 November 2018. Online. https://tinyurl.com/y7pukcgz (accessed 21 May 2020).

Kafer, Alison. *Feminist, Queer, Crip*. Bloomington: Indiana University Press, 2013.

Liebowitz, Cara. 'DIS Representation: How the Wide Feminist Movement Forgets Disabled Women'. Thebodyisnotanapology.com, 2019. Available at https://thebodyisnotanapology.com/magazine/dis-representation-how-the-wider-feminist-movement-forgets-disabled-women/ (accessed 3 April 2019).
Lister, Ruth. *Citizenship: Feminist Perspectives*. Basingstoke: Palgrave Macmillan, 2003.
Lloyd, Moya. 'The Ethics and Politics of Vulnerable Bodies'. In *Butler and Ethics*, edited by Moya Lloyd, 167–92. Edinburgh: Edinburgh University Press, 2015.
McRuer, Robert. *Crip Theory: Cultural Signs of Queerness and Disability*. New York and London: New York University Press, 2006.
Mann, B.W. 'Rhetoric of Online Disability Activism: #Crip the Vote and Civic Participation', *Communication, Culture and Critique* 11/4 (2018): 604–21. Online. https://doi.org/10.1093/ccc/tcy030 (accessed 21 May 2020).
Marshall, Judi. 'Centre for Action Research and Professional Practice'. In *The Sage Encyclopedia of Action Research*, edited by David Coghlan and Mary Brydon-Miller, 91–2. Thousand Oaks, CA: Sage, 2014. Online. https://dx.doi.org/10.4135/9781446294406.n46 (accessed 21 May 2020).
Minnich, Elizabeth K. *Transforming Knowledge*. Philadelphia: Temple University Press, 2005.
Morley, Louise and Walsh, Val. *Feminist Academics: Creative Agents for Change*. London: Taylor and Francis, 1995.
Morris, Jenny. 'Feminism and Disability', *Feminist Review* 43 (1993): 57–70. Online. https://doi.org/10.1057/fr.1993.4 (accessed 21 May 2020).
Oakley, Ann. *Women, Peace and Welfare: A Suppressed History of Social Reform, 1880–1920*. Bristol: Policy Press, 2018.
Parsons, Talcott. 'The Professions and Social Structure', *Social Forces* 17/4 (1939): 457–67. Online. https://doi.org/10.2307/2570695 (accessed 21 May 2020).
Percy, S.L., Zimpher, N.L. and Brukardt, M.J. *Creating A New Kind of University, Institutionalising Community-University Engagement*. San Francisco: Jossey-Bass, 2006.
Redinger, Michael J., Crutchfield, Parker, Gibb, Tyler S., Longstreet, Peter and Strung, Robert. 'Conversion Disorder Diagnosis and Medically Unexplained Symptoms', *American Journal of Bioethics* 18/5 (2018): 31–3. Online. https://doi.org/10.1080/15265161.2018.1445317 (accessed 21 May 2020).
Reid, Colleen and Gillberg, Claudia. 'Feminist Participatory Action Research'. In *The Sage Encyclopedia of Action Research*, edited by David Coghlan and Mary Brydon-Miller, 343–6. Thousand Oaks, CA: Sage, 2014. Online. http://dx.doi.org/10.4135/9781446294406.n141 (accessed 21 May 2020).
Ryan, Frances. '"It's Not Only Steps That Keep Us Out": Mainstream Feminism Must Stop Ignoring Disabled Women', *New Statesman* 20 May 2014. Online. https://www.newstatesman.com/society/2014/05/its-not-only-steps-keep-us-out-mainstream-feminism-must-stop-ignoring-disabled-women (accessed 2 April 2019).
Schuller, Tom and Watson, David. *Learning Through Life: Inquiry into the Future for Lifelong Learning*. Leicester: National Institute of Adult Continuing Education, 2009.
Shah, Mahsood, Bennett, Anna and Southgate, Erica. *Widening Higher Education Participation, A Global Perspective*. Sawston, Cambridge: Chandos Publishing, 2015.
Sépulchre, Marie. 'Tensions and Unity in the Struggle for Citizenship: Swedish Disability Rights Activists Claim "Full Participation! Now!"', *Disability and Society* 33/4 (2018): 539–61. Online. https://doi.org/10.1080/09687599.2018.1440194 (accessed 21 May 2020).
Syfret, Wendy. 'Disabled Women Are Calling out Australian Feminist Website Destroy the Joint', I-D vice.com, 23 November 2015. Online. https://i-d.vice.com/en_au/article/9kb8kz/disabled-women-are-calling-out-australian-feminist-website-destroy-the-joint (accessed 2 April 2019).
Tremain, Shelley L. *Foucault and Feminist Philosophy of Disability*. Ann Arbor: University of Michigan Press, 2017. Online. https://doi.org/10.3998/mpub.8504605 (accessed 21 May 2020).
Tremain, Shelley L. 'Philosophy of Disability as Critical Diversity Studies', *International Journal of Critical Diversity Studies* 1/1 (2018): 30–44. Online. https://www.academia.edu/37034458/Philosophy_of_Disability_as_Critical_Diversity_Studies (accessed 21 May 2020).
Tremain, Shelley L. 'Feminist Philosophy of Disability: A Genealogical Intervention', *Southern Journal of Philosophy* 57/1 (2019):132–58.

Wendell, Susan. 'Toward a Feminist Theory of Disability', *Hypatia* 4/2 (1989): 104–24. Online. https://doi.org/10.1111/j.1527-2001.1989.tb00576.x (accessed 21 May 2020).

Wendell, Susan. *The Rejected Body: Feminist Philosophical Reflections on Disability*. London and New York: Routledge, 1997.

Whipps, J.D. 'Feminist-Pragmatist Democratic Practice and Contemporary Sustainability Movements'. In *Contemporary Feminist Pragmatism*, edited by Maurice Hamington and Celia Bardwell-Jones, 115–27. New York: Routledge, 2012.

Witz, Anne. *Professions and Patriarchy*, 2nd ed. International Library of Sociology. London and New York: Routledge, 2004.

Yoak, Stuart D. and Brydon-Miller, Mary. 'Ethics and Moral Decision Making'. In *The Sage Encyclopedia of Action Research*, edited by David Coghlan and Mary Brydon-Miller, 306–9. Thousand Oaks, CA: Sage, 2014. Online. http://dx.doi.org/10.4135/9781446294406.n128 (accessed 21 May 2020).

2
I am not disabled: Difference, ethics, critique and refusal of neoliberal academic selves

Francesca Peruzzo

Who is entitled to talk about disability? Does the direct experience of disability entitle self-identified disabled researchers more than non-self-identified researchers to talk about disability? This debate has been running since the 1970s, when disability emerged as a political issue and a matter of social, civil and human rights. With the role of the 'expert' being put into question (Foucault 2006), feminist criticism emphasising the validity of personal experience over 'scientific methods' (Morris 1996), and the critique of ableism as a set of practices that exclude disabled people in academia (Campbell 2001; Brown and Leigh 2018), the voice of disabled scholars on their academic experience of disability has become stronger and stronger.

I bring to this chapter my experience as a researcher who does not identify herself as disabled, yet has been researching disability for more than ten years. By drawing upon post-structural analytical tools (Foucault 1982; Butler 1993) and debates in critical disability studies (Davis 2013; Tremain 2001, 2015; Price and Shildrick 2002), the chapter addresses the work of the non-disabled academic as a necessary critique of ableist assumptions regarding the academic subject in the neoliberal university. In an academia that requires us to make ourselves agile, economical and highly performing to keep up with a national, international and global race on knowledge, non-disabled academics are, in fact, a constitutive part of the discourse of ableism as a new set of truths and power relations regarding what constitutes the academic body.

However, power cannot be exercised without freedom. By engaging with the work of critique as a practice of ethical freedom, this chapter advances disability research in academia as a practice of care located at the subjective limits set by the present ableist condition of neoliberal academia. The ethical work of critique, then, becomes necessary to expose the intolerable exercise of power upon disabled bodies, to refuse the modalities in which ableist truths *make* certain academic subjects, and to redesign academia as a democratic space in which difference is the expression of self-stylisation and co-existence.

In March 2018, I attended the 'Ableism in Academia' conference. As a doctoral researcher in critical disability studies who does not self-identify as disabled, I was eager to be involved in such a crucial space for discussion on ableist, exclusionary processes in academia. The conference could not have been more compelling: in neoliberal times, the number of disabled academic professionals is still very low (3.9 per cent according to HESA statistics in 2017), with disabilities, chronic conditions, invisible illnesses and neurodiversity among academic staff still highly under-represented (Brown and Leigh 2018). The conference was set to draw attention to current ableist processes in academia, defined by 'discrimination in favour of able-bodied people', and then to mobilise the participants and the wider public (the conference was live-streamed and stimulated a lively debate as a Twitter trend) towards the writing of a policy-facing manifesto, which would have challenged 'the existing notions of able-bodied perfection and provide impetus for change' (conference website, http://www.ucl.ac.uk/live/ableism-in-academia-2018).

Following a morning session in which disabled academics shared different stances on ableist processes in academia, in the afternoon a workshop was scheduled to discuss ideas that would have informed the proposed manifesto. We were divided into table-groups and asked to generate practical knowledge by discussing five questions, in which the disabled status constituted the first framework for answers. This fact made me question my place as a researcher who does not self-identified as disabled investigating disability in academia. To what extent is my account valid? How can I position myself in the discursive realm of ableism and disableism in academia? I quickly realised that my questions did not stem from a social justice approach as a matter of identity politics and recognition (Kudlick 2013). Neither were they connected to the insider/outsider divide that critical anthropologists (Britzman 1995; Youdell 2006) challenged. Upholding the co-construction of the researcher and the researched in an attempt to reject objectifying and salvific empowerment strategies (Tamboukou and Ball 2003), I felt that my questions dwelled in a rather under-explored terrain in social sciences and philosophy, swinging between epistemological rejections and ontological stances. Here I was not referring to my subject of research: my feelings were addressing an uneasiness in the construction of my own identity as a non-disabled researcher and my possibility of being, rather than researching, something else.

The terrain of disability has been a contested one since the late 1970s, when disabled activists refused the medical understanding of the experience of disability and divided the biological difference of the impairment from the social construct of disability. Disability became the product of social practices that did not allow for the participation of disabled people in society. Feminist scholarship developed this criticism further, beginning to argue for a more subjective and embodied experience of disability (Morris 1991), which blurred the dyadic division between impairment and disability, and investigated the lived experience of disabled people in their impaired bodies. In a more poststructuralist fashion, authors such as Shildrick (2012), Tremain (2001), Corker (1999) and Thomas (1999) challenged the stark division between disability and impairment, creating parallelisms with the feminist critique of gender and sex. By drawing upon Michel Foucault, Judith Butler and other poststructuralist scholars began to investigate the performative and discursive formation of the nature/culture divide and the operation of power in *creating* certain subjects of ability and disability.

In trying to provide a contingent answer to my questions, in my present chapter, I position myself in this poststructuralist discussion, in which disability becomes fluid, relational, discursive and performative. I place my investigation in the present of academia, in which a neoliberal reason allows for certain contingent truths on disability to be pronounced and performed. Using Foucault's performative and productive notion of power, I see academia as an ontological field of government, intending government as 'not referring only to political structures [...] but] rather, designat[ing] the way in which the conduct of individuals or groups might be directed' (Foucault 1982, 790). Neoliberal academia as a field of government becomes a performative and discursive space in which certain academic subjects and subject positions are formed and reformed (Ball et al. 2012), invited to act, speak, think, produce and behave in modalities informed by an economic reason. The aim is to disentangle the productive relations between power as government, knowledge and ableist truth constitutive of the subject of academia, so as to fight against the market as a site of veridiction on setting the limits of who can be, and be part of, the academic body.

Power, however, can always be applied when freedom is involved. To develop ways of refusing the ableist processes that make up the present neoliberal university and certain disabled subjects of academia, in my last section I show how freedom can inform the role of the academic in ethically engaging with a critique of the limits of our present in academia as a practice of care. Non-disabled academics' practice of critique thus becomes a practice of reflection on their subjective limits, and on the limits of the field in which they work, which is necessary to refuse a neoliberal regime of truth that, through comparative, performative and ableist practices, not only excludes specific modalities of being, but also precludes different ways of engaging with others. By reflecting on the production of ableist processes and subjectivities in academia as limits of our present, the aim of my chapter is to contribute to the fight for diversity in the university, suggesting how non-disabled academics can contribute to the opening up of spaces for academic self-stylisation as ethical engagement with the diversity of human beings (Price and Shildrick 2002). The account of non-disabled academics then becomes as crucial as that of disabled academics in the ethical struggle for freedom in imagining and practising a different academia.

Modernism, postmodernism and the troubled divide

> In the most recent upheaval, the intellectual discovered that the masses no longer need him [sic] to gain knowledge: they know perfectly well, without illusion; they know far better than he [sic] and they are certainly capable of expressing themselves. (Foucault and Deleuze 1977, 207)

'Disability', Lennard Davis (2013, 263) maintains, '[in] its present form as a political and cultural formation has only been around since the 1970s, and has come into some kind of visibility since the late 1980s'. The political and identitarian struggles that characterised those years in the UK brought the social model of disability into existence (Finkelstein 1981; Oliver 1990; Barnes 1991). These struggles were aimed against a capitalist system that excluded people whose bodies could not conform to the requirements of the economic system. Disabled people asked to be recognised as part of society, as a matter of social, civil and human rights against exclusionary processes. Those exclusionary processes produced disability out of the politically, materially and culturally inaccessible environments, and disabled people's struggles broke the gates of enclosed settings such as asylums and questioned the stigma attached to impaired bodies (Goffman 1968). Those categories of classification, created and decided by clinical experts, were based on medical knowledge (see International Classification of Diseases and Related Health Problems, ICD-9; Classification or the International Classification of Impairments, Disability and Handicap, 1980, ICIDH-1), locating disability within the individual and not taking into account disabled people's accounts, nor the context around them. Disabled people embraced this as a question of voice, visibility and empowerment: 'Nothing about us without us', Charlton (1998) affirmed, in a sentence that became the motto of disabled people's struggles for power and recognition. As a consequence, the English social model of disability emerged as grounded in a modernist scholarship in which the dichotomous conception of impairment (biological) and disability (social) constituted the universal grand narrative that described disability as a result of oppressive, external power relations imposed over people with impairments.

A challenge to this binary and superimposed division between impairment and disability came from feminist scholarship. Morris (1991) began to question the clear-cut distinction between impairment and disability by taking into account disabled people's personal and everyday experience of living with impairment. Crow (1996) criticised the lack of consideration that the social model dedicated to embodied pain and struggles linked to the impairment (Shakespeare and Watson 2002). Corker and French (1999) explored the narratives of disabled women and how a universalising approach to disability and impairment had overshadowed disabled women's voices. The emphasis on the validity of personal experience and on individual voices in disability research, the claiming for individual affirmation to be a rightful part of society and the intimate experience of pain and exclusion spurred a consequential question: who better than people that were being disabled by disabling environment and practices, as well as by their bodies and minds (Shakespeare and Watson 2002, 17), could understand and speak about disability?

However, if disability and impairment as theoretical tools were first defined to claim disabled people's political and social rights to be part of a society that excluded certain bodies, they also had a productive and performative effect on people experiencing those exclusions. In fact, political and medical definitions such as disabled, invalid and ill, while being crucial to access resources and services, were also individualising, divisive and performative: they constrained and allowed for recognition and self-recognition of individuals in those specific definitions (Slee 2013; Youdell 2006). Here poststructuralist and postmodern approaches come to help. By rejecting the existence of an inner, personal, individual self, a legacy of the Enlightenment thought, they began to question the role of power and knowledge in the shaping those categories and their *active* formation of subjects and selves.

Poststructuralists defined the subject as constituted by fleeting historically, socially and culturally contingent truths, observing that subjects are always 'multiple, [...] political and bound up in power relations' (St Pierre 2000, 25). Butler's nominalist position contributed to highlighting the performative nature of power and language, in that 'discursive performativity appears to produce that which it names, to enact its own referent, to name and to do, to name and to make. [... G]enerally speaking, a performative functions to produce that which it declares (Butler 1993, 107; quoted in Youdell 2006, 42). Following this perspective, Thomas (1999) argued that the impairment itself was an entity that could exist only in the discourse of disability as a political construction, in which the terminology is political, therefore supported by certain kinds of disciplines, such as sociology and political sciences, in the very same way in which a diagnosis can exist in the domain of medical sciences. Furthermore, Tremain (2001; 2015) pointed out how 'being disabled' needs constant practice to be reaffirmed, inscribing the ontological division between disability and impairment within a discourse of disability, and maintaining that this was a discursive reworking on the body that objectified and created (subjectified) disabled subjects. Therefore, the shift from an oppressive conception of power over disabled bodies, as it was denounced through the social model, came to be redefined in a more productive fashion. Individuals, according to Foucault (1982, 212), are made subjects through the operations of power/knowledge relations, through a

> [F]orm of power [that] applies itself to immediate everyday life which categorizes the individual, marks him by his own individuality, attaches him to his own identity, imposes a law of truth on him which he must recognize and which others have to recognize in him. It is a form of power which makes individuals subjects. (Foucault 1982, 781)

According to poststructuralist approaches, then, disability and disabled subjects became the effects of discursive and performative operations of power and knowledge in mobilising certain truths, which 'work[ed] both in inhibiting and productive ways, implying a play of prescriptions that designate both exclusions and choices' (Foucault 1981 in Hook 2001, 6). Subjects are produced by power, not oppressed by it. As Butler neatly puts it,

> [W]e are used to thinking of power as what presses on the subject from outside […] But if, following Foucault, we understand power as forming the subject as well, as providing the very condition of its existence and the trajectory of its desire, then power is not simply what we oppose but also, in a strong sense, what we depend on for our existence and what we harbour and preserve in the beings that we are. (Butler 1997, 2)

The strategic operations of power and knowledge allow for certain truths to be said on disability and to materialise disabled bodies. Power makes visible (objectifies) certain bodies and creates certain subjects (subjectifies) through 'dividing practices', regulated by the operations of a norm, which separate subjects 'both by a process of division either within himself [sic] or from others' (Foucault 1982; quoted in Rabinow 1984, 8). By normatively separating subjects, power designs limits on bodies, which discursively and performatively materialise a divide between the Same and the Other of ability. These operations of power, shaping contingent truths on bodies, demarcate an inescapable grid in which subjects are relentlessly made and remade according to the contingent, historical and normalising truths of their bodies. The body becomes the limits of our present selves, a 'body totally imprinted by history' (Foucault and Deleuze 1977, 83), in which the performative, the discursive and history write the Same/Other division.

And it is the historicity of truth and the complex reciprocal relations of power upon the body that bring me back to academia and disability. Was my feeling of displacement prompted by the questions in the workshop produced by another re-elaboration of ableist power/knowledge discursive practices in neoliberal academia upon the body of non-disabled researchers? If power relations both create and constrain, materialise and exclude bodies in a mutual and inseparable process, would that mean that non-disabled researchers are discursively formed and exist only through the mutual constitution of disability?

By focusing on the embodiment of disability and the notion of the self, Janet Price and Margrit Shildrick recognised the irrevocable bond that links human bodies as well as the role that ethics play in the definition of that bond. They questioned the binary division that describes approaches in disability studies, rejecting 'the suggestion that disability is not an issue for non-disabled people, and that there is some privileged standpoint from which disabled people alone can speak – as though theirs is the only "authentic" understanding of the specific embodiments in question' (Price and Shildrick 2002, 68). They call for a 'suspension of authority to speak' and explore how the process of recognition of a non-disabled subject can only happen with the re-conjunction with a disabled subject, its Other. This reflection calls for a dual process of critique, by the disabled and the non-disabled academic, as both constitutive of the present of neoliberal academia. The work of critique, Foucault maintains, is in 'the movement by which the subject gives himself [sic] the right to question truth on its effects of power and questions power in its discourses of truth', 'the art of not being governed quite so much' (Foucault 2007, 45–7).

Hence, I want to use my feeling of displacement to address the problematic of the disabled and abled academics divide using critique in a three-fold fashion. First, I operate a diagnosis of the present of neoliberal academia as a point of departure to analyse ableism as a new discursive formation, a new objectifying reworking of power relations over disabled bodies that necessarily situates myself in this continuous discursivity. Disability then becomes problematised as an ontological question, a 'question of what' (Corbetta 2003, 17): what counts as a body in academia, what counts as ability in academia? Second, I use my performed and discursive non-disabled academic position to argue for the reconciliation of disability and ability research in neoliberal times. This is an ethical endeavour that suggests that perhaps a solution to this divide sits exactly in the work of critique of questioning the forms of government that produce disabled and non-disabled academics, forms that emerge from the economy of power/knowledge relations that sustains the present condition of academia. 'This history of the present', O'Farrell (2005, 72) maintains, 'is not simply a diagnosis, it is also an intervention [...] it is only in the present that one can make changes'. Third and last, I use the work of critique of non-disabled researchers to engage with a critical and ethical practice on the limits that neoliberal academia writes on their bodies and selves. It is only by doing so that certain ways of being made and spoken as able and disabled academic subjects can be jointly refused, being 'guided by a concern for freedom as requiring an endless exploration of the possibilities for the always-to-be-reinvented activity of individual and collective self-creation' (Burchell 1996, 34).

The limits of the academic body: A history of the present of academia

> The question I start off with is: what are we and what are we today? What is this instant that is ours? Therefore, if you like, it is a history that starts off this present day actuality. (Foucault 1988, 411)

The work of critique starts with a question of the present. What is disability in academia today? As Eggins explains, the current higher education situation sees

> [O]n the one hand, the pull towards co-operation, social cohesion, social harmony, transparency, equity and to enabling greater numbers to participate in higher education. On the other hand are the financial issues, the neo-liberal agenda that calls for competition, free trade, the dominance of the market. The flows of change move first one way, then in another: equity, inequality, convergence, divergence; change, non-change; inclusion, exclusion; the global, the local. (Eggins 2003, 8; quoted in Riddell 2005, 12)

While practices of inclusion were promoted as a means for cohesion and recognition of diversity in higher education, a discursive and performative reworking of individualising and divisive practices were perpetrated through neoliberalism as a new regime of truths. Neoliberalism is 'a complex, often incoherent, unstable and even contradictory set of practices that are organized around a certain imagination of the "market" as a basis for the universalisation of market-based social relations, with the corresponding penetration in almost every single aspect of our lives' (Shamir 2008; quoted in Ball 2012b, 3). Competition subsumes the principle of exchange constitutive of classical liberalism (Burchell 1996; Ball and Olmedo 2013), rewriting the way in which the state operates within the university as well as how academics work in universities. 'Central to this neoliberal view of higher education is a market-driven paradigm' (Giroux 2014, 17) that, through international classifications and comparisons, let a new academic normal emerge: the institution that can keep up with a potentially limitless race of rankings and performance rates, and consequently the academic subject that is suitable to be part of this institutional race. Comparisons – systems for assessing the quality of research and teaching in UK higher education institutions such as the Research Excellence Framework (REF) and the Teaching Excellence Framework (TEF) – as materialisations of institutional and self-control operate in there, in the institutional structure and administration, as well in here (cf. Peck and Tickell 2002) in the way in which I am made an academic, in which I marketise my being academic. In an age of cuts, being economical has become an imperative and a new form of government, promoting a sort of enterprise form of governing institutions and ourselves. 'Economical' here has a double meaning: 'economical' in terms of time, resources to invest; in terms of autonomy, a frugal, cheap academic suitable for these austere times; as well as 'economical' in terms of calculability, able to make the institution and oneself visible on the academic market, in order to be calculable, and therefore comparable.

The institution makes itself attractive, concerning funding, resources, customers/students and attention, and simultaneously asks us to make ourselves agile (Gillies 2011), marketisable, highly performative and presentable. The history of the present of academia is a regime of truth in which the market is the site of veridiction (Foucault 2008), in which a technology of performativity controls people's government by means of comparisons and judgements (Ball 2003), in which individualisation is bound up with performance and with a certain kind of quality, the quantifiable quality (the more I do, the higher the quality bar; Lazzarato 2009). That is an outstanding output! We are produced by discourses of academic excellence, impact and productivity; we are again animated by power, not oppressed (Ball 2012a). There is a 're-invention of professionals themselves as units of resource whose performance and productivity must constantly be audited so that it can be enhanced' (Shore and Wright 1999; quoted in Ball 2012a, 18). In today's fast-paced academia, in which numbers are the best means of visibility and each piece of in-line production has been substituted by a new (REF-*able*) publication, new ways of representing impact, new modalities of marketising ourselves and therefore benefiting the institution invite a new involvement with ourselves and a reconceptualisation of abilities. This calcul-*ability* of ourselves clashes when 'the measured pace of research sometimes impacts quantity, but not necessarily the quality of the work' (Kosanic et al. 2018). We should make ourselves 'more calculable than memorable' (Ball 2012a, 17).

In fact, 'the price of this involvement' is that we 'must assume active responsibility for these activities, [...] and in so doing [we] are required to conduct [our]selves in accordance with appropriate (or approved) models of action' (Burchell 1996, 29). Being able becomes a new requirement for being in academia, a new set of practices mobilised by performative relations of power informed by an economic reason. Ability becomes a discourse of efficiency, fashioning our bodies and getting into 'our minds and our souls, into the ways in which we think about what we do, and into our social relations with others' (Ball 2012a, 18). The discourse of ability creates a new normal, able Same, and an abnormal, non-able Other; it operates new dividing practices upon certain bodies; it reproduces new exclusions and new subjects.

This new ableist normal Same in academia becomes what Butler describes as the *we*, which 'instrumentalizes violence to maintain the appearance of its collectivity' (Butler 2005, 4–5). The institutional we is the new neoliberal *academic body*, cheerful, *show yourself happy to be here*, healthy – *sickness slows you down* – productive – *how many papers this year? Oh look, your citation index has gone up!* – attractive – *make funds come to you*, agile – *flexi-hours*, malleable – *flexi-morals*. And by defining the able *we* of academia, the discourse of ableism casts again new forms of exclusions, operating as

> [A] network of beliefs, processes and practices that produces a particular kind of self and body (the corporeal standard) that is projected as the perfect, species-typical and therefore essential and fully human. Disability is then cast as a diminished state of being human. (Campbell 2001, 44)

Neoliberal academia and the discourse of ableism are drawing new limits on bodies. The divisive operations of power in terms of 'losers and winners' produced by this regime of performativity and competition open up for statements to be pronounced and for actions to be performed as 'violence against [what it defines and makes] disabled bodies' (McGuire 2010, 13), producing new forms of marginalisation. Ableism creates new visibilities and allows only certain subjectivities to be visible. The only way in which neoliberal academia *enables* subjects to be part of the *academic body* is by being high-performing and marketisable, casting outside subjects that are not 'economic', not calculable enough, not able enough.

The point of departure, then, for the critique of academia as being ableist is exactly the place in which the recognition of a subject that identifies and is identified as disabled dissatisfies the possibilities for being in academia, allowing us to interrogate the available norms that make academia.

However, as Foucault reminds us, the work of critique 'is not so much a matter of what we are undertaking, more or less courageously, than it is the idea we have of our knowledge and its limits' (Foucault 2007, 49). The work of dividing practices in a discourse of ableism in academia, and their formation of certain academic subjects, also constrains what non-disabled academics can become in academia. 'What can I become, given the contemporary order of being?' Butler (2005, 24) defiantly asks. The only Other that non-disabled academics can become in the present academia is an able Other. The neoliberal order conditions possibilities of becoming. Academics can only become more successful, *more winner*; they cannot be anything else. To reinstate my ableist condition, I need to relentlessly perform my ableist performance against a disableist one, as there is no Same without the Other. If I cannot become anything else, and the only thing my Other can do is to strive to become the Same – what Campbell (2009) defines as 'internalised ableism' – then this condition constitutes a problem of ethics as well as of responsibility towards my Other. The ground in which *the we* can be reunited is the violence that neoliberal academia produces in subjects of measurement and comparisons, in the marketisation of bodies. And here it is no longer a question of recognition; it becomes a question of refusal of forms of subjectification, a reconciliation of disability as two forms of government sustained by the neoliberal regime of truth in academia. Researching disability by non-disabled academics becomes, then, an endeavour on the limits of present academia, denouncing its exclusionary processes, as well as a way of freeing bodies by the only way they could operate: by being able. And here I go back to my previous question, to begin to provide an answer to it. The sense of displacement that I felt during the 'Ableism in Academia' conference was provoked by the materialisation of my limits in academia, and by a feeling of the impossibility of being something different. I found myself 'other to myself precisely at the place where I expect to be myself' (Butler 2004; quoted in Ball 2012a, 19).

And it is from this position, from this feeling of uneasiness, loss, discomfort and impossibility, that I want to find a reconciliation of being, refusing to be made, spoken, constrained and animated in certain ways as an academic subject. The work of critique is the one that 'would ensure the desubjugation of the subject in the course of what we could call, in a word, the politics of truth' (Foucault 2007, 47). By researching disability in academia, I am researching my Other, my limits, which are an indissoluble part of my self, but that can also allow me *to go beyond myself*, as an insistence of thinking lived presents and imagined futures differently in academia (Kafer 2013).

Through the work of ethics, we can develop a process of becoming something different altogether or, perhaps, just becoming together. It is a concern for co-existence (cf. Burchell 1996). Thinking in this way, we can *make* ourselves freer than we think, as 'imminent ontolog[ies]' (Bailey 2013, 812) that are always in the process of being made and remade. Therefore, in the final part of my chapter I talk to power, and I argue for an ethical approach to researching neoliberal academia by disabled and able researchers as a space for the re-conjunction of the *we*, so as to constitute an analytical process from which 'we can develop a position […] to look and notice – to "live with" one another – differently' (McGuire 2010).

Going beyond and caring: The ethical refusal of neoliberal academic subjective limits

> [I]n the historically contingent limits of present thought and action, attention is drawn to what might be called the costs of these limits: what does it cost existence for this truth to be produced and affirmed in this way? What other possibilities of existence are necessarily excluded, condemned, constrained, etc.? (Burchell 1996, 33)

In my last section, I want to try to trace what could be a contingent, ethical, political escape from the relentless entanglement of power/knowledge networks and the constitution of prescriptive subjectivities. I will start from the freedom that is descriptive of the liberal and neoliberal styles of government. 'Power', Foucault maintains, 'is exercised only over free subjects, and insofar as they are free' (Foucault 1982, 790). The kind of freedom that Foucault talks about is not in a zero-sum game with power. It is a freedom that opens up new modalities of living, that calls for experimentation, that attends to our present while pointing at our possibilities of change, of being freer than we think. Here I need to remark on a difference in the word 'power' that exists in French but not in English. Foucault distinguishes between *pouvoir* (subjectification/*assujettissement*) and *puissance* (subjectivation). While the first term means 'power over' and is linked to relations of domination and subjection, the second means 'power to', entailing capacities for self-creation and desubjectification (Milchman and Rosemberg 2011). By considering power as 'power to', then, a different engagement with our subjectivities is possible, grounding the conditions for change in the economic, social, cultural and political conditions in which we find ourselves. This conception, then, moves beyond just resisting the present situation in academia. As Foucault militantly suggests,

> [M]aybe the target nowadays is not to discover what we are but to refuse what we are. We have to imagine and to build up what we could be to get rid of this kind of political 'double bind', which is the simultaneous individualization and totalization of modern power structures. (Foucault 1982, 785)

This implies not refusing neoliberalism *in itself*, and therefore a pre-existing neoliberal subject, but *of itself*, refusing how this present manifestation of neoliberal reason is making ourselves able subjects of academia (power exerted upon bodies). By considering power as an ethical practice aimed at self-stylising our bodies in the present, we can strive to escape the tale of progress that preaches the future as better than the 'now'. In fact, the operations of power/knowledge in a new discourse of ableism are the manifestation of the reworkings of power, proving how the future is not necessarily better than either the past or the present. And we must challenge these relentless power/knowledge operations.

This ethical practice of self-stylisation of subjects is discussed in Foucault's later work. By drawing upon Foucault's ethical account, Oksala defines ethics as 'the manner in which one forms oneself as a subject of a morality, acting in reference to its prescriptive elements; the modes by which subjects problematize their activity' (Oksala 2005, 158). Challenging the regime of truth that governs academia, and that makes academia what it is, means to call into question the truths about myself, as 'any relation to the regime of truth will at the same time be a relation to myself' (Butler 2005, 22). And these truths open a political space in the reflection on the self, with 'ethics [being] the considered form that freedom takes when it is informed by reflection' (Foucault, 1997, 284), transforming subjectivity into a practical process of becoming (Tamboukou and Ball 2003), a practice of care, more about 'what I do' than 'what I am'. As a non-disabled academic in neoliberal academia, what kind of academic do I want to become? How can I care for myself as an academic and necessarily for the community of academics that constitutes the space in which I work, am, belong and become? It is the problematisation of what non-disabled academics do and of the limits of their activity in academia that can open up a critique of the present and different possibilities of becoming. However, this implies adopting 'an attitude, an ethos, a philosophical life in which what we are is at one and the same time the historical analysis of the limits that are imposed upon us and an experiment in going beyond them' (Foucault; quoted in Rabinow 1984, 50).

In fact, it is on these limits that I always encounter my Other, and the endless modalities through which I can become other. This process of self-formation 'is ethical itself, but it implies complex relationships with the others insofar as this ethos of freedom is also a way of caring for others' (Foucault 2000, 288). The care for the other is an integral part of the self I was, I am and I will become, therefore 'who I am affects another's self-construction' (Infinito 2003, 156). This ethical practice of freedom and reflection is, therefore, indissolubly individual and collective. Caring for the self becomes a present concern for the others, both through the refusal of institutional practices and because the Other is a constitutive part of what I am. Caring for the others becomes caring for myself and for what I can become. In this way, this approach to ethics eliminates the binary division through ability and disability.

The work of critique starts with the practice of reflection on my and therefore our limits, the work of critique on myself as a practice of care of what academia has made me become, how I am made to use *my* freedom, which is a shared struggle on the ground of neoliberal inequities of the academic race to excellence and quality. Performativity constructs the self against our Other's self, rather than with it, not only limiting our imagination, but also preventing us from becoming together. While through this ethical work on ourselves we explore the ways in which we can self-stylise our academic subjectivity, it also has implications not only for those with whom we share our academic life, but also what academia represents for our present, what kind of citizens we want to become and what community of citizens we want to live with. The academic must act, and act precisely insofar as they are both an academic and a citizen (cf. Foucault 2010). And insofar as caring for myself and others is a political action, researching disability becomes a democratic task.

> [T]he agonistic character of democracy upon which Foucault insisted [...] opens a path to a politics of care of self and care of others by its constant effort to expand the scope for new modes of subjectivity, by creating the space for the flourishing of a multiplicity of arts of living. A democratic politics would maximize those spaces, and provide a critique of all those practices and discourses that seek to homogenize subjectivity, to make it uniform, and to narrow the scope of freedom. (Milchman and Rosenberg 2011, 12)

The non-disabled researcher, then, by means of self-critique works on an ethical endeavour that 'emerges at the limits of our schemes of intelligibility, the site in which we ask ourselves what it might mean to continue in a dialogue where no common ground can be assumed' (Butler 2005, 21). Self-stylisation necessarily leaves us without a common ground, without a norm to fashion our practices and subjectivities, but it gives us a much greater thing: the respect for the myriad modalities in which we can become, which can actually be practised as a radical democratic project that provides the basis for imagining a life beyond the dreamworld of capitalism' (Giroux 2014, 12). This suggests collectively embarking on the creation of academic and public spaces in which neoliberalism can be challenged and refused, and bodies can be restyled, become together and co-exist. These practices of refusal cannot happen if both non-disabled and disabled academics questions disability and ability in academia. As Giroux powerfully reminds us,

> [C]onnective ties are essential for developing intellectual practices that are collegial rather than competitive, refuse the instrumentality and privileged isolation of the academy, link critical thought to a profound impatience with the status quo, and connect human agency to the idea of social responsibility and the politics of possibility. (Giroux 2014, 23–4)

I hope my words stimulate a pause, a process of reflection on what we are and what we might become in academia, beginning now with a political refusal of a discourse of ableism that inhibits practices of care for ourselves and others in neoliberal academia. This statement defiantly challenges the idea that 'performance has no room for caring' (Ball 2003, 224), suggesting how the academic should act as a means for caring for the creation of a space in which we all, as part of an academic community, can imagine endless modalities in which we can become, co-exist, research and care.

Conclusion: What's the voice of the non-disabled academic?

In this chapter, I explored the discursive and performative formation of disablism and ableism in academia, and I suggested the ethical work of critique and reflection as a modality to care for myself and for others and to refuse the limits that neoliberal academia places on our bodies. Going back to those questions for the manifesto that left me with a feeling of helpless exclusion, I can now say that they sit precisely in this use of critique: they were guided by a concern for freedom and care. They showed me my limits and made me question the limits of the community to which I feel I belong and I care for.

To conclude, I want to consider how Foucault's work of critique can contribute to the 'working within to go beyond' the dichotomous division between ability and disability in neoliberal academia. Foucault's tools do not provide answers or solutions to the relentless practices of self-division and subjectification. However, as I have argued in this chapter, his tools can allow for a critical engagement with the limits of the academic dispositif, the 'arrangement of elements and forces, practices and discourses, power and knowledge' (Foucault 2008, xxiii) that make up the current neoliberal university and constitutive of those feelings of exclusion and discomfort that I experienced during the workshop on 'Ableism in Academia'. To embrace Foucault's ethical and analytical tools implies dissecting our present in academia: challenging, fashioning and reworking ourselves through positive practices of freedom and self-stylisation, and realising that the only way in which we can be done and undone by our other(s) is by refusing the marketisation of bodies and knowledge. And this can only happen by modifying our relation to the present as a practice of care. For this exact reason, this chapter calls for the work of non-disabled academics in disability studies as a necessary practice of critique of the limits of neoliberal academia, as a practice of care of their selves, and for the selves of other academics – both the ones they share their space and knowledge with, and those who are excluded by the neoliberal discourse of ableism. This is a practice that necessarily needs to be conducted together.

Foucault's tools, then, can be deployed to take the accounts of non-disabled academics and, through critique and reflection, introduce different ways of asking questions and invent 'new rules for the game of truth in relation to which we conduct ourselves individually and collectively' (Burchell 1996, 34). They can open new spaces for the democratic self-stylisation of academic bodies, making the production of knowledge and selves an exploration of the endless possibilities in which we can as individuals and as a collectivity reinvent ourselves.

References

Bailey, Patrick L. J. 'The Policy Dispositif: Historical Formation and Method', *Journal of Education Policy* 28/6 (2013): 807–27. Online. https://doi.org/10.1080/02680939.2013.782512 (accessed 21 May 2020).

Ball, Stephen J. 'The Teacher's Soul and the Terrors of Performativity', *Journal of Education Policy* 18/2 (2003): 215–28. Online. https://doi.org/10.1080/0268093022000043065 (accessed 21 May 2020).

Ball, Stephen J. 'Performativity, Commodification and Commitment: An I-Spy Guide to the Neoliberal University'. *British Journal of Educational Studies* 60/1 (2012a): 17–28. Online. https://doi.org/10.1080/00071005.2011.650940 (accessed 21 May 2020).

Ball, Stephen J. *Global Education INC. New Policy Networks and the Neo-liberal Imaginary*. Abingdon and New York: Routledge, 2012b.

Ball, Stephen J., Maguire, Meg and Braun, Annette. *How Schools do Policy: Policy Enactments in Secondary Schools*. Abingdon and New York: Routledge, 2012.

Ball, Stephen J. and Olmedo, Antonio. 'Care of the Self, Resistance and Subjectivity Under Neoliberal Governmentalities', *Critical Studies in Education*, 54/1 (2013): 85–96. Online. https://doi.org/10.1080/17508487.2013.740678 (accessed 21 May 2020).

Barnes, Colin. *Disabled People in Britain and Discrimination*. London: Hurst, 1991.

Britzman, Deborah P. '"The Question of Belief": Writing Poststructural Ethnography', *Qualitative Studies in Education* 8/3 (1995): 229–38. Online. https://doi.org/10.1080/0951839950080302 (accessed 21 May 2020).

Brown, Nicole and Leigh, Jennifer. 'Ableism in Academia: Where are the Disabled and Ill Academics?' *Disability and Society* 33/6 (2018): 985–9. Online. https://doi.org/10.1080/09687599.2018.1455627 (accessed 19 May 2020).

Burchell, Graham. 'Liberal Government and the Techniques of the Self'. In *Foucault and Political Reason*, edited by Andrew Barry, Thomas Osborne and Nikolas Rose, 19–36. Abingdon: Routledge, 1996.

Butler, Judith. *Bodies that Matter*. London: Routledge, 1993.

Butler, Judith. *The Psychic Life of Power*. Stanford, CA: Stanford University Press, 1997.

Butler, Judith. *Giving an Account of Oneself*. New York: Fordham University Press, 2005.

Campbell, Fiona Kumari. 'Inciting Legal Fictions: "Disability's" Date with Ontology and the Ableist Body of the Law', *Griffith Law Review* 10/1 (2001): 42–62.

Campbell, Fiona Kumari. *Contours of Ableism: The Production of Disability and Abledness*. Basingstoke and New York: Palgrave Macmillan, 2009.

Charlton, James I. *Nothing About Us Without Us: Disability Oppression and Empowerment*. Berkeley: University of California Press, 1998.

Corbetta, Piergiorgio. La icercar sociale: metodologia e tecniche. I. I paradigm di riferimento. Bologna: Il Mulino, 2003.

Corker, Mairian. 'Differences, Conflations and Foundations: The Limits to 'Accurate' Theoretical Representation of Disabled People's Experience?' *Disability and Society* 14/5 (1999): 627–42. Online. https://doi.org/10.1080/09687599925984 (accessed 19 May 2020).

Corker, Mairian and French, Sally, eds. *Disability Discourse*. Buckingham: Open University Press, 1999.

Crow, Liz. 'Including All of Our Lives'. In *Encounters with Strangers: Feminism and Disability*, edited by Jenny Morris. London: Women's Press, 1996.

Davis, Lennard J. 'The End of Identity Politics: On Disability as an Unstable Category'. In *The Disability Studies Reader*, 4th ed., 263–77. New York: Routledge, 2013.

Eggins, H., ed. *Globalization and Reform in Higher Education*. Maidenhead: Society for Research in Higher Education and Open University Press, 2003.

Finkelstein, Vic. 'To Deny or Not to Deny Disability'. In *Handicap in a Social World*, edited by A. Brechin, P. Liddiard and J. Swain, 34–6. Sevenoaks: Hodder and Stoughton, 1981.

Foucault, M. 'The Order of Discourse'. In *Untying the Text: A Post-structural Anthology*, edited by R. Young, 48–78. Boston: Routledge and Kegan Paul, 1981.

Foucault, Michel. 'The Subject and Power', *Critical Inquiry*, 8/4 (1982): 777–96. Online. https://doi.org/10.1086/448181 (accessed 19 May 2020).

Foucault, Michel. 'What Our Present Is'. In *Foucault Live (Interviews, 1961–1984)*, edited by Sylvère Lotringer, 407–15. New York: Semiotext(e), 1988.

Foucault, Michel. 'The Ethics of the Concern of the Self as a Practice of Freedom', in *Ethics: Subjectivity and Truth: Essential Works of Foucault, 1954–1984*, vol. 1, edited by P. Rabinow, 281–302. New York: The New Press, 1997.

Foucault, Michel. 'The Ethics of the Concern of the Self as a Practice of Freedom'. In *Ethics, Subjectivity and Truth: Essential Works of Foucault, 1954–1984*, vol. 1, edited by P. Rabinow. London: Penguin, 2000.

Foucault, Michel. *Psychiatric Power: Lectures at the Collège de France, 1973–74*, edited by Jacques Lagrange. Basingstoke and New York: Palgrave Macmillan, 2006.

Foucault, Michel. 'What is Critique?' In *The Politics of Truth*, 2nd ed., edited by Sylvère Lotringer, 41–81. Cambridge, MA: MIT Press, 2007.

Foucault, Michel. *The Birth of Biopolitics. Lectures at the Collège de France, 1978–79*, edited by Michel Senellart. Basingstoke and New York: Palgrave Macmillan, 2008.

Foucault, Michel. *The Government of Self and Others. Lectures at the Collège the France, 1982–83*, edited by Frédéric Gros. Basingstoke and New York: Palgrave Macmillan, 2010.

Foucault, Michel and Deleuze, Gilles. 'Intellectuals and Power'. In *Language, Counter-memory, Practice: Selected Essays and Interviews*, edited by Donald F. Bouchard 205–17. Ithaca: Cornell University Press, 1977.

Gillies, Donald. 'Agile Bodies: A New Imperative in Neoliberal Governance', *Journal of Education Policy* 26/2 (2011): 207–23. Online. https://doi.org/10.1080/02680939.2010.508177 (accessed 22 May 2020).

Giroux, Henry A. 'The Swindle of Democracy in the Neoliberal University and the Responsibility of Intellectuals', *Democratic Theory* 1/1 (2014): 9–37. Online. https://doi.org/10.3167/dt.2014.010102 (accessed 22 May 2020).

Goffman, Erving. *Stigma: Notes on the Management of Spoiled Identity*. London: Penguin Books (1968, originally 1963).

HESA (Higher Education Statistics Agency). Online. https://www.hesa.ac.uk/data-and-analysis (accessed 22 June 2020).

Hook, Derek. 'Discourse, Knowledge, Materiality, History: Foucault and Discourse Analysis', *Theory and Psychology* 11/4 (2001): 521–47.

Infinito, Justen. 'Ethical Self-formation: A Look at the Later Foucault', *Educational Theory* 53/2 (2003): 155–71. Online. https://doi.org/10.1111/j.1741-5446.2003.00155.x (accessed 22 May 2020).

Kafer, Alison. *Feminist, Queer, Crip*. Bloomington: Indiana University Press, 2013.

Kosanic, A., Hansen, N., Zimmermann-Janschitz, S. and Chouinard V. 'Researchers With Disabilities in the Academic System', *American Association of Geographers*, 1 September 2018. Online. http://news.aag.org/2018/09/researchers-with-disabilities-in-the-academic-system/ (accessed 29 April 2019).

Kudlick, Catherine. 'Comment: On the Borderland of Medical and Disability History', *Bulletin of the History of Medicine* 87/4 (2013): 540–59. Online. https://doi.org/10.1353/bhm.2013.0086 (accessed 22 May 2020).

Lazzarato, Maurizio. 'Neoliberalism in Action: Inequality, Insecurity and the Reconstitution of the Social' *Theory, Culture and Society* 26/6 (2009): 109–33. Online. https://doi.org/10.1177/0263276409350283 (accessed 22 May 2020).

McGuire, Anne. 'Disability, Non-disability and the Politics of Mourning: Reconceiving the "We"', *Disability Studies Quarterly* 30/3/4 (2010). Online. http://dx.doi.org/10.18061/dsq.v30i3/4.1282 (accessed 22 May 2020).

Milchman, Alan and Rosenberg, Alan. 'Michel Foucault. An Ethical Politics of Care of Self and Others'. In *Political Philosophy in the Twentieth Century: Authors and Arguments*, edited by Catherine H. Zuckert. Cambridge: Cambridge University Press, 2011. Online. https://doi.org/10.1017/CBO9781139028530.016 (accessed 22 May 2020).

Morris, Jenny. *Pride against Prejudice*. London: Women's Press, 1991.

Morris, Jenny, ed. *Encounters with Strangers: Feminism and Disability*. London: Women's Press, 1996.

O'Farrell, Clare. *Michel Foucault*. London: Sage, 2005. Online. http://dx.doi.org/10.4135/9781446218808 (accessed 22 May 2020).

Oksala, Johanna. *Foucault on Freedom*. Cambridge: Cambridge University Press, 2005. Online. https://doi.org/10.1017/CBO9780511597923 (accessed 22 May 2020).

Oliver, Michael. *The Politics of Disablement*. Basingstoke: Macmillan, 1990.

Peck, Jamie and Tickell, Adam. 'Neoliberalizing Space', *Antipode* 34/3 (2002): 380–404. Online. https://doi.org/10.1111/1467-8330.00247 (accessed 22 May 2020).

Price, Janet and Shildrick, Margrit. 'Bodies Together: Touch, Ethics and Disability'. In *Disability/Postmodernity: Embodying Disability Theory*, edited by Mairian Corker and Tom Shakespeare, 63–75. London: Continuum, 2002.

Rabinow, Paul. *The Foucault Reader*. New York: Pantheon Books, 1984.

Riddell, Sheila, Tinklin, Teresa and Wilson, Alastair. *Disabled Students in Higher Education: Perspectives on Widening Access and Changing Policy*. London: Routledge, 2005.

Shakespeare, Tom and Watson, Nicholas. 'The Social Model of Disability: An Outdated Ideology?' In *Exploring Theories and Expanding Methodologies: Where We Are and Where We Need To Go* (Research in Social Science and Disability, vol. 2), edited by S.N. Barnartt and B.M. Altman, 9–28. Bingley: Emerald, 2002. Online. https://doi.org/10.1016/S1479-3547(01)80018-X (accessed 22 May 2020).

Shamir, R. 'The Age of Responsibilization: On Market-embedded Morality', *Economy and Society* 37/1 (2008), 1–19.

Shildrick, Margrit. 'Critical Disability Studies: Rethinking the Conventions for the Age of Postmodernity'. In *Routledge Handbook of Disability Studies*, edited by Nick Watson, Alan Roulstone and Carol Thomas, 30–41. London and New York: Routledge, 2012.

Shore, C. and Wright, S. 'Audit Culture and Anthropology: Neo-liberalism in British Higher Education', *Journal of the Royal Anthropological Institute* 5/4 (1999): 557–75.

Slee, Roger. 'How Do We Make Inclusive Education Happen When Exclusion is a Political Predisposition?' *International Journal of Inclusive Education* 17/8 (2013): 895–907. Online. https://doi.org/10.1080/13603116.2011.602534 (accessed 22 May 2020).

St Pierre, Elizabeth Adams. 'The Call for Intelligibility in Postmodern Educational Research', *Educational Researcher* June–July (2000): 25–8. Online. https://doi.org/10.3102/0013189X029005025 (accessed 22 May 2020).

Tamboukou, Maria and Ball, Stephen J. *Dangerous Encounters: Genealogy and Ethnography*. New York: Peter Lang, 2003.

Thomas, Carol. *Female Forms: Experiencing and Understanding Disability*. Buckingham: Open University Press, 1999.

Tremain, Shelley. 'On the Government of Disability', *Social Theory and Practice* 27/4 (2001): 617–36. Online. https://doi.org/10.5840/soctheorpract200127432 (accessed 22 May 2020).

Tremain, Shelley, ed. *Foucault and the Government of Disability*. Ann Arbor: University of Michigan Press, 2015. Online. https://doi.org/10.3998/mpub.8265343 (accessed 22 May 2020).

Youdell, Deborah. *Impossible Bodies, Impossible Selves: Exclusions and Student Subjectivities*. Dordrecht: Springer, 2006. Online. https://doi.org/10.1007/1-4020-4549-2 (accessed 22 May 2020).

3
Disclosure in academia: A sensitive issue

Nicole Brown

In an age where social activist movements for increased awareness and tolerance are commonplace, it is interesting to observe that there are still huge gaps in our knowledge and experience. The social model of disability (Oliver 2013) has certainly helped develop the understanding that disabilities are not 'a person's fault' but a matter of and for society and societal values. In the last decade there has been an increased interest in making public life more accessible. In the United Kingdom this is evidenced in initiatives such as the 'offer me a seat' campaign (Transport for London n.d.), the Accessible Travel Policy (Office of Rail and Road 2019) and the widening of the blue badges system (BBC News, 15 June 2019). Conversations on social media, however, highlight that despite the increased awareness relating to the experiences of the disabled, chronically ill and/or neurodiverse, misconceptions and misunderstandings still prevail, leading to fundamental crises for individuals (BBC News, 15 January, 7 August, 19 November 2018; Coleman 2018; Rimmer 2019).

In this chapter, I draw on my research into academics' lived experience of illness to consider individuals' sensitivities and the sensibility required in communicating with disabled, chronically ill and/or neurodiverse academics. I commence this chapter with a brief introduction to the research upon which this chapter is based. Subsequently, drawing on the research data analysis and using specific examples from the research, I focus on sensitivity demanded of all of us. I discuss sensitivity around our use of language and individuals' experiences of illness that may directly impact conversations and or processes, such as the research on hand. Further, I highlight how sensitivity helps deepen understanding when considering the situation of those needing to disclose a disability or illness, or more specifically an invisible, potentially contested condition. Finally, I emphasise the need for sensitivity in relation to the emotional labour involved in being ill and/or disabled.

The construction of academic identity under the influence of fibromyalgia

The premise of this research project was the understanding that illness and/or disability as a lived experience impacts a person's understanding of self and thus will influence their construction of their academic identity. The focus on fibromyalgia is particularly pertinent, as fibromyalgia as a condition is contested. Fibromyalgia is characterised by chronic, widespread pain, fatigue, sleep disturbances, cognitive dysfunctions (often described as 'brain fog' or 'fibro fog'), increased sensitivity and psychological disorders (White and Harth 2001) and it is associated with a wide range of somatic symptoms (Wolfe et al. 2010). The range of symptoms on its own makes the condition difficult to grasp. Moreover, fibromyalgia symptoms typically wax and wane, change and move. These shifts of kinds of symptoms, their distribution and their severity happen over the space of longer periods such as months and weeks, but often occur within days or even hours. A person with fibromyalgia may get up early in the morning struggling to move for the pain, but then several hours later may be well enough to engage in exercise programmes, work routines or other everyday activities, only for the body to then crash under the strain, to the point where the person will experience debilitating fatigue and pain, sometimes for several days before getting better again. Therein lies the main problem for individuals diagnosed with fibromyalgia. The lack of a definite process for diagnosis and the variability of the condition make it a doubtful and contested condition within the medical professions, too (Ehrlich 2003; Wolfe 2009; Mengshoel et al. 2018; Häuser and Fitzcharles 2018).

For this research, I recruited 28 academics from all career stages who had been diagnosed with fibromyalgia. Academic roles ranged from early-career researchers currently undertaking their PhD studies, via mid-career academic practitioners and lecturers, to professors in later career stages. Participants' working conditions ranged from independent research positions and self-employment to hourly paid lecturers and those in part- and full-time employment in further education and higher education contexts. The fibromyalgia diagnosis as inclusion criterion was more clearly defined and led to fewer variabilities. All participants had received a formal diagnosis at some point in their lives, with the time lived with a formal fibromyalgia diagnosis between 3 and 10 years. During the course of my research and work with participants, two participants' fibromyalgia diagnoses were re-evaluated and refined. The fibromyalgia diagnosis was not entirely revoked but reframed within the context of Ehlers-Danlos syndrome and central sensitisation disorder, respectively. As the fibromyalgia diagnosis continued to be relevant and both participants' treatments for fibromyalgia were also continued, the participants' contributions to the research were not excluded. Participation varied among and across participants, with some starting the research and dropping out and others temporarily withdrawing from the research tasks but then returning to them in order to complete them. Of the 28 academics signed up, eight participants can be considered as having dropped out entirely.

The research approach has been published elsewhere (Brown 2018a; 2018b; 2019). Suffice it to say, data was generated through arts-based approaches combined with interviews conceptualised as conversations between the researcher and participants (Brinkmann and Kvale 2015). Data analysis drew on artistic approaches as well as on traditional coding processes through an iterative process of sense-making through employing hermeneutics (Smith et al. 2009) and thematic analysis (Braun and Clarke 2006; 2019). For the following sections, I have extrapolated some data from the research that referred to the themes of interruptions, correct language, disclosure and emotional labour in order to highlight the broader topics of sensibility and sensitivity. Participants' names used in the following are pseudonyms.

Interruptions and disruptions

Throughout the process I encountered interruptions and disruptions to the data generation and analysis stages. Due to the variability of fibromyalgia, academics drifted in and out of participating in the research. They were keen to tell their stories, share their experiences and be heard; but the reality of life with fibromyalgia and pressures of academic work led to flare-ups and complications, which in turn resulted in the increased need for pacing. Within the hierarchy of academics' priorities, participation in my research was often the first thing to be abandoned or cut back on. During the course of my study two participants interrupted their PhD studies, one participant decided not to continue her PhD studies and forfeited her scholarship, and three further participants contemplated reducing working hours and workloads, accepting diminished salary. Out-of-office messages were a constant reminder of the fluctuation of illness and long-term absences.

> So 19.03.2017 10:26
>
> Automatic reply: Thank you
> To Brown, Nicole
>
> I am currently on sick leave. If your message requires a reply I will do so as soon as possible once I return.
>
> Best wishes

Figure 3.1: Screenshot of an email sent to Nicole Brown.

But as someone with fibromyalgia myself, I too encountered flare-ups and periods of increased pain. Mostly I was able to maintain composure and it would not impact the conversations with the participants so that they specifically asked about my health status:

> And so, what about you? Do you have it as well? And is that why you started to look into it?
> Jackie
>
> Nicole
> I never asked but, if I may know (don't worry if you can't answer) do you yourself suffer from fibromyalgia?
> Carmen

In all honesty, being able to maintain public face and composure was only possible because many of the conversations happened by email. Indeed, my participant Carmen's query started a whole conversation around my being ill, carrying out research and balancing work with the doctorate and family commitments:

> From Nicole to Carmen:
> Dear Carmen,
> I saw your message earlier, but was rushed, so didn't want to reply straight away. The short answer is yes, I do. The full story is somewhat longer, but I was initially diagnosed in 2003. However,

I didn't accept the diagnosis and so continued the journey from doctor to doctor, until in 2012 I was diagnosed again. This was the point where I started accepting the diagnosis. But with hindsight I showed the first signs of fibromyalgia when I was a teenager, so probably around 1990. So, yes, I have a long story myself. Feel free to ask away… [smile emoji].

From Carmen to Nicole:
Hi Nicole, thank you so much for sharing your stories
I appreciate it
And well done to you that you have worked hard so far for your phd and other things in your career
I just…….. I've been finding the phd hard as I'm ill a lot
I have constant headaches, sore throat, fatigue and fever
And it's just….. people around me start to adapt with my pain I think as I'm always ill
And like with panels and examinations etc. it's done after 8 months, 1 year etc. and it's just that my 8 months seem to be different than a healthy student's
As I am not capable of 8 hours a day of work, for example
And in the end my PhD is assessed by my thesis
And not say my thesis and the situation where I'm working on my thesis with this illness
Sometimes I feel like it's a huge struggle cause I can't work as much as other people in the way that I have limited time and energy
That's why I asked.

From Nicole to Carmen:
I fully understand. And it doesn't come easy for me either. I am usually asleep by 10 pm, and don't do much after 8 pm actually. For me the worst thing is the brain fog, which really upsets me. But I am ill a lot, too.

From Carmen to Nicole:
I'm just worried that I won't finish my PhD, I think.

This conversation disrupted the natural flow of the interview and we ended the conversation on a leisurely note, only to take up the interview on another occasion. However, these interruptions demonstrate the reality of being a researcher and trying to work through an illness. Similarly, there is ample evidence throughout all interviews of how individuals, including myself, started struggling after a certain amount of time, finding it difficult to focus thoughts, not being able to prevent brain fog from setting in:

> [Pause]. Right. I tell you, tell you what Alison, I'm starting to struggle now. Umm, umm, I mean, I think it's been roughly an hour anyway, that we've been talking. If it's okay with you, I'd, I'd like to ask you back for another chat, cos I, I've actually written down a, a few questions, and I've got a few questions that I want to, to ask, but I really, I'm starting, I know that I'm starting to, yeah, not be able to focus.
> Nicole

> Sorry Nicole, I'm fucked, I'm really tired. Lost my train of thought, going to lie down for a second, yes.
> Hanna

> Thank you for changing it this afternoon, but I, I slept for 12 hours when I got, because I got back yesterday [from an international conference]. I was, I was so behind and, I appreciate you being able to adjust it.
> Jackie

Once I had coded all the data and had gone over all of the interviews, I realised that one particular conversation between Angela and myself epitomises the severity and immensity of the task of balancing work and life with an illness, of carrying out research and maintaining a relatively normal work schedule while having fibromyalgia:

> Nicole: And at the same time to be very, very honest, I'm finding myself, that I'm now starting to struggle to make the connections that I need to make [laughs].
> Angela: Oh no. Okay, yeah, it's hard when you're focusing.
> Nicole: I'm coming to the limits of my concentration span, I think.
> Angela: I understand, yeah. I totally get it. I do. Believe me.
> Nicole: It's really frustrating cos, yeah, it's lovely to hear you talk, and, and it kind of makes a lot of sense, of the things that you say in it, and I, I get the drift of, you know, like, some jobs being more, sort of, related to status and reputation,

and therefore not as welcoming or accommodating to people like ourselves basically.

Some of the interruptions were also signs of minds drifting off, but at the same time a way for the participants to engage me in their personal environments:

> I don't mind [wearing a headset and standing out from other colleagues]. [Waves]. Sorry, I'm just waving to some, my neighbours. [Laughter]. But I don't mind wearing a headset, in fact I think it's great.
> Jackie

> There was a couple of years really of doing sort of small courses. I did a Spanish course, I did a course in soft furnishings in curtain making. I made these curtains, I'll show you my curtains. They are pretty good curtains. See? Look, those curtains there [moves the screen round to show curtains].
> Hanna

It was situations like these that made the research process particularly difficult. Sensitivity and sensibility were required in order to respond appropriately to the needs of individuals. I was constantly trying to distance myself from my own experience as an academic with fibromyalgia in order not to become known as 'the fibromyalgia patient', not to be leading in my questioning and to maintain objectivity regarding the thoughts and experiences of others. However, through engaging with the participants on such a personal level, being shown around their houses, meeting colleagues, friends, husbands and partners, I felt drawn into the participants' world in a way that I feared would disrupt my analysis and my understanding of what was happening. For some participants, like Hanna, the conversations through the research process would constitute their only social contact for a week, sometimes two. In this sense, dismissing individuals' stories, even if they would not necessarily be the focus of the research, would have been detrimental to the individuals and consequently to my relationship with them.

The correct language and terminology

The research showed how the academic participants in this research made sense of academic identity and their work in academia, but also their experiences with the fibromyalgia diagnosis. Throughout this sense-making process academics engaged in a scholarly debate and considered their experiences on a personal level but through a somewhat academic lens. It is this scholarly and academic endeavour to reach understanding that has led to the all-important debate around terminology and language. The importance of language and terminology was highlighted in an informal conversation at a very early stage of this research project, when I spoke to a participant about being a fibromyalgia patient, but corrected myself to say a person diagnosed with fibromyalgia:

> Nicole: So, one of the questions relates to how you feel as a fibromyalgia patient, I mean, a person diagnosed with fibromyalgia.
>
> Patricia: I'm not a person diagnosed with fibromyalgia, or a patient. I am a sufferer.

Within the wider discourse around illness, disability and neurodiversity, language and terminology are a hotly debated topic. There are advocates who would like to see language to reflect that the person is more important than the person's disability, for example. Then again, there are specific groups advocating terminologies used to reflect the person's identity that is encapsulated in language. According to this debate, it should therefore be unthinkable to say 'the disabled' or 'the handicapped', but would be desirable to use 'the Deaf' or 'the Autistic' (Sinclair 2013). Language here is seen as a powerful tool to convey thought processes. A person using a wheelchair, for example, would primarily want to be seen as the person rather than the disabled person (Ward and Meyer 1999). This interpretation is closely aligned with the social model of disability (Oliver 2013) that sees disability as a barrier imposed by society and its members. In contrast to this, proponents of the use of 'the Deaf' or 'the Autistic' are generally advocates of the affirmation model (Swain and French 2000). For them, being ill, disabled or neurodiverse is not a negative, non-normal experience. Instead, they embrace their illness, disability or neurodiversity as part of their identity. In this sense, offering a hearing aid to those who are deaf is an affront to their identity: the inherent experience of being deaf is taken away from them (Leigh 2009).

Similarly, the term 'patient' is charged with connotations and reminders of a person's passivity and victimisation within the medical realm, as patients are objects within doctor–patient relationships, whose experiences are validated by doctors and who are supposed to endure treatments prescribed to them. Most participants in this research were very precise regarding the terminology they used and they wanted to be used. Even if most participants did not express their preferences as clearly as Patricia had done, the most widely used terminology around fibromyalgia was to do with suffering:

> I go through phases of this, and so therefore, I must be lucky, that I'm not one of those people that suffers all the time but, no it comes and goes.
> Jackie

> I have just seen [a tweet] which reminded me that I had not responded to your DM [direct message]. Please accept my apologies. This is the way it is with FM sufferers, or at least me. I have been going through a very bad patch for about the last 8 months or so.
> Patricia

> One of the, my colleagues, she was talking about fibromyalgia, she was talking about how she was suffering […] I said I feel the same.
> Kate

> Did we really need to talk to pain sufferers? Like, yes, also pain sufferers is a really problematic term [thumbs up sign]. So there has been a fair amount of political juggling.
> Alison

The language that participants and I have used throughout the project was therefore largely agreed upon on an individual basis. After all, not only are these terms politically and culturally charged and as such represent signs of oppression and victimisation, they also encapsulate personal experiences and feelings in relation to being ill. The conversation quoted above highlights very clearly how politically correct language may sometimes be inappropriate exactly because it takes away that charged connotation. With fibromyalgia the concern around the right use of language and terminology is even more complex, as fibromyalgia is badly understood and therefore not clearly classifiable as an illness, disease or disability. Overall, all participants described fibromyalgia as a disabling condition, although most were reluctant to refer to themselves as disabled. Sensitivity regarding which language to use and how to approach individuals was key for the development of a long-lasting relationship with individuals.

Considerations of disclosing fibromyalgia in academia

Where hidden or invisible conditions like fibromyalgia are concerned, individuals have a choice to disclose, pass or conceal (Goffman 1990/1963) and therefore more control over their identity (Kundrat and Nussbaum 2003). The decision on whether or not to disclose fibromyalgia is closely linked to academics' personal attitude towards the condition, and as such rests on a number of factors. Age plays a particularly important role in this connection. Individuals who are older or who have more experience with illnesses tend to cope better with managing issues around their conditions and the broader concerns of disclosure (Kundrat and Nussbaum 2003). Before being able to publicly announce and stand by an illness, the person needs to have come to terms with the condition at a very personal level. For some participants, being ill with fibromyalgia was very strongly connected with the feeling of being held back and slowed down. This emotional response also determines how participants act and react towards others knowing about their condition. Participants generally consider fibromyalgia as disabling and are not shying away from considering themselves as being disabled or referring to fibromyalgia as a disability.

> For me a disability is something except for which you would be able to perform at full capacity and participate fully, in your, in your life, however you want that to be. [...] Mine is a thing that reduces my potential performance and that needs accommodations to bring me up, to the level of everybody else. No, I think, I think mine's a disability.
> Sian

And yet, having lived with fibromyalgia for a long time and attempting to make sense of the condition does not necessarily mean that one has accepted and fully come to terms with it to such an extent that a public disclosure is acceptable. To be confident enough to tick the 'I am disabled' box means that this person would have accepted his/her dysfunction, disability or illness, a rather advanced stage in the moral career of a discredited person (Goffman 1990/1963), as it means learning to accept chronic illness, neurodiversity or disability as a normal experience of life or even as an asset, an outlook on disability that is at odds with internalised ableism:

> I think I would disclose if I needed any reasonable adjustments, or if I could put those in place I would not disclose maybe, it depends, it depends. I know now that I couldn't go for a full-time teaching post, lecturing post, because I wouldn't have the stamina. Unfortunately. And that's very sad to have to say that or admit that.
> Kate

In addition to this very personal interpretation and understanding of disability, a public disclosure brings further risks. Academics, specifically early-career academics, worry about the consequences of being identified as someone dealing with health issues and conditions. In an environment where temporary, as-and-when contracts are more prevalent than permanent, tenured positions, employees are concerned about job insecurity. Individuals fear that by admitting to health conditions or disabilities they may be worsening their chances for employment. For them, the rewards of passing (Goffman 1990/1963) are greater than the consequences of disclosing. Some participants told of occasions when they had shared their diagnosis with colleagues whose lack of understanding had led participants to change their views on disclosing and to generally hold back:

> What I've found interesting this year is, I've had three students come to me telling me they've got it [fibromyalgia]. And it was really interesting, when I said I understood because I had it, and they said, but you're so full of energy, how do you keep going? Because they'll sit in lectures and then say, I've got to leave, and I'll go home, and they won't see me go ooh [does flopping exhausted action].
> Jackie

> I've told four people at work that I have fibromyalgia and I think, two of them kind of understand.
> Yasmin

Whether or not academics choose to disclose their disabilities and illnesses is, in practice, a risk-benefit analysis of consequences associated with the specific concern or issue. In order to access support, workplace adjustments, potential financial benefits and allowances, academics do need to disclose their conditions. Another potential benefit of disclosing a condition is the opportunity to have an ally and companion, someone to share the same identity with (Defenbaugh 2013). However, disclosing more commonly means being categorised as a deviant within the normed and normalised society, which in turn leads to being stigmatised (Goffman 1990/1963). Within academia it is this stigmatisation that causes particular concerns. Invisible, lesser-known or contested conditions are dismissed as a fabrication, malingering and the act of a fundamentally lazy or overwhelmed worker seeking validation. Considering such strong views, the act of disclosing automatically links the personal and private to the public. Participants talk about how disclosing fibromyalgia as an illness or potentially as a disability could result in an increased risk of being stigmatised and discriminated against, particularly as fibromyalgia itself is a contested condition and not widely understood or accepted. At the same time, this risk is weighed up against the potential support and help they would receive.

> I now do put in that I have a disability, because, well, I mean with, with that sort of thing it's because I might need access to some form of service.
> Bernie

> Well I'm always honest about it, so for example I submitted a grant application on Monday and there was the equalities disabilities monitoring form and so in a box it said, you know, 'do you have any special concerns' and I'm always honest, and I put on there, you know, multiple chronic medical conditions that require accommodations, so I don't hide it in terms of submitting my work.
> Sian

The decision about whether to disclose or to hide a condition is therefore an act of self-preservation, information control and impression management (Goffman 1990/1959; 1990/1963) – thus it is identity work. For most participants, disclosing to colleagues and immediate line managers did not equate to disclosing to the university at institutional level; and they felt more comfortable with completing the monitoring and disability review forms than with explaining themselves to colleagues:

> They [colleagues] can't help me, you know, so it's basically, like, why would I want a pity party. There's nothing they can do, they can't take my work from me, they can't give me any less work, they can't do my work for me, they can't give me the career progression that I want, erm, with the record I have, without it there is no such thing as a mitigating circumstances form, for career progression, erm, and people don't have an ability to forget what you tell them. They will just constantly be asking me how am I feeling, and, you know, how are you doing and I don't want to talk about it with them if they can't help me.
> Sian

Sian's words in relation to what colleagues can and cannot give her exemplify this cost-benefit analysis. She does not want her colleagues to feel pity, commiserate with her or focus on her illness more than on practical work and solutions. A 'pity party' would have a serious impact on her academic identity: not only how she sees herself, but also how others within academia see her.

Being an academic means more to individuals than a mere profession or role. For the participants, being an academic is a lifestyle choice that allows them to indulge in their personal curiosity and thirst for knowledge. In this sense, disclosing fibromyalgia would be seen as an admission of weakness. It is this element of weakness that also determines the tendency towards not disclosing fibromyalgia. For some participants, considering themselves as ill or disabled is a self-fulfilling prophecy and the beginning of a downward spiral of failure that will be more difficult to escape. Therefore, instead of admitting defeat the academics push themselves through episodes of illness, pretending that everything is fine:

> Some days I have no idea how I've got to the end of a lecture because you put so much energy into it, especially on those days, when you've got more and more tired […] I do sometimes get to the end and think, I don't actually remember the last part of the lecture, but we got there.
> Jackie

> People see me as being able, and yeah, they see the image I portray; they see me as being able and energetic and mostly on and up.
> Yasmin

In the conversations, participants highlighted that even once they have personally come to terms with being ill, the disclosure of that illness in academia is still contentious. Attitudes and expectations in relation to productivity and ways of working are such that deviation from that norm is practically impossible, especially in an environment where precarious contracts and job insecurity are rife:

> I don't think you can, you can like openly disclose.
> Kate

> You're breaking protocol because you're being vulnerable, personal and interpersonal, and intrapersonal; and you're asking for something different, you're asking to be assisted, you're asking for help, you're actually displaying the need for assistance, which is really not welcomed all the time, and actually it's irritating.
> Angela

> There are kinds of disabilities that are easier to disclose, that have different kinds of stigma that do affect workplace politics, so I think it is, I'm not at all talking about the lived experience, but I think it is easier, say, you'd get a better reaction if you're a woman and you say 'I have breast cancer' than if you say 'I am a woman and I have', I don't know, 'borderline personality issues'.
> Alison

Many participants discussed disclosing to colleagues and the university in relation to and connection with their contractual conditions. Participants on fixed-term contracts or on support staff or teaching fellow contracts were less likely to disclose their fibromyalgia diagnosis. The question around when people were told of, found out or knew about her life with fibromyalgia prompted Dana to contemplate her privileged professorial position:

> Most people only know about me having fibromyalgia once I became a professor. [...] It wasn't a conscious hiding of it, but it might have been unconscious. And also remember, it also goes with the research because before that research was 'fibromyalgia's a psychosomatic disorder', so did you want people to think it's in your head, and things like that; or is it the influence of research then in the last four or five years talking about, you know, neurological conditions or sort of, sort of biochemical sort of aspects of it. So,

> I don't know whether it's the, having that professor identity, or something, or if it is to do with the research [that] is now, if you like, validating my experience as not just being in my head, but having a physical cause. […] I remember when I, or we had HR paperwork being reviewed and we were renewed and we were being asked to update them, and I put about fibromyalgia and one of my colleagues, I don't know why he knew that, said 'Are you sure? Are you sure you want people to know that?'
> Dana

Dana goes on to explain that she had eventually come to terms with the diagnosis on a personal level and is now using her privileged position as a professor to advocate for and support others with fibromyalgia. Her moral career has taken a turn towards being a professional within her group of the 'discredited' (Goffman 1990/1963, 38). For her, fibromyalgia is now no longer merely an illness she has to deal with, but also the focus of her research and public engagement activities. In her own words, she is now in a position where she can indulge in more freedom and flexibility:

> If I don't have a class, and if I'm not well, if I decide I'm going, not going to start work at nine o'clock, I'll start at 12 o'clock and I'll carry on for my, whatever number of hours I want to work, or I can work from my bed, so I'm in pain, but my brain's working, so I'll work from my bed. I can do that.
> Dana

Other participants, especially those in the early stages of their career, find being ill in academia taxing and demanding. In their view, getting the balance right between work and private life is often difficult because academia is experienced and interpreted as an all-encompassing lifestyle choice and identity. Participants therefore regularly refer to their emotional experiences, and managing their self-worth and feelings of isolation. Being diagnosed with a chronic illness is in itself life-changing and isolating (Charmaz 1991; Frank 2013). But then the feeling of not being able to be completely open, honest and transparent about the body's needs and therefore the adjustments required also leads to a wide range of emotional responses. Participants express their experiences and feelings of isolation and having to work through their needs by themselves, especially if they have not disclosed their condition to those around them, and so they have to deal with their illness on their own and thus become even more isolated:

> At the moment I just feel like I'm just a, a mess. I feel like, like, people are avoiding me from my course, maybe not deliberately but they're just, they're so busy and involved with what they are doing. And I think extended illness of this type makes people very uncomfortable. They, they don't know what to say, they don't know what they can do. It's not like an acute illness where they can come and visit you with a bunch of flowers and, you know, you're in bed looking all poorly and then next week you're not so bad and then the following week you're back in the office. I think it's very confusing for other people and, and, yeah, I think it makes them feel uncomfortable, and I feel like people who were very supportive, say, six months ago, the last, this last spell of illness since March, I've hardly heard from them at all, not seen them, so I do feel a bit abandoned. And, and, you know, I, I have made an effort to keep in touch with people, it's not that I've put myself off, I understand that they're really, I mean, they are insanely busy, they could, you know, they're in the midst of their PhDs, but it's, I do feel a bit hurt.
> Hanna

> You know, and then the really annoying part is that when I do want any social interaction or I want to go and see people or talk about ideas nobody has any time for me, right.
> Sian

Thought processes around disclosure therefore relate to physical, material manifestations as well as emotion work. In effect, individuals analyse and calculate whether disclosing the condition is a risk worth taking. Individuals are more likely to disclose their health concerns if they feel that disclosure facilitates continued employment and explains absences or conditions (Butler and Modaff 2016). Women with fibromyalgia have also been found to be more likely to disclose when fluctuating work commitments or changes in work relationships occur (Oldfield et al. 2016). The difference between the general public and academics is manifested in the dimension of disclosure. Non-academics choose to disclose illness and impairments to provide information about the contested illness or to selectively reveal invisible impairments (Oldfield et al. 2016).

'Disclosure dances' in academia

In order to understand what it means to be disabled or ill in academia, higher education must be seen in the context of the processes towards increased marketisation, internationalisation and bureaucratisation (Hussey and Smith 2002; Tilak 2008; Gewirtz and Cribb 2013). Through their ability to critically reflect and analyse, academics identify the working conditions as a contemporary academic in the neoliberal university as a source of aggravation for their symptoms. However, academics do not interpret the academy as a source or cause for the condition. Instead, working in academia continues to be romanticised (Lovin 2018) and is still seen as worth striving for, and so the participants' focus lies on managing their emotions and bodies in an attempt to compete with non-disabled colleagues.

In an environment where, as discussed, the culture of overwork is endemic, the academic who becomes ill or disabled faces the decision on whether they disclose their 'weaknesses'. This choice around disclosure is open to anyone who has a so-called 'invisible' disability, and even individuals who have more obvious physical disabilities can often choose the extent to which they disclose their effects. For example, they may have no option but to disclose that they are in a wheelchair or use a mobility aid, but could decide whether to disclose the fact they also have a diagnosis of fibromyalgia and the additional pain, fatigue and brain fog they suffer. At the same time, disclosure is a form of information management and controlling what kind of information is shared (Goffman 1990/1963). Openly admitting to having brain fog – a cognitive dysfunction – in an employment that prides itself for cerebral work is not the same as openly admitting to having pain. The selection of what is shared at which point, under which circumstances and with whom, and the subsequent sharing of details are 'dances rather than declarations' (Oldfield et al. 2016, 1451), as, like dancers, individuals respond to circumstances and persons when they share particular experiences or details. This is because disability or illness are often not interpreted or felt as fixed states, but as fluid, liminal spaces or continua. Within the lived experience of a disabled or chronically ill body individuals go through phases of 'feeling normal' and 'feeling disabled' within their bodies (Deegan 2010, 30ff.). Apart from the fact that conditions often fluctuate and therefore disability or chronic illness does not take on permanency, the narratives of individuals with disabilities and chronic illnesses highlight that personal circumstances, external factors and environments impact the conception of whether or not the body is experienced as 'normal'. Disability is not dichotomous, but a fluid state (Barnartt 2010), where one's experience of cognitive dysfunction, pain and fatigue is more or less pronounced. With this in mind it is not surprising that disclosure is complex.

Ultimately, within academia three core conditions need to be met for a person to be able to disclose their 'otherness'. First, the person with the diagnosis needs to have reached a state of personal acceptance. For example, if we use the example of an individual academic with fibromyalgia, they would first need to learn to accept that there is something 'wrong'. It is perhaps easier to accept an illness than to accept disability, but then it is not so easy to accept an illness that does not have an outcome – unlike cancer, for example, where the narrative is one of heroism (Frank 2013) for those who fight and survive, but also for those who are brave knowing that they cannot survive. Second, those with a fibromyalgia diagnosis need to experience acceptance at their workplaces. The culture at the workplace must be such that individual differences are accepted and understood. Medically unexplained or contested conditions like fibromyalgia and chronic fatigue syndrome, in particular, are not met with the right levels of understanding. For example, a visible disability requiring wheelchairs, walking canes and guide dogs is more easily understood than disabilities that cannot actually be seen. 'But you don't look sick' is commonly heard. Finally, in order to be able to fully disclose the fibromyalgia diagnosis, an academic needs to be sure that there will not be any repercussions. In reality, many academics, especially those with hidden disabilities and illnesses, experience discrimination in one form or another – not necessarily as a malicious act, but because of lack of understanding (Brown and Leigh 2018). As society is discriminating in that sense, academics with illnesses worry that their workplace will be equally discriminating if it becomes clear that they have health needs, and so they end up not disclosing their condition. With this in mind, the disclosure issue is really about how comfortable academics are within their own skins. Disclosure therefore needs to be discussed as a personal, private event as much as it needs to be considered as a public event.

When disclosure is considered within the public realm, it tends to be discussed in the context of stigma. Many academics with invisible conditions or disabilities have got an opportunity to navigate their image and control if and how much they would like to divulge of their condition, and hence their 'otherness'. Their bodies do not openly display their issues and are not inscribed with any stigmatising features (Goffman 1990/1963). This is obviously a concern because they may be treated as 'normal' in relation to productivity and effectiveness although they may not be able to meet these high expectations due to their bodily limitations. At the same time, not disclosing a condition does mean that academics may pass and not be subjected to stigma (Goffman 1990/1963). General awareness and understanding of the lived experiences are so limited that individual symptoms do not tend to come up within everyday interactions with others. Academics may struggle with brain fog, lack of concentration and focus, but these are personal experiences, not public ones. In the case of conditions like fibromyalgia that are contested and medically unexplained, individuals are often doubted and indeed start doubting themselves. But even conditions that are visible or disclosed through stigma symbols (Goffman 1990/1963) such as back rests, wheelchairs and hearing aids lead individuals to question themselves. Sensitivity is therefore the key component in an empathetic approach to communicating with disabled and chronically ill academics.

The emotional labour of disclosure

In the previous sections I have shown how negotiating fibromyalgia in the academy is not only a public but also a private endeavour. I have also highlighted how the research process as a whole and individual conversations in particular have been shaped by the condition and external factors surrounding it. In this final section, I would like to return to the theme of disclosure as a sensitive issue. Ultimately, any work relationship with others but also with oneself requires the negotiation of emotions.

For example, the choice of whether or not to disclose a condition is as much emotional as it is logical and rational. On the one hand, there are benefits to disclosing illness, in that as the person disclosing a condition, you can share your experiences and explore a support network of others with the same identity. Disclosing therefore leads to having an ally and companion through illness (Defenbaugh 2013). On the other hand, trying to contain the important information around one's illness results in individuals needing to manage their conditions, but also trying to 'hide' key components of who they are. This information control (Goffman 1990/1963) is fraught with the potential risk of being exposed involuntarily or of being blackmailed into disclosing a condition one may not necessarily be ready to share publicly. The most recent examples of such journeys relate to the Welsh rugby player (Davies 2019) and *Queer Eye* presenter Jonathan Van Ness (BBC News, 22 September 2019), whose HIV diagnoses suddenly entered the public domain. With hidden or invisible conditions individuals normally have a choice to conceal or disclose and therefore have more control over their identity. Age is often thought to be relevant for how individuals deal with illness and disabilities, as older people are more experienced in dealing with illness. Age here is not understood as the chronology of life and time; it is rather the space, state of mind and mindset within one's lifespan that relates to whether an individual has had more or less experience with being ill (Kundrat and Nussbaum 2003). However, in reality, coming to terms with a condition on one's personal level and subsequently managing the information about oneself in social networks are detailed processes of knowing who to tell what and ensuring that different groups of peers do not necessarily meet each other in order to be able to maintain the chosen secrecy in the workplace, for example. As this information management requires careful staging of one's identity as well as the containment of emotions, information control needs to be seen as a form of emotional labour (Goffman 1990/1959; 1990/1963).

Although emotional labour and emotion work within academia are still poorly researched (Constanti and Gibbs 2004), several strategies and factors for emotion management have been identified (Archer 2008; Morris and Feldman 1996; Frost 2003). The strategies range from 'playing the game' and speaking out about what is wrong through to lowering one's own expectations or, in the worst case, 'quitting the game' (Archer 2008). The emphasis in all these works lies on the fact that the requirement to manage and control information about oneself leads to emotional pain. If no active countermeasures are taken to alleviate this emotional pain, it has the potential to become toxic 'to the point that it can be contained no longer and finally erupts' (Ward and McMurray 2016, 88). This eruption may then manifest itself as an aggravation of symptoms, stress or worsening mental health, which in turn will increase the emotional impact on individuals. Knowing that these are the experiences of individuals with disabilities or chronic conditions, we return to sensitivity. In an ableist society such as academia, this kind of sensitivity and empathy is often foregone – not necessarily because of malicious intent, but because of lack of understanding and awareness of different ways of living and working.

References

Archer, Louise. 'The New Neoliberal Subjects? Young/er Academics' Constructions of Professional Identity', *Journal of Education Policy* 23/3 (2008): 265–85. Online. https://doi.org/10.1080/02680930701754047 (accessed 22 May 2020).
Barnartt, Sharon N. 'Disability as a Fluid State: Introduction'. In *Disability as a Fluid State* (Research in Social Science and Disability, vol. 5), edited by Sharon N. Barnartt, 1–22. Bingley: Emerald Group, 2010. Online. https://doi.org/10.1108/S1479-3547(2010)0000005003 (accessed 22 May 2020).
BBC News. 'Airport Turns Away Wheelchair User'. 7 August 2018. Online. https://www.bbc.co.uk/news/av/45106446/airport-turns-away-wheelchair-user (accessed September 2019).
BBC News. 'Heathrow Airport Wheelchair Failure "A Disgrace"'. 19 November 2018. Online. https://www.bbc.co.uk/news/uk-england-tees-46253991 (accessed September 2019).
BBC News. 'Model With No Bowel Denied Toilet Access in Manchester'. 15 January 2018. Online. https://www.bbc.co.uk/news/uk-england-manchester-42693760 (accessed September 2019).
BBC News. 'Blue Badge Permits: People With "Hidden disabilities" to be Eligible'. 15 June 2019. Online. https://www.bbc.co.uk/news/uk-48640448 (accessed September 2019).
BBC News. 'Queer Eye's Jonathan Van Ness Says He's HIV Positive'. 22 September 2019. Online. https://www.bbc.co.uk/news/newsbeat-49786893 (accessed September 2019).
Braun, Virginia and Clarke, Victoria. 'Using Thematic Analysis in Psychology', *Qualitative Research in Psychology* 3/2 (2006): 77–101. Online. https://doi.org/10.1191/1478088706qp063oa (accessed 22 May 2020).
Braun, Virginia and Clarke, Victoria. 'Reflecting on Reflexive Thematic Analysis', *Qualitative Research in Sport, Exercise and Health* 11/4 (2019): 589–97. Online. https://doi.org/10.1080/2159676X.2019.1628806 (accessed 22 May 2020).
Brinkmann, Svend and Kvale, Steinar. *InterViews: Learning the Craft of Qualitative Research Interviewing*, 3rd ed. Thousand Oaks, CA: Sage, 2015.
Brown, Nicole. 'Video-Conference Interviews: Ethical and Methodological Concerns in the Context of Health Research'. *SAGE Research Methods Cases* (2018a). Online. https://dx.doi.org/10.4135/9781526441812 (accessed 22 May 2020).
Brown, Nicole. 'Exploring the Lived Experience of Fibromyalgia Using Creative Data Collection', *Cogent Social Sciences* 4/1 (2018b). Online. https://doi.org/10.1080/23311886.2018.1447759 (accessed 22 May 2020).
Brown, Nicole. 'Identity Boxes: Using Materials and Metaphors to Elicit Experiences', *International Journal of Social Research Methodology* 22/5 (2019): 487–501. Online. https://doi.org/10.1080/13645579.2019.1590894 (accessed 22 May 2020).
Brown, Nicole and Leigh, Jennifer. 'Ableism in Academia: Where are the Disabled and Ill Academics?' *Disability and Society* 33/6 (2018): 985–9. Online. https://doi.org/10.1080/09687599.2018.1455627 (accessed 19 May 2020).
Butler, Jennifer A. and Modaff, Daniel P. 'Motivations to Disclose Chronic Illness in the Workplace', *Qualitative Research Reports in Communication* 17/1 (2016): 77–84. Online. https://doi.org/10.1080/17459435.2016.1143387 (accessed 25 May 2020).
Charmaz, Kathy. *Good Days, Bad Days: The Self in Chronic Illness and Time*. New Brunswick, NJ: Rutgers University Press, 1991.
Coleman, Clive. 'Paraplegic Man Drags Himself Through Airport'. BBC News. 2 November 2018. Online. https://www.bbc.co.uk/news/uk-45765767 (accessed September 2019).
Constanti, Panikkos and Gibbs, Paul. 'Higher Education Teachers and Emotional Labour', *International Journal of Educational Management* 18/4 (2004): 243–9. Online. http://dx.doi.org/10.1108/09513540410538822 (accessed 25 May 2020).
Davies, Daniel. 'Gareth Thomas: Ex-Wales Rugby Captain has HIV'. BBC News. 15 September 2019. Online. https://www.bbc.co.uk/news/uk-wales-49675303 (accessed September 2019).
Deegan, Mary Jo. '"Feeling Normal" and "Feeling Disabled"'. In *Disability as a Fluid State* (Research in Social Science and Disability, vol. 5), edited by Sharon N. Barnartt, 25–48. Bingley: Emerald Group, 2010. Online. https://doi.org/10.1108/S1479-3547(2010)0000005004 (accessed 25 May 2020).
Defenbaugh, Nicole L. 'Revealing and Concealing Ill Identity: A Performance Narrative of IBD Disclosure', *Health Communication* 28/2 (2013): 159–69. Online. (accessed 25 May 2020).

Ehrlich, George E. 'Fibromyalgia is Not a Diagnosis', *Arthritis and Rheumatism* 48/1 (2003): 276. Online. https://doi.org/10.1002/art.10636 (accessed 25 May 2020).

Frank, Arthur W. *The Wounded Storyteller: Body, Illness, and Ethics*, 2nd ed. Chicago: University of Chicago Press, 2013.

Frost, Peter J. *Toxic Emotions at Work*. Boston: Harvard Business School Press, 2003.

Gewirtz, Sharon and Cribb, Alan. 'Representing 30 Years of Higher Education Change: UK Universities and the *Times Higher*', *Journal of Educational Administration and History* 45/1 (2013): 58–83. Online. https://doi.org/10.1080/00220620.2013.730505 (accessed 19 May 2020).

Goffman, Erving. *The Presentation of Self in Everyday Life*. London: Penguin Books, 1990, originally 1959.

Goffman, Erving. *Stigma: Notes on the Management of Spoiled Identity*. London: Penguin Books, 1990, originally 1963.

Häuser, Winfried and Fitzcharles, Mary-Ann. 'Facts and Myths Pertaining to Fibromyalgia', *Dialogues in Clinical Neuroscience* 20/1 (2018): 53–62. Online. https://www.ncbi.nlm.nih.gov/pmc/articles/PMC6016048/ (accessed 25 May 2020).

Hussey, Trevor and Smith, Patrick. 'The Trouble with Learning Outcomes', *Active Learning in Higher Education* 3/3 (2002): 220–33. Online. https://doi.org/10.1177/1469787402003003003 (accessed 25 May 2020).

Kundrat, Amanda L. and Nussbaum, Jon F. 'The Impact of Invisible Illness on Identity and Contextual Age Across the Life Span', *Health Communication* 15/3 (2003): 331–47. Online. https://doi.org/10.1207/S15327027HC1503_5 (accessed 25 May 2020).

Leigh, Irene. *A Lens on Deaf Identities. Perspectives on Deafness*. Oxford: Oxford University Press, 2009. Online. https://doi.org/10.1093/acprof:oso/9780195320664.001.0001 (accessed 25 May 2020).

Lovin, C. Laura. 'Feelings of Change: Alternative Feminist Professional Trajectories'. In *Feeling Academic in the Neoliberal University: Feminist Flights, Fights and Failures*, edited by Yvette Taylor and Kinneret Lahad, 137–62. Palgrave Studies in Gender and Education. Cham, Switzerland: Palgrave Macmillan, 2018. Online. https://doi.org/10.1007/978-3-319-64224-6_7 (accessed 19 May 2020).

Mengshoel, A.M., Sim, J., Ahlsen, B. and Madden, S. 'Diagnostic Experience of Patients with Fibromyalgia – A Meta-Ethnography', *Chronic Illness* 14/3 (2018): 194–211. Online. https://doi.org/10.1177/1742395317718035 (accessed 25 May 2020).

Morris, J. Andrew and Feldman, Daniel C. 'The Dimensions, Antecedents and Consequences of Emotional Labor', *Academy of Management Review* 21/4 (1996): 989–1010. Online. https://doi.org/10.5465/amr.1996.9704071861 (accessed 25 May 2020).

Office of Rail and Road. *Accessible Travel Policy – Guidance for Train and Station Operators*. July 2019. Online. https://orr.gov.uk/__data/assets/pdf_file/0018/41517/accessible-travel-policy-guidance-for-train-and-station-operators.pdf (accessed September 2019).

Oldfield, M., MacEachen, E., Kirsh, B. and MacNeill, M. 'Impromptu Everyday Disclosure Dances: How Women with Fibromyalgia Respond to Disclosure Risks at Work', *Disability and Rehabilitation* 38/15 (2016):1442–53. Online. https://doi.org/10.3109/09638288.2015.1103794 (accessed 25 May 2020).

Oliver, Mike. 'The Social Model of Disability: Thirty Years On', *Disability and Society* 28/7 (2013): 1024–6. Online. https://doi.org/10.1080/09687599.2013.818773 (accessed 25 May 2020).

Rimmer, Monica. 'Student with Stoma Accused by Wetherspoons Staff of Taking Drugs'. BBC News. 8 September 2019. Online. https://www.bbc.co.uk/news/uk-wales-49556333 (accessed September 2019).

Sinclair, Jim. 'Why I Dislike "Person First" Language', *Autonomy, the Critical Journal of Interdisciplinary Autism Studies*, 1/2 (2013). Online. http://www.larry-arnold.net/Autonomy/index.php/autonomy/article/view/OP1 (accessed 25 May 2020).

Smith, Jonathan A., Flowers, Paul and Larkin, Michael. *Interpretative Phenomenological Analysis: Theory, Method and Research*. London: Sage, 2009.

Swain, John and French, Sally. 'Towards an Affirmation Model of Disability', *Disability and Society* 15/4 (2000): 569–82. Online. https://doi.org/10.1080/09687590050058189 (accessed 25 May 2020).

Tilak, Jandhyala B. 'Higher Education: A Public Good or a Commodity for Trade?' *Prospects* 38/4 (2008): 449–66. Online. https://doi.org/10.1007/s11125-009-9093-2 (accessed 25 May 2020).

Transport for London. 'Please Offer Me a Seat'. N.d. Online. https://tfl.gov.uk/transport-accessibility/please-offer-me-a-seat (accessed 25 May 2020).

Ward, Jenna and McMurray, Robert. *The Dark Side of Emotional Labour*. Abingdon and New York: Routledge, 2016.

Ward, Michael J. and Meyer, Roger N. 'Self-determination for People with Developmental Disabilities and Autism: Two Self-advocates' Perspectives', *Focus on Autism and Other Developmental Disabilities* 14/3 (1999): 133–9. Online. https://doi.org/10.1177/108835769901400302 (accessed 25 May 2020).

White, Kevin and Harth, Manfred. 'Classification, Epidemiology, and Natural History of Fibromyalgia', *Current Pain and Headache Reports* 5/4 (2001): 320–9. Online. https://doi.org/10.1007/s11916-001-0021-2 (accessed 25 May 2020).

Wolfe, Frederick. 'Fibromyalgia Wars', *Journal of Rheumatology*, 36/4 (2009): 671–8. Online. https://doi.org/10.3899/jrheum.081180 (accessed 25 May 2020).

Wolfe, F., Clauw, D.J., Fitzcharles, M.A., Goldenberg, D.L., Katz, R.S., Mease, P., Russell, A.S., Russell, I. J., Winfield, J.B. and Yunus, M.B. 'The American College of Rheumatology Preliminary Diagnostic Criteria for Fibromyalgia and Measurement of Symptom Severity', *Arthritis Care and Research* 62/5 (2010): 600–10. Online. https://doi.org/10.1002/acr.20140 (accessed 25 May 2020).

4
Fibromyalgia and me

Divya Jindal-Snape

Through poetic inquiry Divya Jindal-Snape offers a moving expression of the narrative I's self-doubts linked with the experience of having a contested, invisible illness. In her poem the author acknowledges the significant role the illness experience plays but at the same time emphasises that there is more to self – and an academic self – than an illness.

The pain you are causing me is driving me to my bed
But do you exist or are you just in my head
Should I resist you and carry on with life
Am I looking for an excuse for being a bad mother and wife

Am I just lazy
And a bit crazy
To think I need my bed
When you are just in my head

New research does suggest that you are real and not 'just in my head'
What a relief as the psychosomatic label used to fill me with dread
However does everyone understand that the pain and fatigue are here to stay
Any amount of exercise, rest or medication won't take them away
At least not fully but maybe enough to take off the edge
So that I can carry on without wanting to jump off the ledge

I hope no one has to go through such pain and fatigue
As even now for some medics you are full of mystique

What hurts more is that people who don't have a clue
Give me advice on what I should or shouldn't do
Good support from family and friends over the years
Strong shoulders to rely on helped deal with you with minimal tears

You are however only a small part of me
I will acknowledge you but won't allow you to become my identity

5
A practical response to ableism in leadership in UK higher education

Nicola Martin

In 2017 Boucher observed that 'Disability has been almost totally ignored in the leadership literature' (2017, 1005). This chapter aims to make an evidence-based contribution to the discussion, focusing specifically on leadership by disabled people in higher education and informed by a report commissioned by the Leadership Foundation for Higher Education (LFHE) and undertaken by the author (Martin 2017). Disabled academics such as Campbell (2009), Oliver (2009) and Shakespeare (2013) provide numerous illustrations which show that disabled people are often by necessity strategic, entrepreneurial problem solvers with the ability to see the bigger picture. These scholars and many others, including Bass (1999), Black (2015) and Logan and Martin (2012) suggest that abilities associated with good leadership develop as a result of a lifetime of having to find creative ways to address myriad socially constructed everyday difficulties.

In a report commissioned by the LFHE, Bebbington (2009) provides compelling arguments in favour of diversity in leadership from social justice and business perspectives, and suggests practical ideas for taking this agenda forward. Equality data from 2016–17 quoted later indicates that the majority of leaders in higher education are still non-disabled white men between the ages of 46 and 55, so progress since Bebbington wrote her report can hardly be described as rapid. Rather than being problematised, disability is viewed here and in Martin's (2017) LFHE report as a valuable aspect of diversity. Barriers are considered, such as lack of access to leadership training and ableism in many forms, including 'the tyranny of low expectations'. Enablers are also explored in depth, including organised supportive environments and the personal characteristics of disabled people who often bring exceptional strategic and team development skills to the table. The expression 'nothing about us without us' (Charlton 1998) underpins the approach taken in this research, which identifies and reflects on emerging themes from insights generously provided by participants. Key terms are explained in the following sections.

Defining disability versus impairment

Given that impairments covered by legislation including the Equality Act 2010 are not always recognised as such by people affected, and the definitions of disability and impairment are not always understood, some clarification is required. English, Scottish and Welsh higher education institutions (HEIs) are subject to the Equality Act 2010 (www.legislation.gov.uk/ukpga/2010/15/contents, accessed 11 June 2020), which absorbed and replaced various aspects of previous equalities legislation including the 1995 Disability Discrimination Act (DDA) and subsequent amendments. (In Northern Ireland the DDA still operates.) The Equality Act requires public bodies including HEIs to go beyond reasonable adjustments and proactively promote equality of opportunity (Ewens and Williams 2011). Section 6 of the Equality Act 2010 arguably employs what some participants described as 'an ableist definition describing impairment rather than disability': 'A person has a disability if they have a physical or mental impairment, and the impairment has a substantial and long-term adverse effect on his or her ability to carry out normal day-to-day activities.'

'Ableism' is a term deployed by Campbell (2009), Goodley (2013; 2014) and others to denote attitudes and societal constructs that impact negatively upon disabled people. Loja et al. equate ableism with 'The invalidation of impaired bodies and the constant struggle to establish credibility' (2013, 193). Viewing disability through the lens of ableism is also in keeping with the definition given by the Department of Disability Studies at the University of Leeds (https://tinyurl.com/y3szqf2k, accessed 13 December 2018): 'the result of negative interactions that take place between a person with an impairment and her or his social environment. Impairment is thus part of a negative interaction, but it is not the cause of, nor does it justify, disability.'

Defining leadership

Bebbington (2009) cautions that leadership is theorised in various ways and means different things to different people. Trait theory characterises a contested, possibly ableist approach in which leaders are 'born not made' and have qualities such as vision, creativity and charisma. Opportunity does not seem to feature and participants in this study reflected on their own experiences of opportunities being curtailed during their education and working life. Potentially concerns around heteronormativity, ageism and sexism might also apply in trait theory. Corlett and Williams (2011) and Williams (2011) highlight the absence of disability within mainstream organisational and identity literature, reflecting ableist assumptions and potentially unconscious bias away from the idea of disabled people as leaders towards the idea of the mythical norm (Lorde 1984). With reference to Bass (1999), Bebbington (2009) contrasts traditional leader–follower structures with transactional and transformational concepts of leadership. Transformational leadership is characterised by motivation through collaboration, social exchange and sharing of power. Transactional leadership involves managing compliant followers through contingent reward.

Distributed leadership is discussed by Bolden et al. (2008) and Bennett et al. (2003) in terms of interactions between members working together and generating an additional cooperative dynamic which facilitates conjoint activity. The advantages of distributed leadership include 'Pooling of initiative and expertise, [and] the outcome is a product or energy which is greater than the sum of their individual actions' (Bennett et al. 2003, 8).

Equality data

The contested term 'disclosure' is used in descriptors of Higher Education Statistics Agency (HESA) datasets, which ask people to identify with various impairment labels. The HESA staff record for 2016–17 (figure 5.1, charts 10a–d) indicates that the most commonly reported impairments amongst academic and professional and support staff were 'a longstanding illness or health condition' and 'a specific learning disability'. A slight increase in 'disclosure' is apparent year on year from 2002–3 (Equality Challenge Unit 2015). More interestingly, HESA revealed very few disabled people in senior roles in the sector. As we will see later in this article, accuracy of reporting is potentially an issue.

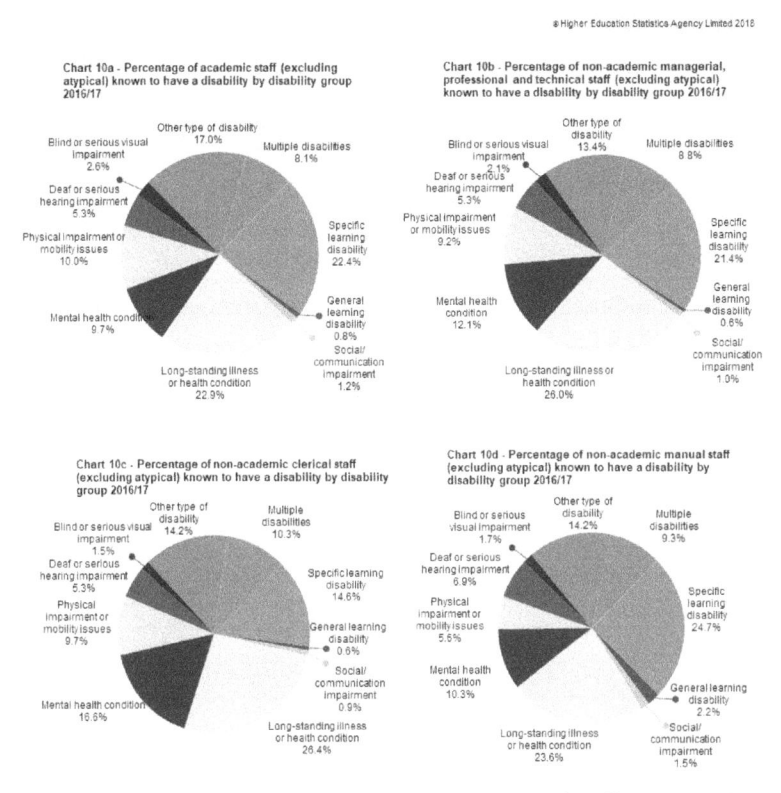

Figure 5.1: Four charts depicting the percentages of staff known to have a disability. Source: HESA 2018

The Equality Challenge Unit's in-depth analysis of HESA datasets in 2015 revealed that fewer professors than academics below professorial level identified themselves as having an impairment (2.7 per cent compared to 3.4 per cent). Only 5 of the 170 heads of institutions (2.4 per cent) identified as disabled, compared with 5 per cent of staff in support roles.

It is estimated that there are 11.9 million disabled people in the UK – 19 per cent of the total population (https://tinyurl.com/y6esnqwf, accessed 13 December 2018). Of these, 16 per cent are of working age. The proportion of people disclosing a disability in higher education seems low by comparison, though it is difficult to ascertain the extent to which this is due to limited disclosure rather than low levels of actual employment of disabled people in the sector. Structural ableism may well play a part, but without being able to rely on the data it is not possible to draw firm conclusions about whether this is so. The HESA figures from 2016–17 presented in table 5.1 below do not provide an encouraging picture in relation to the representation of women, ethnic minorities or disabled people among senior leaders, who appear still from this data to be mainly white British non-disabled men between the ages of 46 and 55.

Table 5.1: Academic staff, managers, directors and senior officials by age, disability, ethnicity and gender, 2016/17

Characteristics	Managers, directors and senior officials	Total academic staff
Age group		
25 and under	5	5,245
26–35	35	54,410
36–45	110	56,600
46–55	215	52,015
56–65	165	31,515
66 and over	20	7,090
Disability status		
Known to have a disability	25	8,195
No known disability	520	198,675
Ethnicity		
White	495	161,255
Black	5	3,445
Asian	20	17,595
Other (including mixed)	10	7,545
Not known	15	17,030
Nationality		
UK	485	143,335
Other EU	35	35,920
Non-EU	20	25,660
Not known	0	1,955
Sex		
Female	225	94,475
Male	315	112,395
Total staff	**540**	**206,870**

Source: HESA, 2016/17

Ontological risk

'Identity-based devaluation' is an expression utilised in a discussion of 'stigmatised leaders' (Avery et al. 2016, 1111). Intersectionality is a theme in Avery et al.'s work and that of other authors, including Boucher (2017), Deegan (2018) and Lorde (1984), who discuss the ordinary inter-relatedness of facets of multiple identity. This thinking is in keeping with the ethos of the Equality Act 2010, which identifies various protected characteristics that can apply to a single individual. 'Protected' refers to protection from discrimination and the Equality Act is cognisant of the potential for discrimination on the grounds of, for example, disability and gender. Higher education leadership demographics illustrate an entrenched non-disabled white male privilege and recent discussions about the gender pay gap, in which men do better than women by a long way in UK universities, do not inspire confidence (Guilbourg 2019).

For people with invisible impairments there is often an element of choice about whether to make information about this public. Roulstone and Williams (2014) identified concerns beyond the university sector about the 'riskiness' of disclosure among 42 disabled managers. Stigma was an aspect of this consideration, but often more pressing was the idea that alternative features of identity would become deprioritised in the eyes of other people, as if 'disabled person' negated further aspects of self. Much the same was found by Nash (2014) among participants in a large study of more than 2,000 disabled employees. Feelings of riskiness were also uncovered by Sayce (2011); these were specifically associated with identifying with hidden impairments, especially mental health issues. Women leaders with visible impairments were also found by Boucher (2017) to feel the need to underplay and minimise impairment effects at work. Behaviours utilised in the workplace by women leaders with physical impairments identified by Boucher included 'using surface acting to present an optimistic demeanour' and 'approaches such as passing' in her interview-based study of twenty women managers with physical impairments (Boucher 2017, 7). While participants could not choose to hide their impairments, they often found themselves minimising the challenges they were navigating as a result of pain, fatigue and poorly organised inaccessible environments.

Ambivalence about disclosure (Roulstone and Williams 2014) renders numbers unreliable. HESA data includes only information volunteered by staff, some of whom may not realise that their long-term health condition is covered by equalities legislation. The number of disabled people who do not make it through ableist recruitment procedures is currently impossible to capture. Nash (2014) and others argue that the idea of waiting for accurate figures before addressing disability equality at work defies logic, particularly as reasonable adjustments under the 2010 Equality Act should be anticipatory rather than retrospective.

Universal design for learning (UDL) is built on the idea of planning ahead for a diverse group of people with various requirements that can usually be accommodated most easily when strategically and operationally factored in from the beginning. The universality of the concept of UDL means that it is relevant to staff, students and all stakeholders. Arguably UDL diminishes the necessity for ontologically risky disclosure procedures because the infrastructure is effectively better for everyone, which means that reasonable adjustments are therefore required less frequently by individuals.

Research approach

A steering group of disabled staff was drawn from the National Association of Disabled Staff Networks (NADSN) and National Association of Disability Practitioners (NADP). Members of the steering group did not claim to be neutral bystanders but acknowledged a personal interest in disability equality in the workplace (Bryman 2006). Emancipatory research methodology underscored the project, ensuring control by and usefulness to disabled people of the findings as well as accessibility of approach (French and Swain 1997; Barton 2005).

Following ethical clearance, email contact was made with networks and organisations aimed at higher education staff, including the Equality Challenge Unit (ECU), NADP, the Disability Equality Research Network (DERN) and NADSN. Participants were invited to be part of a focus group, have a one-to-one interview or respond anonymously to a questionnaire. Six one-to-one interviews and four focus groups, covering 45 respondents in total, took place and 46 questionnaires were completed. In each situation, open-ended questions were asked that covered the following topics:

- Demographic information including role
- Experiences of impairment
- Identity and disclosure
- Values, influences, strengths and leadership style

- Barriers and frustrations
- Strategies, resources and advice
- Positive suggestions

Results from interviews, focus groups and questionnaires were combined and thematically analysed together. On the advice of the steering group, the data was not broken down according to impairment category in order to avoid 'homogeneity by impairment label' (Madriaga et al. 2008). Grouping responses according to job titles was also avoided, similarly because of the danger of over-generalisation from small numbers. Often people said 'I am only speaking for myself', and this perspective was treated with respect.

Summary of findings

Demographic information

Although giving out personal information without a clear understanding of why they should or how doing so could be of personal benefit made participants feel quite uncomfortable generally, they reported understanding the rationale for doing so within the context of this research. In other situations this request has not seemed neutral or unthreatening to participants, who naturally find themselves questioning the uses to which such information might be put. Many participants felt that the ontological risk of telling the institution outweighed the benefit, particularly if there was no obvious appropriate assistance available. Some commented on thinking very carefully about disclosure during recruitment and not necessarily trusting the non-discrimination statements that accompanied recruitment information.

Of the 91 participants, 46 gave detailed (optional) demographic information. Twenty-one were female, 29 said they were white British nationals and ten characterised themselves as non-white British nationals. Seven were not British nationals. Three stated their religion and ten their sexual orientation; two identified as gay. Ten participants were aged under 40 and three over 60. Thirty-three were in the 40–60 age range. Thirty-four had higher degrees. Twenty-nine had held two or more previous leadership roles. Only seven reported being in their first leadership role. Sixteen worked in Russell Group and red-brick universities and 21 were from universities that prior to 1992 were polytechnics which typically specialised in technical and vocational courses.

Participation was open to people currently or previously in leadership roles and those aspiring to promotion. Participants were self-selecting and contacted via disabled staff networks (Robson et al. 2016), disability-focused JISCMAIL lists and email. Despite best efforts, vice-chancellors and members of university governing bodies are not represented. Participants described their leadership roles as follows:

- Professor
- Principal Lecturer
- Senior Lecturer
- National Teaching Fellow
- Head of Research Centre
- Senior Research Fellow
- CEO
- Senior HE administrator
- Head of Service
- Consultant (post senior HE roles).

In broad terms participants identified their impairments as follows:

- <u>Unseen impairments:</u>
  - Dyslexia
  - Dyspraxia
  - Asperger syndrome
  - Autism
  - Mental health issue
  - Chronic health condition
  - Epilepsy
- <u>Visible impairments:</u>
  - Hearing impairment
  - Visual impairment
  - Mobility impairment
  - Restricted growth.

Ten people stated that they had more than one impairment. Researchers within critical disability studies face criticism for excluding participants identified with intellectual impairment, particularly those who do not communicate conventionally (Goodley 2010). Insights were gathered from one individual who self-identified with intellectual impairment but people with this label are conspicuously absent in higher education. Limited relevant literature exists (for example Caldwell 2011; Schalock and Verdugo 2012), and highlights the need to support without compromising leader autonomy and criticises the paucity of appropriate opportunities for leadership development for this group.

Relevant equalities legislation

Limitations of the Equality Act 2010 were frequently cited, although a small number of participants showed enthusiasm for the intersectional nature of the legislation: for example, 'The Equality Act is good in principle but really – does it have any teeth?' Many recommended the ECU as a source of information about the enactment of equalities legislation, some specifically referencing the report *Enabling Equality: Furthering Disability Equality for Staff in Higher Education* (Ewens and Williams 2011), commissioned jointly by the Leadership Foundation for HE and ECU.

Several participants found the Equality Act's definition of disability to be based too much on the medical model with its emphasis on diagnosis and difference (see for example Gabel and Peters 2004; Palmer and Harley 2012). One participant directly equated the medical model with ableism and the pathologising of difference: 'with all its ableist assumptions, the medical model serves to pathologise, diagnose, try to fix, and in so doing, manages to oppress people deemed to be deviant in some way from the mythological norm'.

Medical model thinking was problematised by participants at all career stages including initial recruitment and promotion. Particularly irritating was the perceived tendency to make assumptions that someone with x medical label would not be able to do y. Some participants felt that this sort of attitude had reduced their promotion chances.

Disabling barriers

Participants focused far more on disabling barriers than impairment but some acknowledged the inter-relationship between both. Seven people described impairment-related pain and fatigue, which was exacerbated by environmental factors. Someone returning from cancer treatment talked about having difficulty in coping with the change in their energy levels after treatment and feeling that the institution had done very little to support their return to work.

Overcoming barriers was a recurring theme. Participants generally thought that their own tenaciousness and problem-solving abilities had enabled them to address disabling barriers for themselves. In relation to supporting colleagues, participants talked more about the application strategy in order to plan effectively to eradicate barriers for others by, for example, ensuring equitable recruitment practices and accessible development opportunities. Positive personal attributes were also acknowledged by participants, particularly in relation to 'thinking outside of the box'. Strengths associated with neurodiversity included creativity, problem-solving skills and an ability to see the bigger picture, a point reiterated in the literature, particularly by dyslexic entrepreneurs (Logan and Martin 2012). One participant commented: 'All my life I have had to solve problems. I'm a disabled person navigating a world designed by non-disabled people. I think laterally and encourage other people to do the same. My approach to leadership is inevitably informed by my approach to life.'

People talked far more about disability than impairment. Many participants referred directly to adopting a social model perspective to circumventing barriers. One specifically referenced the elaborated definition developed by Oliver: 'The social model of disability is about nothing more complicated than a clear focus on the economic, environmental and cultural barriers encountered by people who are viewed by others as having some form of impairment' (Oliver 2009, 47). Shakespeare's (2013) post-social model was evoked by some when discussing the inter-relationship of physical impairment, chronic pain and difficult or inaccessible environments.

The affirmative model (Cameron 2011; Swain and French 2000), which acknowledges the ordinariness of impairment, appealed to many participants. Nash (2014) found that UK disabled employees mainly acquired impairments during their working life, often through getting older. Planning for this eventuality would be in keeping with intersectional approaches to enacting equalities legislation in practical terms.

> I get tired and I have a clear sense of how I can conserve my energy and apply myself effectively. The infrastructure at [institution] is frustratingly inadequate in terms of systems and admin backup, therefore exhausting, for everyone, not just disabled staff.

Participants in this study favour an ontological position that is alive to ableism and the social construction of disability. Among their responses were numerous examples of barriers being created in the workplace for reasons that included ableist attitudes of others. The importance of eradicating or helping other people over these barriers was a recurring theme.

Ableism and identity

Participants emphasised the nuanced nature of the intersection of disability with other aspects of identity such as gender, poverty, race, opportunity and sexual orientation:

> Acknowledge differential experiences of disability discrimination when this oppression is combined with others: the self-advocacy frustrations of a white middle-class woman with anxiety disorder may not be the same as a South Asian working class male with Asperger's, and if both of those individuals are cisgendered or heterosexual their experiences might differ again from LGBTQIA persons.

Several were annoyed by their identity being subsumed by others under an impairment category (e.g. 'the deaf man in library services'). Particularly infuriating were comments like 'I know what you need. We had someone who was wheelchair-bound here before.' Many examples of colleagues using language that may be deemed offensive (such as 'wheelchair-bound') were given, but in the main disabled people expressed understanding of individuals while pointing to institutional gaps in disability equality action and training. Some commented that racist language would not be tolerated by the institution while everyday ableist terms, such as 'mad', 'crazy', 'turn a blind eye' or 'fell on deaf ears', were commonplace at work. Two autistic participants were particularly infuriated by colleagues saying 'we are all on the spectrum' or 'everybody is a bit autistic'.

> Echoing Morley's (2013) findings of women's leadership experiences in higher education, one participant spoke of not fitting into the management 'mythical norm': 'I don't look like any of our senior leadership team. I'm not an old white dude in a grey suit.' Her perspective is supported by the demographic information about leadership in higher education that was quoted earlier.

Examples of judgements based on a single visible facet of someone's identity were evidenced in this and other studies (Campbell 2009; Goodley 2013; 2014). These are illustrative of the day-to-day ableism that disabled people report experiencing: 'They seem to see my physical impairment, not my impressive track record. It is so infuriating to feel that I have to continually justify my place at the leadership table.'

Leadership style

Enactment of the principles of distributed leadership was common among participants. Approaches included: empathising with and encouraging colleagues, collaboration, proactively developing diverse, cohesive, organised teams with a shared vision and not taking credit for the work of others. Inclusive practice and UDL underpinned the ways in which participants were leading. Humility and concern for others characterised their responses but disabled leaders were also able to recognise and describe their own abilities. Strengths included having a clear overview, being organised, planning strategically, acting with integrity and proactively enacting inclusive practices.

> I see the bigger picture while not losing sight of detail. I am strong in working with group dynamics, power relations, inequalities, diversity and inclusion. I have vision and think outside the box. I am not afraid to try new approaches but at the same time I am not too attached to my own perspectives and ideas. Instead, I prefer to work through community and cooperation, while appreciating and providing space for people's uniqueness. I work hard and am committed and invested. I am much organised.

Participants were enthusiastic about facets of distributed leadership without necessarily being aware of the term. The idea of openness of leadership boundaries to enable a broader range of individuals and groups to contribute a variety of expertise, thus enabling numerous, distinct, germane perspectives and capabilities, was described in various ways. Disabled leaders offered examples in which ideas were developed by staff with the relevant skills, then adopted, adapted and improved by other team members within a culture of trust and collaboration.

Leadership behaviours described by participants translated into practical operational examples as well as strategic-level engagement, with good practice often being informed by their own less positive experiences. These included helping colleagues to identify opportunities for development and ensuring equity in recruitment and appropriateness and accessibility of training opportunities.

Strategically, participants were committed to planning for diversity rather than retrofitting reasonable adjustments. Many talked enthusiastically about UDL as an underpinning and overarching framework within which to develop a functional equitable organisation.

Barriers and frustrations

Key themes that emerged were ableist attitudes and assumptions, poor infrastructure and administration, technology and leadership training:

> Other people's attitudes create barriers: I found that often colleagues make assumptions about what is right and what can help the disabled person without asking them.

> I'm nearly 60 and I've had cancer. I get the distinct impression that people above me have decided that an older disabled woman would not be interested in promotion.

UDL principles were seldom in evidence in HEIs and the infrastructure was often inadequate. Participants repeatedly reported having to work hard to ensure their own access to necessary reasonable adjustments:

> Above all, I am tired of the lack of understanding of reasonable adjustments and the energy spent educating people over and over again.

> Our campus is on a hill and I'm timetabled to get from one side to the other in five minutes. I can't do this in my wheelchair. There are no automatic doors. It's a failure of timetabling and estates planning which leaves me frustrated and exhausted.

Several participants commented that leadership programmes were not routinely designed with UDL principles in mind:

> I really find it astonishing that organisers don't anticipate that there may be disabled people present.

> Ironically I could not get to the session I was delivering because the lift wasn't working.

Frustration was expressed about translating access-to-work (AtW) support into arrangements that were hassle-free within the institution:

> Getting support from AtW can be a very slow process. Disabled people usually know what they require. Assessment processes can take time and are not always helpful as the disabled person already knows what type of support and equipment they need. I am at my most productive when I do not have to undertake endless administrative tasks. In a senior role I need a PA!

The availability of assistive technology varied, and this created considerable irritation:

> When ICT systems change there does not seem to be any coherent planning about maintaining accessibility.

> I left one university where assistive technology was networked, promoted and well used by staff and students. It was a nasty surprise when I found I had to start all over again because it was not available as standard in my new place. What followed, inevitably, was months of negotiation with the institution and AtW at a time when I should have been settling into quite a demanding senior role.

The Equality Act 2010 described duties to make reasonable adjustments for disabled employees as anticipatory. Arguably the experience of the participant who did not have appropriate technology for nine months contravenes the anticipatory duty and therefore breaches the Equality Act.

What can be done?

A striking congruence is apparent between the findings of this research and those of the much larger study by RADAR (2010). In both, disabled people reject ableist assumptions and provide insights into the sort of societal constraints that can and do hinder their career progression. Recommendations for action from this study are grouped into four broad themes:

- Strategic-level action
- Inclusive design, UDL, reasonable adjustments and access to work

- Leadership recruitment and development
- Peer support and networks

Strategic-level action

Participants were generally positive about the intersectional principles underpinning the Equality Act 2010 but felt that legislation in isolation would make no difference unless there was high-level commitment to bringing about organisational change. Many recommended visibly championing and strategically planning for disability equality alongside other equalities, and emphasised the importance of acknowledging and rectifying institutional discrimination. A degree of cynicism was apparent about the exercise of writing policies in isolation. Involvement of stakeholders was identified as important (Löve et al. 2018), as was the translation of strategy into action. Policy practice gaps irritate participants, who often articulated practical ways of actually making things work:

> Do the work to understand how your own policies might be perpetuating disableism.[1]

> I would like the fact that I am a disabled parent caring for a disabled child taken into consideration, resulting in a slight reasonable adjustment to my expected output for the next Research Excellence Framework submission. Nobody seems to have thought about this and I would rather not have to point it out myself. It's really awkward.

Benchmarking and equality impact assessment were recommended as ways in which to analyse existing policies and practices, as a precursor to coherent planning for cultural and practical changes (Draffan et al. 2017):

> Organisations should undertake benchmarking (such as the Disability Standard) to analyse existing policies and practices and identify how these can be revised to support more diverse leadership. Ensure that the recruitment policy and procedure has been through an equality impact assessment, is monitored and reviewed regularly to make sure it's practical and fair.

> A systematic cultural change programme within and beyond HE is needed around under-representation and disadvantage of disabled people in employment and other aspects of life, i.e. beyond legal compliance.

Some participants commented on global concerns and were mindful of the privileged position of minority-world countries, in relation to disability equality (an issue that has been explored by Grech 2011, Martin 2011 and others):

> The Disability Discrimination Act, followed by the Equality Act, definitely changed things for the better in this country but this protection is not available all over the world. I'm not sure how aware university staff in the developing world are of the UN Convention on the Rights of People with Disabilities.

Inclusive design, UDL, reasonable adjustments and access to work

Access to work (AtW) was frequently mentioned in this study as having the potential to make a very positive difference to disabled people's working lives, echoing Sayce (2011).

Participants flagged the requirement to raise institutional and individual awareness of AtW and to embed procedures institutionally in order to make the system work in-house. Something seemed to be getting lost in translation, making AtW hard to use in universities. It even felt a bit risky for some, because of compromises in confidentiality and ableist attitudes. Lack of control of the process annoyed many participants, some of whom gave examples of worrying breaches in confidentiality through the forwarding of emails between departments and an 'I hope you don't mind but I've told x and y…' approach. At least one person thought that this sort of ableist attitude had resulted in their missing out on a promotion (and the institution missing out on their talent). Some people sidestepped promotion because setting up the required support was just too much of a three-act drama.

> AtW should be married up with whatever policies we have in place or contracts, you know … for instance, the procurement that goes into getting equipment, getting support workers, all that. There has got to be a more streamlined way of doing it. It's very difficult to get continuity with AtW when moving from one job to another.

> Nobody had any sort of useful conversation with me about my work when I returned from cancer treatment.
>
> Successful people who work for themselves, such as dyslexic entrepreneurs, have control of [the] support they arrange. The university and AtW should listen to me and put in place reasonable things I need. At the moment it's too convoluted and inconsistent. I don't feel able to control the situation adequately. This causes me unnecessary stress.

Many participants were worried that cuts in wider disability benefits would compromise working life. The Independent Living Fund (ILF) closed on 30 June 2015, from which point enquirers were redirected to local councils.

> AtW is part of a wider package. I am concerned about the way things are going with disability benefits generally. The Independent Living Fund is part of the story for many and this is under threat. Proposed Disabled Student Allowance (DSA) changes might discourage potential disabled students and ultimately limit opportunities to get graduate level employment. A joined-up approach is necessary. Moving from DSA to AtW ought to be much simpler.

The benefits to everyone of UDL, including networked assistive technology, came through strongly:

> Universal design isn't about disability. If the university took a good hard look at all its systems from the perspective of the end users and streamlined everything so that the administrative structure was much better, everyone would benefit.
>
> I would not be able to do any of what I do without computers and electronic technology! Much 'assistive technology' is good for everyone. The sector does need a bit of a technological revolution to make best use of it. Networking assistive technology and not associating it specifically with disability would be a start.

Visibility of diverse leadership role models and a high-level commitment to a workplace culture in which diversity was celebrated, rather than problematised, was suggested by many participants. The feeling was that people would be more likely to be open about their requirements in an open and accepting climate, and UDL principles would be more likely to underpin strategy, policy and practice if championed from the top:

> We need to address the policy/practice gap and be very clear about the benefits of diversity in leadership.

Infrastructure and organisational concerns were a thorn in the side of many. Lack of control of such things in the workplace was a major irritation that was also highlighted by Nash (2014) and Roulstone and Williams (2014). Participants in this study were clear that routinely functional administration systems, which would be of benefit for all, would also save universities a lot of money. Some felt that disabled students got a better deal than staff. The expertise in UDL and reasonable adjustments focused on the student experience was not fully available to staff, which seemed somewhat counter-intuitive and wasteful:

> I need about four hours' clerical assistance a week and for that person to do things like format my documents in probably ten minutes. If I was given £50 a week to organise my own clerical support I would be quite happy and a lot less worn out.

> Disability services for students are quite separate from services for staff and usually much better. Joint provision would make sense. There is expertise and resources in universities which staff can't access.

Leadership recruitment and development

Echoing the findings of Nash (2014), participants provided numerous worrying examples of situations in which they considered that ableist attitudes in recruitment and line management and a lack of role models, together with uncertainty about the portability of effective support, had limited their career progression. Roulstone and Williams (2014) used the expression 'glass partition' to reflect the feeling that it was often just too difficult to move on. Waters talked about 'the subtle bigotry of low expectation' (quoted in Nash 2014, 19). The subtle bigotry of ableism appears to be rearing its ugly head too. The first comment below reveals concerns that intersectional approaches to bigotry may well also be in evidence. It is followed by a more positive solution-focused suggestion about diversity in leadership:

> Stop hiring white, abled men. I mean this seriously, it is embarrassing. There should be more women, more disabled people and more people of colour in leadership positions.

> Acknowledge that leadership exists in many forms at many levels and leaders are not all non-disabled white men in grey suits.

Leadership development activities came in for some criticism for their ableist approaches, with a few notable exceptions that seemed to be more in tune with UDL approaches.

Disability Rights UK offers 'A career development programme for people in employment, living with a disability or health condition' (www.disabilityrightsuk.org/disabled-people-leading-career-development, accessed 12 June 2020). Delivery by disabled people is highlighted as a strength in models of good practice mentioned by participants, which also included Frontrunners, Churchill and the Calibre leadership programme:

> Frontrunners and Trailblazers and other similar initiatives are starting to encourage young disabled people to think about leadership. This is a good thing. Churchill and Calibre offer bespoke leadership training for disabled people which is also highly regarded and quite rightly so.

Peer support and networking

Peer support, supportive colleagues and disabled staff networks were valued by participants, although some commented that they felt that the university sometimes hijacked visible initiatives in order to showcase their equality-promoting credentials (Boucher 2017). Embedding groups into structures that could affect strategic-level change was recommended (Robson et al. 2016). Some groups included people indirectly affected by disability through, for example, caring responsibilities.

> It's really important to maintain control and confidentiality so you can be yourself. I do not want my being part of a network to give the university the impression that I necessarily want to be a visible 'face of disability'. I certainly don't want to be 'The Chair'.

> Our disabled staff network is a sub-committee of the Diversity and Equal Opportunities Committee which is chaired by the

> vice-chancellor. It fits into the structure in a real way and this helps us to get our voices heard.
>
> Peer support is really important. I became disabled about six or seven years into the job and I came to you for advice because I felt vulnerable, isolated and lost and didn't know what to do. I still remember I said how I may end up in a wheelchair and you said, 'Don't worry, you'll have more energy!'
>
> I am staying in this job because I am surrounded by supportive colleagues.

Participants engaging in blue-sky thinking thought that a national network for disabled university leaders would be fantastic. NADSN includes members in leadership roles (Robson et al. 2016). Meeting disabled peers at NADP, NADSN, ECU and similar conferences, all of which have been complimented on their attention to accessibility, was discussed in terms of 'providing a sense of solidarity'. Nash (2014) has developed 'Purple Space', described on its website as 'the network for promoting disabled talent in business' (www.purplespace.org, accessed 12 June 2020).

The way ahead?

Ideas for further research emerging from this study include:

- Embedding equality and diversity considerations into future research around leadership practice, and developing a better understanding of the constraints of ableism (Corlett and Williams 2011).
- Evaluating leadership training through the lens of ableism.
- Considering in greater depth the impact of ableism during transitions between work roles and organisations.
- Encompassing intersections with disability and age equality into research on ageing and ageism in the workplace.
- Ensuring consideration of inclusion of insights from participants who do not use speech as their primary means of communication and/or have the label of intellectual impairment (Goodley 2010).

- Being aware of the findings of Nash (2014) and others that people with long-term health conditions may not identify as disabled and facilitating the inclusion of people to whom this applies.
- Engaging in longitudinal study of the leadership trajectories of disabled people.
- Considering barriers to getting to first base in employment in higher education by scrutinising the equitability of recruitment processes.

No grand claims are made for this study, which simply engages with the limited available literature and captures views of willing volunteers at a particular point in time. Voices will inevitably have been missed, including individuals who do not realise that they are protected as a disabled person under the Equality Act 2010 and people who could not access the processes used for gathering data.

Concluding thoughts

Many decision makers within the sector may never have heard the word 'ableism', but disabled people who responded to this research provided ample evidence of its existence in UK universities. Experiences of disabled leaders and aspiring leaders, gathered by questionnaires, focus groups and interviews, highlighted workplace ableist barriers but also suggested potential straightforward and inexpensive solutions to practically all of them. These were mainly based around UDL principles but required decision makers to understand and want to utilise a UDL strategy. Participants felt that a culture change was required to move institutions closer to understanding and addressing ableism and embedding UDL into policies, practices and procedures. Recommendations included avoiding ableism in initial recruitment, promotion and leadership development, ensuring the visibility of positive senior disabled role models, and recognising and encouraging the skills disabled leaders can bring to the party. Simple changes to make the infrastructure and administration processes more efficient were suggested and would benefit everybody. No one thrives in chaos. Disabled leaders had a clear understanding of the sort of arrangements that would help them and these were often systemic rather than individualised. Networking assistive technology was given as an example that would not just benefit disabled people. On a practical level, disabled leaders wished for more control over how processes like

AtW played out. Some commented that lack of control also felt like lack of respect. Having a narrow idea about what a leader should look like can result in institutions missing out on talented disabled leaders, who have often developed immense problem-solving skills through having to navigate disabling barriers in everyday life. Characteristics associated with effective distributed leadership were amply demonstrated. These included thinking strategically, communicating effectively, encouraging and developing diverse teams and acting with integrity. The advantages of encouraging diversity in the workplace, including at the most senior level, are well documented. Disability is an ordinary part of diversity. In an ableist culture disability can be problematised while other diversity strands are encouraged. Clearly this is just not good enough.

Acknowledgement

Thank you to Joanna Krupa for the provision of expert disability-related assistance and to the participants who gave freely of their time.

Note

1 See Sara Ahmed's 'On Being Included' for a useful discussion of this in relation to race (2012, 44–50).

References

Ahmed, S. *On Being Included: Racism and Diversity in Institutional Life*. Durham, NC: Duke University Press, 2012.

Avery, Derek R., McKay, Patrick F. and Volpone, Sabrina D. 'Blaming the Building: How Venue Quality Influences Consumer Bias Against Stigmatized Leaders', *Journal of Applied Psychology* 101/8 (2016): 1111–21. Online. https://doi.org/10.1037/apl0000117 (accessed 25 May 2020).

Barton, Len. 'Emancipatory Research and Disabled People: Some Observations and Questions', *Educational Review* 57/3 (2005): 317–27. Online. https://doi.org/10.1080/00131910500149325 (accessed 25 May 2020).

Bass, Bernard M. 'Two Decades of Research and Development in Transformational Leadership', *European Journal of Work and Organizational Psychology* 8/1 (1999): 9–32. Online. https://doi.org/10.1080/135943299398410 (accessed 25 May 2020).

Bebbington, Dianne. *Diversity in Higher Education: Leadership Responsibilities and Challenges*. London: Leadership Foundation for Higher Education, 2009. Online. https://www.lfhe.ac.uk/en/components/publication.cfm/S2-02 (accessed 25 May 2020).

Bennett, Nigel, Wise, Christine, Woods, Philip A. and Harvey, Janet A. *Distributed Leadership: A Review of Literature*. Nottingham: National College for School Leadership, 2003.

Black, Simon A. 'Qualities of Effective Leadership in Higher Education', *Open Journal of Leadership* 4/02 (2015): 54–66. Online. https://doi.org/10.4236/ojl.2015.42006 (accessed 26 May 2020).

Bolden, Richard, Petrov, Georgy and Gosling, Jonathan. *Developing Collective Leadership in Higher Education*. London: Leadership Foundation for Higher Education, 2008.

Boucher, Carlene. 'The Roles of Power, Passing, and Surface Acting in the Workplace Relationships of Female Leaders with Disability', *Business and Society* 56/7 (2017): 1004–32. Online. https://doi.org/10.1177/0007650315610610 (accessed 27 May 2020).

Bryman, Alan. 'Integrating Quantitative and Qualitative Research: How Is It Done?' *Qualitative Research* 6/1 (2006): 97–113. Online. https://doi.org/10.1177/1468794106058877 (accessed 27 May 2020).

Caldwell, Joe. 'Disability Identity of Leaders in the Self-Advocacy Movement', *Intellectual and Developmental Disabilities* 49/5 (2011): 315–26. Online. https://doi.org/10.1352/1934-9556-49.5.315 (accessed 27 May 2020).

Cameron, Colin. 'Not our Problem: Impairment as Difference, Disability as Role', *The Journal of Inclusive Practice in Further and Higher Education* 3/2 (2011): 10–25.

Campbell, Fiona Kumari. *Contours of Ableism: The Production of Disability and Abledness*. Basingstoke and New York: Palgrave Macmillan, 2009.

Charlton, James I. *Nothing About Us Without Us: Disability Oppression and Empowerment*. Berkeley: University of California Press, 1998.

Charmaz, Kathy. 'Grounded Theory Methods in Social Justice Research'. In *The Sage Handbook of Qualitative Research*, edited by Norman Denzin and Yvonna S. Lincoln, 4th ed., 359–80. London and Thousand Oaks, CA: Sage, 2011.

Corlett, Sandra and Williams, Jannine. 'The Effects of Discourse and Local Organising Practices on Disabled Academics', Identities and Critical Management Studies. Stream 29. Newcastle: Northumbria University, 2011.

Deegan, Mary Jo. 'Multiple Minority Groups: A Case Study of Physically Disabled Women'. In *Women and Disability*, edited by Mary Jo Deegan and Nancy A. Brooks, 37–55. Abingdon and New York: Routledge, 2018, originally 1985. Online. https://doi.org/10.4324/9781351318082 (accessed 27 May 2020).

Draffan, E.A., James, A. and Martin, N. 'Inclusive Teaching and Learning: What's Next?' *Journal of Inclusive Practice in Further and Higher Education* 9/1 (2017): 23–34.

Equality Challenge Unit. *Equality in Higher Education: Statistical Report 2015 Part 1: Staff*. London: Equality Challenge Unit, 2015.

Ewens, David and Williams, Jannine. *Enabling Equality: Furthering Disability Equality for Staff in Higher Education: Literature Review*. London: Equality Challenge Unit and Leadership Foundation for Higher Education, 2011.

French, Sally and Swain, John. 'Changing Disability Research: Participating and Emancipatory Research with Disabled People', *Physiotherapy* 83/1 (1997): 26–32. Online. https://doi.org/10.1016/S0031-9406(05)66107-X (accessed 27 May 2020).

Gabel, Susan and Peters, Susan. 'Presage of a Paradigm Shift? Beyond the Social Model of Disability Toward Resistance Theories of Disability', *Disability and Society* 19/6 (2004): 585–600. Online. https://doi.org/10.1080/0968759042000252515 (accessed 27 May 2020).

Goodley, Dan. *Disability Studies: An Interdisciplinary Introduction*. London: Sage, 2010.

Goodley, Dan. 'Dis/entangling Critical Disability Studies', *Disability and Society* 28/5 (2013): 631–44. Online. https://doi.org/10.1080/09687599.2012.717884 (accessed 27 May 2020).

Goodley, Dan. *Dis/ability Studies: Theorising Disablism and Ableism*. Abingdon and New York: Routledge, 2014.

Grech, Shaun. 'Recolonising Debates or Perpetuated Coloniality? Decentring the Spaces of Disability, Development and Community in the Global South', *International Journal of Inclusive Education* 15/1 (2011): 87–100. Online. https://doi.org/10.1080/13603116.2010.496198 (accessed 27 May 2020).

Guilbourg, Clara. 'Big University Gender Pay Gap Revealed'. BBC News. 29 March 2019. Online. https://www.bbc.co.uk/news/business-47723950 (accessed 11 April 2019).

Higher Education Statistics Agency (HESA). 'Higher Education Statistics for the UK 2016/17'. Online. https://www.hesa.ac.uk/data-and-analysis/publications/higher-education-2016-17 (accessed 11 April 2019).

Higher Education Statistics Agency (HESA). 'Data Intelligence'. Online. www.hesa.ac.uk/support/data-intelligence?data_streams=5&year=3&field=All (accessed 13 Dec 2016).

Logan, J. and Martin, N. 'Unusual Talent: A Study of Successful Leadership and Delegation in Entrepreneurs who have Dyslexia', *Inclusive Practice* 4/1 (2012): 57–76.

Loja, Ema, Costa, Maria E., Hughes, Bill and Menezes, Isabel. 'Disability, Embodiment and Ableism: Stories of Resistance', *Disability and Society* 28/2 (2013): 190–203. Online. https://doi.org/10.1080/09687599.2012.705057 (accessed 27 May 2020).

Lorde, Audre. *Sister Outsider*. Freedom, CA: Crossing Press, 1984.

Löve, Laufey, Traustadóttir, Rannveig and Rice, James G. 'Achieving Disability Equality: Empowering Disabled People to Take the Lead', *Social Inclusion* 6/1 (2018): 1–8. Online. https://doi.org/10.17645/si.v6i1.1180 (accessed 27 May 2020).

Madriaga, M., Goodley, D., Hodge, N. and Martin, N. 'Enabling Transitions into Higher Education for Students with Asperger Syndrome'. Higher Education Academy, 2008. Online. http://shura.shu.ac.uk/id/eprint/1004 (accessed 27 May 2020).

Martin, Nicola. 'Progressing Disability Equality in Further and Higher Education in the Majority World. Could NADP Help?' *Journal of Inclusive Practice in Further and Higher Education* 3/1 (2011): 18–25. Online. https://nadp-uk.org/wp-content/uploads/2015/02/JIPFHE.ISSUE-3.1.pdf (accessed 27 May 2020).

Martin, Nicola. 'Encouraging Disabled Leaders in Higher Education: Recognising Hidden Talents'. Stimulus paper. London: Leadership Foundation for Higher Education, 2017. Online. https://www.lfhe.ac.uk/en/components/publication.cfm/MartinST36 (accessed 27 May 2020).

Morley, Louise. 'Women and Higher Education Leadership'. Stimulus paper. London: Leadership Foundation for Higher Education, 2013. Online. https://www.lfhe.ac.uk/en/components/publication.cfm/MorleyST10 (accessed 27 May 2020).

Nash, Kate. *Secrets & Big News. Enabling People to be Themselves at Work*. Codsall: Kate Nash Associates, 2014.

Oliver, Michael. *Understanding Disability*, 2nd ed. Basingstoke and New York: Palgrave Macmillan, 2009.

Palmer, Michael and Harley, David. 'Models and Measurement in Disability: An International Review', *Health Policy and Planning* 27/5 (2012): 357–64. Online. https://doi.org/10.1093/heapol/czr047 (accessed 27 May 2020).

RADAR. *Doing Seniority Differently. A Study of High Fliers Living with Ill Health, Injury or Disability*. RADAR, 2010. Online. https://www.disabilityrightsuk.org/sites/default/files/pdf/doing-senioritydifferently.pdf (accessed 27 May 2020).

Robson, Linda, Patel, Mona and Nicholson, Jacquie. 'National Association of Disabled Staff Networks (NADSN) – "Our Stories: Experiences from our Disabled Staff Networks across the UK"', *Journal of Inclusive Practice in Further and Higher Education* 7 (2016): 28–33.

Roulstone, Alan and Williams, Jannine. 'Being Disabled, Being a Manager: "Glass Partitions" and Conditional Identities in the Contemporary Workplace', *Disability and Society* 29/1 (2014): 16–29. Online. https://doi.org/10.1080/09687599.2013.764280 (accessed 27 May 2020).

Sayce, Liz. *Getting In, Staying In and Getting On. Disability Employment Support Fit for the Future*. London: Department for Work and Pensions, 2011. Online. https://assets.publishing.service.gov.uk/government/uploads/system/uploads/attachment_data/file/49779/sayce-report.pdf (accessed 27 May 2020).

Schalock, Robert L. and Verdugo, Miguel Á. *A Leadership Guide for Today's Disabilities Organizations: Overcoming Challenges and Making Change Happen*. Baltimore, MD: Brookes, 2012.

Shakespeare, Tom. *Disability Rights and Wrongs Revisited*, 2nd ed. Abingdon and New York: Routledge, 2013.

Swain, John and French, Sally. 'Towards an Affirmation Model of Disability', *Disability and Society* 15/4 (2000): 569–82. Online. https://doi.org/10.1080/09687590050058189 (accessed 27 May 2020).

Williams, J. 'What Can Disabled Academics' Career Experiences Offer to Studies of Organization?' PhD diss., Northumbria University, 2011.

Appendix: Questionnaire

Demographic information

Name (optional):
Email (optional):
Position held:
Institution (optional) or type of institution:
Further background information you consider relevant, e.g. age, gender, ethnicity, qualifications, previous roles (optional)

Consent for information to be used anonymously on the understanding that I can withdraw prior to publication (Signature)

Open-ended questions

1. How would you describe your contribution to higher education?
2. How would you characterise your leadership style?
3. What influenced your development as a leader? (Prompt: include comments on specific leadership training, if any.)
4. What are your strengths?
5. What do you enjoy about your role?
6. How would you describe the values that underpin your work?
7. What are your ambitions?
8. What would make your work life easier?
9. What is your greatest achievement?
10. What could make you even more productive?
11. What aspects of your role do you find particularly dull and why? Could this be changed? How?
12. What is your greatest frustration about work?
13. What aspects of your role do you find particularly rewarding and why?
14. What, if anything, would you like to say about your impairment (in broad terms)?
15. What are the main barriers you experience in relation to your role and what might help to reduce these? (Prompt: own actions, other people, systems.)
16. What aspects of your role do you find particularly challenging and why?

17. What sort of policy, practice, legislation, support or assistance would make or has made a positive difference to you at work, and how? (Prompt: in relation to access-to-work funding, membership of networks and/or interest in networks, in which case, what would these look like, sources of useful information, union support, mentoring etc.).
18. What advice might you give to your 25-year-old self about career development and/or leadership? (Question to be adjusted if interviewing anyone younger than 30.)
19. What would be your three top tips to aspiring leaders?
20. What would be your three top tips to institutions in relation to recruiting, retaining and supporting leaders?
21. What would be your three top tips to institutions in relation to recruiting, retaining and supporting disabled leaders (if there is any difference from your answers to question 20)?
22. Have you got any practical suggestions for existing resources, resource development, useful training, training that would be useful but does not exist, policy etc.?
23. Any other comments you have not had the opportunity to make?

6
Autoimmune actions in the ableist academy

Alice Andrews

Behind me, all down my back, joints, tendons and ligaments stiffen and tighten. At the back of my mind I sense that the woolly incoherence of my thoughts is worsening. My guts clench. It is hard to write these words. The medical complex offers a diagnosis that brings the problem(s) to the fore: autoimmune diseases causing systemic inflammation, pain, stiffness, fatigue, mood swings, brain fog; my immune system is attacking *me*. 'I' have turned on and against 'myself'. I work harder to try to keep up; symptoms worsen. Losing control of myself, my life, my work, I sense that I need to live and work differently. But my backbone is paralysed. I don't have the guts (metaphors abound!) to admit to not being in control. I need help.

> Here is where the cruel autoimmunity with which sovereignty is affected begins, the autoimmunity with which sovereignty at once sovereignly affects and cruelly infects itself. […] It is not some particular thing that is affected in autoimmunity but the self, the ipse, the autos that finds itself infected. As soon as it needs heteronomy, the event, time and the other. (Derrida 2005, 109)

Out of the experience of a hyper-immune body that painfully attacks itself comes the experience of the autoimmunity of the self itself. Jacques Derrida employs the biomedical term autoimmunity as a further name for the deconstructive trace that inscribes a paradoxical opening (from) closure of the sovereign self, where the sovereign self *requires* others in order to 'be' (that is protect/immunise) that which it 'is'.[1] The sense of self as whole, autonomous, rational and able, which is presumed within much academic labour, is inherited from Western modernity's bias towards rationality and immunity from difference. And yet, as I work to find a position within autoimmune illness from which to work, this academic self struggles to assert itself.

For Derrida, in order to protect (immunise) the *autos* one must oneself destroy (autoimmunise) one's own unity by admitting difference (Derrida and Borradori 2003). As my body attacks itself, protection of the notion of myself as an able, autonomous, whole, healthy and secure self is demanded; and yet the more I defend this notion of myself, the more I destroy it – the harder I work the less I *work*. The process is a cruel, painful and even terrifying one, and risks 'paralysis' (Derrida and Borradori 2003, 188). And yet, according to Derrida, it is also the threat of this petrifying autoimmunity that necessarily forces one to open to difference, the event and the future, *for better as well as worse* (Derrida and Borradori 2003, 124).

This chapter begins from the subjective experience of autoimmune illness in the academy. It begins from desire to survive academia and the autoimmunities of the attempts to do so. This autoimmunity forces me to seek assistance from others, to locate the problem not within the suffering individual but within the hyper-immunisations of ableist norms, which are inherited from Western modernity and maintained within the neoliberal present. The intention is to suggest that the academy's attempts at self-defence are autoimmune – particularly with regard to its attempts to eradicate illness, disability and difference – and that this autoimmunity might force an opening to ways of working together that could move beyond a logic of survival.

The term 'autoimmunity' recalls legacies of Western modernity that continue to inform the contemporary academy and this chapter. In addition to the sense of 'self' and 'other' inherent within biological and conceptual understandings of immunity, immunity also locates a juridico-political context concerning the sharing or the refusal of the gifts and the duties of the *munus*, that is, the inclusions or exclusions within communities. The mechanisms of community/immunity are often based on norms such as nationality, race, ability, etc., and is a mechanism that readily exposes itself to autoimmune destruction.[2] But further, autoimmune illnesses – sometimes dubbed 'Western diseases' – have been linked to the effects of industrial capitalism with its production of increasingly toxic global environments, on both a material level of pollutants and an affective level of anxiety, depression and stress – which trigger over-the-top immune responses as a consequence of this fragility (Nakazawa 2008; Velasquez-Manoff 2013; Berlant 2011; Puar 2017, Cvetkovich 2012; DiAngelo 2011). Though there is not the space to unpack all of these complications here, it is essential to note that these histories effect the bodyminds of those working within – or excluded from – the academy, and thus affect the capacity of the academy to engage with its colonial and ableist past and present, and its capacity to call for imagining new futures. Autoimmune bodyminds in the academy, like canaries in the coalmine,[3] add a further important perspective to demands for engaging in the labour of institutional change: if we fail to challenge ableist norms, debilitated bodyminds risk continuing to fail to perform this essential work.

Deconstructive autoimmunity offers a way of thinking, I would suggest, that works not *against* risk, incoherence, pain, suffering, paralysis and loss of control (sovereign decision-making), but rather finds, with and within these, suggestions for living and working differently. It is in this sense that affinities can be marked between Derridean autoimmunity and the perspectives of crip theory, another body of thought to which I open for assistance. The term 'crip', following Robert McRuer (2006), Alison Kafer (2013) and others, is a redeployment of the disparaging term 'cripple' as a social, political and theoretical agitator. As a verb form 'cripping' marks an action that deconstructs the rigid identifiers 'disability' and 'ability' to indicate the fluid and constructed character of disability's entanglements within material, social, cultural and political systems that work to privilege certain abilities over others. Crip theory therefore employs deconstructive gestures in order to resist the exclusion of disability, pain, suffering and illness – which persist as criteria for elimination in many societies and institutions – and to argue, from a social justice perspective, for the need to lessen the violence and suffering that such exclusions create. Perhaps, by mobilising crip knowledges, and by cripping knowledge (Johnson and McRuer 2014), the autoimmune self-destruction of the contemporary university might be reconfigured as the self destruction of the *immune system* that protects the neoliberal, racist, ableist and individualist university, with the aim of opening in its place a system of protection, interdependency and mutuality that might take care of *all* forms of suffering.

By deploying a crip autoimmune autobiographical account, I am able to attend to *both* the need to take care and protect oneself within specific, situated and personal problematics of survival and injustice, *and* its autoimmune opening to interdependency and the needs and injustices faced by others. The methodology gives permission to begin from where one is and to resist ableist norms: to be slow, to fumble, to work from within messy contingencies, to acknowledge that analyses will not be perfect and will exclude and misrepresent others' experiences, to face the pain and difficulties of this, while insisting on both continuing the attempt and sharing this with others. The specific site of *this* analysis as an account of an autoimmune academic will be that of the UK university system, examined from the narrow perspective of one able to call themself an ill, white, cis female mother and academic who passes as able-bodied and middle class. My question, from my sickbed, becomes: what might the experiences of autoimmunity and ableism have to teach us about the demands of the university? And might the 'autoimmune illnesses' of the university – which are not only a metaphor – be that which, in Derrida's words, '[risks] paralyzing and thus [calls] for the event of the interruptive decision' (2005, 35)?

Autoimmune identifications

Having given myself permission to speak from where I am, the question of *how* to speak arises, of how '*I am*', and to whom I am able to speak. In order to unpack the autoimmunities of the academy I begin with the question of identification. Living and working with chronic illness, with fluctuating energy and pain levels and uncertainty regarding the future, can be isolating. Usually such experiences enter discussions in the academic workplace only through acts of individual disclosure (Price and Kerschbaum 2016). The workforce is presumed able-bodied and able-minded until proven otherwise. The onus is, therefore, placed on individuals to navigate support through obtuse administrative networks. This results in the non-disabled not being required to consider the effects of dis/ability (until they may experience disability themselves). It further results in individuals who find themselves to be in tension with the abled norm to negotiate processes and politics of identification alone. Answering Corbett O'Toole's (2013) call for greater disclosure of one's relationship to disability within disability studies, I outline here an incomplete account of my developing relationship to identifications with disability – and the (auto)immunities of these – in order to add my voice to those who are working to resist this isolating experience.[4]

As soon as the word identity appears, protective battles, conflicts and disagreements are evoked, and wherever defensive battles are evoked, so too is the possibility of a self-destructive autoimmune rebound – or potential autoimmune openings. This is certainly true with regard to disability identity, which – when experienced by many to be an identity policed by medical certifications, normative representations and attitudes, and political positions – can lead to recurring questions: am I disabled enough? Am I disabled in the 'right way' to employ this identifier? How might my experience of illness (and by extension pathologised forms of neurodiversity, mental distress, etc.) communicate within the languages of disability?

As Susan Wendell (2001, 17) has argued, many disability activists involved in the political struggle to secure disability rights in the West have resisted the identification of disability with illness due to the fact that this association risks contributing to the medicalising of disability. Medical models often view disability as an individual misfortune that medicine can and should remedy or mitigate, constructing it as shameful, pitiable and radically undesirable (Siebers 2008, 3). To counter this pathologising individualisation of disability, activists have worked hard to dissociate disability from an individual's physical impairments and locate them firmly instead in disabling social conditions – material, cultural, political, attitudinal. In the 1970s UK-based activists from the Union of the Physically Impaired Against Segregation (UPIAS) produced a foundational definition of what has come to be known as the social model of disability, where disability is considered to be 'something imposed on top of our impairments by the way we are excluded from full participation in society'; 'it is society which disables physically impaired people' (UPIAS quoted in Oliver 1983, 24).

The clarity of the social model has been hugely successful in communicating that much of the suffering experienced by disabled people is a result of systemic oppression, and also in galvanising a disability rights movement that secured legal rights for disabled people in the UK and elsewhere.[5] Yet this activist history, as Wendell reminds us, has tended to exclude the ill disabled in its demands for full participation, for '[f]luctuating abilities and limitations can make people with chronic illnesses seem like unreliable activists […]. Stamina is required for commitment to a cause' (Wendell 2001, 25). Considering, from my sickbed, how to remain committed to an academic cause, to social justice, and the responsible teaching and research that this necessitates, demands that I follow Wendell in challenging these requirements. Indeed, I would suggest that the insistence on any form of political activism that renders impairments, debility, illness and so on as outside its politics risks autoimmune self-destruction. What the social model, with its strict binary between impairment and disability, obscures is the fact that bodyminds fail – they suffer pain, trauma, fatigue; they get worn out – and that this debilitation is disabling in our social world. By excluding such experiences from social and educational environments, we risk excluding the possibility of developing skills of interdependency, of taking care of and with one another through differences, and the central importance of this within any activist movement – or workplace. For Wendell, living with disabilities including 'living with pain, fatigue, nausea, unpredictable abilities, and/or the imminent threat of death creates different ways of being that give valuable perspectives on life and the world' (2001, 31). If we were to agree with Wendell, we would have to concur that this value cannot be indexed to any form of productivity, but must instantiate an alternative understanding of value – the value, perhaps, of always already resisting capitalist demands for individual productivity (Lazard 2017).[6]

However, the particularity of my perspective reminds me to remain attentive to the potential autoimmune rebounds of this move to welcome pathology into disability identity. It feels risky to identify with a stigmatised form of difference such as being one of the unhealthy disabled, for here narratives of disability pride are easily overwritten by narratives of overcoming, eradication and cure that continue to oppress disabled people (Clare 2017). As a straight, white, cisgendered woman with (relatively stable) employment and access to a National Health Service, some of these risks are mitigated. However, for those whose bodyminds continue to be pathologised due to constructions of race, gender, sexuality and class – where queer, black, brown, female and trans bodyminds are biologised – affirmative identifications with disability, illness or suffering might become less easy to imagine (McRuer 2006; Lukin 2013; Erevelles 2005; 2011; Spade 2011).

Metaphors of disability and impairment are deeply ingrained in our language and cultural discourses and have commonly been employed to signify lack of worth, to oppress and exclude already marginalised identities (Lukin 2013, 312). For example, disability metaphors, when intersecting with racist oppressions, result in a greater number of people of colour being identified as disabled (Erevelles and Minear 2010, 357), while trans people are characterised as ill in order to permit access to procedures (Preciado 2013; Spade 2011), and poverty and oppression under global neoliberal capitalism bar many from essential healthcare (Puar 2017). In light of these crossing histories, illness and disability can become a troubled site for easy identification. And within a university system whose colonial, classist and eugenicist histories continue to hold influence, such historical intersections are essential to consider (Bhambra et al. 2018; Dolmage 2017).

Yet according to Nirmala Erevelles and Andrea Minear, many critical race theorists, and radical scholars more generally, 'have mistakenly conceived of disability as a biological category, as an immutable and pathological abnormality' (2010, 358) and have therefore resisted recognising *shared* commitments to resisting disqualifications based on perceived, biologised or essentialised characteristics. Illness and disability, like race or gender, are not essentialisable but are part of a spectrum of life and of experience, and while the aim to lessen suffering is to be affirmed, excluding – or *eradicating* – on the basis of (perceived) suffering *causes* further violence by legitimating eugenicist discourses, whilst also excluding 'cripistemologies' from our collective knowledges and legacies. Indeed, Therí A. Pickens has argued that there is much promise in Arab American and African American narratives that rely on the body's mundane fragilities, where pain and illness need not be read as worthless but instead mobilise these everyday experiences as urgent social and political critique (Pickens 2014). I would suggest that such experiences also have much to offer the social and political critique of the ableist academy. Here forced attention to my own mundane fragilities led me to recognise the mechanisms of identification that oppress not only myself, but also multiple others.

Having spent the last few years experiencing diffused non-specific yet increasingly alarming symptoms – from overwhelming fatigue to poor concentration, from depression to menstrual irregularities – an embodied awareness of the workplace's demands for identification came to light. Initially the banality of the symptoms allowed them to be ignored; when they could no longer be ignored they could be attributed to my autoimmune illnesses, my poor diet or busy life as a working mother, perhaps to the hectic term and the stresses of teaching increasing numbers of struggling students, or to political conditions. When doctors come to be involved early menopause is first assumed; when pathology is investigated 'normal ranges' insist on health – until, as chance would have it, a blood test is secured, an anomaly found, a diagnosis made. My experience of debilitating symptoms exists within a complexity of environmental conditions (including the gender biases of the doctor's surgery and the allocation of caring responsibilities at home and at work) that not only make the symptoms worse – or even cause them in the first place[7] – but also reveal the intrinsic failures of the demand for what Ellen Samuels calls 'biocertification' within 'fantasies of identification' (2014, 12). Regardless of my self-identification as disabled or as chronically ill, with the appearance of new, uncertain symptoms, accommodations at work are difficult to source without a medical certificate, and a medical certificate is difficult to source if one's embodied symptoms do not conform to pre-established 'normal ranges'.

According to Samuels, it was Western modernity's crisis of identification – driven by colonialism, urbanisation, class and geographic mobility, and the rise of the welfare state – that led to a drive for incontrovertible physical evidence to biologically certify, capture and control identity (2014, 1–2). The demand for physical evidence works to naturalise racial and bodymind differences, which not only enforces, but also produces, biological normalcy, producing and maintaining racial and gender oppressions, and the disablement that so often results. Tracing the first appearance of the English word 'normal' to 1840 and the genesis of statistical analysis, the disability scholar Lennard Davis (2013) details how in the nineteenth century statistics combined with socially constructed ideas of the perfect body to determine what counts as healthy or pathological. With regard to disability identity Davis asks: is 'impairment bred into the bone, or can it be a creation of a medical-technological-pharmaceutical complex?' (Davis 2013, 238). We might further add with regard to race or gender identity: is the medical-technological-pharmaceutical complex complicit in the construction of the biocertifications of race and gender that oppress, exclude and disable people of colour and trans people in particular?

In the academy, the biocertification of mobile experiences of illness, distress and disability can, perhaps, be most clearly seen in the case of mental disabilities as an increasing mental health crisis is widely reported. For despite there being no biological markers to determine diagnoses – only a range of mostly behavioural symptoms based on societal norms (Fullagar 2018, 40) – staff and students are required to prove mental disabilities through medical certificates. However, according to the UK psychiatrist Sami Timimi, one can more convincingly consider one's socio-political environment – characterised, as I shall clarify in the following section, as neoliberal – as producing both mental distress *and* its medicalisation:

> the pressures to compete and then deal with perceiving oneself (or being perceived by others) as a 'loser', the individualisation of identity and ambition, the internalisation of anxieties of failing, the mass surveillance of parents/teachers and young people, and the commodification of potential solutions […] all contribute to the rapid numbers of psychiatric diagnoses. (Timimi 2018, 61)

These are diagnoses, I would add, that fall upon certain disabled, gendered and racialised bodyminds more than others (Moodley et al. 2018), and diagnoses one is *encouraged* to seek due to the manner in which these govern access to support. Yet according to Timimi, these 'diagnostic systems used in psychiatry have failed to establish themselves as scientifically credible or clinically useful'. In response to this failure, Timimi's suggestion (based on outcome-based research) is to advocate concentrating on the 'contextual and real-life experiences of patients' rather than diagnoses in order to select treatments (Timimi 2018, 61). I take this to mean, in line with the social model, that one should consider mental disability not in terms of medically certifiable pathology, but within a specific, disabling context. I would agree, yet I further want to insist that it is also necessary to account for the mobility of biological impairments in neoliberal environments as the effects of stress, diet, pollution, toxins, etc. impact on embodied experience and the identifications of health, illness and 'normal ranges'.

Samuels suggests that the civil rights movement and the development of queer and crip resistances, for example, have done little to challenge these 'fantasies of identification' and their demand for biocertifications (2014, 10). And indeed we could suggest that it is precisely when these deconstructions of identity are combined with a period of austerity and the shrinking of the welfare state that the demand to definitively identify and certify disabled, immigrant, queer and trans bodyminds can be seen to be increasing (McRuer 2018). In the university this policing of disability, race and gender becomes immediately clear in the demand for certificates to prove one's right to access accommodations, or the right to work or study, or to access health or wellbeing services. Such practices are clear attempts to immunise the social body through fantasies of identification and the maintenance of ableist norms. I would argue that these immunisations, in their selection in favour of abled bodies and minds, are in fact autoimmune, and as such are forcing us to consider our relations to, and potential identifications with, illness, disability, race and gender – as well as our capacity for collective resistances in the academy and beyond.

Autoimmune abilities

The UK 2010 Equality Act provides legal protections for disabled people, protections secured as a direct result of the activism of disability rights campaigners and their understanding of the social model of disability.

The Act defines disability as 'a physical or mental impairment that has a "substantial" and "long-term" negative effect on your ability to do normal daily activities' (http://www.legislation.gov.uk/ukpga/2010/15/contents). The law offers (to those who can biocertify their impairment) the right to request reasonable accommodations. In the workplace these might be adjustments to working conditions designed to 'level the playing field', modifying the environment in order to enable an individual to engage in 'normal daily activities'. However, this logic of levelling the playing field leads to the question of what the rules of the game might be and what the 'normal daily activities' in the academy have become (Kalfa et al. 2018). And it is a logic that belies the fact that the playing field is experienced by many as a battle field, upon which the metaphors of defence and attack take on a different quality.

Writing in the *Guardian* in 2018, an anonymous academic provides an insight into the rules of the game for UK academia. They ask us to imagine what it is like to be on the hiring committee for a permanent lectureship:

> Imagine working in an industry where entry-level jobs require 'world-leading' research records [...]. [Where the candidates have] gained teaching and admin experience, published books and papers (and planned the next ones), thought about impact and outreach, and earned an impressive set of references and student feedback in addition to their outstanding formal qualifications. [...] They've probably not been paid for all of this work. They've been juggling their considerable achievements with part-time (or sometimes even full-time) jobs outside academia, or they've been relying on financial support from a parent or partner. [...] How lucky the academy is. (*Guardian* 2018)

Acknowledging that the new standard is 'exceptional', the writer of this article proceeds to argue that one should not select from the long list of exceptional applicants 'the most exceptional overachiever', for such individuals are likely to be 'habituated to toxic and even harmful levels of overwork' (*Guardian* 2018). Instead, it is suggested, one should ask who needs the job most, based on precarity, 'age, race, ability, or health', for such individuals might have the skills to be 'adaptable' and think 'beyond the current frameworks'. The current frameworks referred to include the normalising of attainment and pay gaps related to ethnicity, gender and disability, excessive workloads, the use of temporary contracts and the use of performance monitors such as the Research Excellence Framework

(REF) and Teaching Excellence Framework (TEF). Within all of this, in order to survive, students and academics are forced to adhere to ever rising standards, to perform the role of the competent, knowing expert, and to compete with and *out*perform one another in these roles. The implication in the quotation above is that the non-normative academic has value as a potential agitator of these ableist conditions – a point to which I shall return.

These frameworks signify what many have named the neoliberal university (Slaughter and Rhoades 2000; Washburn 2005; Evans 2005; Gill 2009, Radice 2013; Mountz et al. 2015; Nishida 2016). Under neoliberalism cultural values that promote individual performance and competition within a marketplace come to be seen as the only possible method of survival, or signifier of success (Wilson 2018; Cronin 2000). The effects of these survival methods are demonstrably autoimmune at both an institutional and a personal level: institutionally as universities compete with one another only by debilitating their own workforces (Brady 2018; Else 2017; Fisher 2014; Bothwell 2018); individually as workers survive only through finding ever more onerous ways to 'play the game' (Kalfa et al. 2018). I focus here on examples of lived experiences of autoimmune actions in order to suggest that careful methodologies – ones that account for and respond to the pressures on individuated subjects to over-defend themselves – are required in order to construct *sustainable* strategies for thinking 'beyond the current frameworks'.

On a micro-level, then, this autoimmunity is marked within the inevitable experience of failure such an environment produces. The anonymous academic quoted above, for example, confesses that in the light of the hyper-ability of the applicants, 'Whenever I attend job presentations at my own institution, I feel ashamed to have a permanent post' (*Guardian* 2018), while Rosalind Gill makes clear the virulence of such affective responses to neoliberal individualism through a metaphor of illness, an account worth quoting at length:

> This individualising discourse devours us like a flesh-eating bacterium, producing its own toxic waste – shame: I'm a fraud, I'm useless, I'm nothing. It is (of course) deeply gendered, racialised and classed, connected to biographies that produce very different degrees of 'entitlement' (or not). This affective response in turn is profoundly silencing and isolating – and how could it be otherwise; we don't want to 'show' our ugly failure, any more than it might already be evident […]. When students tell me of receiving a rejection from a journal, they have often kept it secret for some time

[…]. When I tell them it has happened to me, and to every academic I know, they are surprised, having immediately and automatically internalised the experience as their own shameful failure. Some will have concluded that they really aren't good enough, they can't 'hack it'. But others will have already devised 'solutions': I must try harder, read more widely, understand theory better, etc. etc. – the solution, then, for 'us' good neoliberal subjects, is simply to work even harder. (Gill 2009, 240)

This discourse of individuated hyper-ability, Gill suggests – like the threatening unseen other of the microbial pathogen – is consuming us: it attacks not only the 'flesh' but also the affective world of the individual to create and maintain 'bad feelings'. Yet rather than resisting this damaging 'pathogen', the neoliberal autoimmune response is either to leave this environment (and likely find the same problems elsewhere) or to 'work even harder', and so transfer this 'pathogen' and worsen its 'symptoms'. The reference to illness here is, of course, not only a metaphor – although for Gill the subject of physical illness is relegated to a footnote, where it is claimed that 'morbidity and mortality rates look bleaker and bleaker for our profession, and colleagues report "I get sick all the time"' (Gill 2009, 243n2). It is clear that there are psychological *and* physical responses to the neoliberal academy that can produce and/or worsen pain, distress and disability.

As evidenced in the quote above from the anonymous academic, the academy has become dependent on what Robert McRuer calls 'compulsory able-bodiedness' (2006, 2) but which, following Alison Kafer, I would further expand to also include 'compulsory able-mindedness' (Kafer 2013), or more simply 'compulsory ableness' (Campbell 2009, 4). This dependency is normalised to the extent that ableness is figured as a non-identity, as 'the natural order of things' (McRuer 2006, 2). And yet this is maintained only via an autoimmune debilitation of the workforce. But, I suggest, it is precisely this autoimmune reaction, where one comes to *feel* the deleterious effects of our own immunisation of ourselves within such competitive environments, that forces an autoimmune *opening* to lived experiences that render visible the structural conditions and oppressions of both ourselves and others. One possible 'treatment' for this 'illness' might involve a process of what Oriana Fox calls 'shame attacking' – as a form of *both* personal therapy *and* consciousness raising that collectively supports individuals in the risky process of challenging socio-political norms and the conditions that isolate and shame (Fox 2018).

Such practices of public shame attacking might, for example, expose how the biographies – and identities – we use to navigate the academic environment position us *differently* in relation to the performance of what we might call, following Lauren Berlant, the (academic) 'good life' (Berlant 2011). The individualising of these stories has obscured the fact that the performance of the 'good academic' – as articulate, self-confident, rational, knowing, etc. – privileges those who have bodyminds and life experiences that have enabled them to internalise the codes of this performance. It obscures the fact that Eurocentric teaching de-legitimates certain forms of knowledge and ways of thinking, and that racism and sexism – from microaggressions to hate speech – on campus and elsewhere is rife (Bhambra et al. 2018; Ahmed 2015).[8] It obscures the fact that academic conventions privilege certain modes of communication (of the extrovert, the coherent essay, normative social interaction), and it privileges those who are not required to hold multiple jobs, or have responsibilities for caring for others, or limited energy. For many the optimistic attachment to the 'good life' of academia is, therefore, what Berlant calls a *cruel optimism*, and which we might figure as an autoimmune attachment to a promise that debilitates as it sustains (Berlant 2011).

The risky act of sharing one's shame of failing to sustain this promise might become an alternative means of self-protection, one that resists attachment to the idea of absolute immunity and *insists* on inter-dependencies with others. Collective shame attacking speaks to the need to listen to others', as much as to share one's own, accounts; but most significantly, perhaps, collective shame attacking might create environments within which to learn how personal experiences/opinions/embodiments might be co-constituted within networks with complex power relations – so that responding to shame and to demands for shaming can be considered a collective rather than an individual responsibility, a responsibility for both care and for learning. Understanding the powerful effects of ableism – including the demand to always be fully able to comprehend, work with and produce within these complexities – is, I suggest, crucial.

By turning to consider our dependence on ability, critical disability studies scholars shift the focus from disabled people (as the problem), towards an analysis of the logic that *produces* the concept of both disability and the concepts of deviance – and therefore shaming and exclusion – in general. According to Fiona Kumari Campbell, *ableism* is 'A network of beliefs, processes and practices that produces a particular kind of self and body (the corporeal standard) that is projected as the perfect, species typical and therefore essential and fully human' (Campbell 2009, 5; 2001, 44); while '[d]isableism is a set of assumptions (conscious or unconscious) and practices that promote the differential or unequal treatment of people because of actual or presumed disabilities' (Campbell 2009, 4). As Dan Goodley makes clear, by essentialising certain abilities ableism *produces* disability. That is, all those who fall short of ableist standards (i.e. all of us), and who, in falling short, strive to achieve this standard, *produce and maintain* the concept of 'species-typical' abilities, and instantiate deviations from this norm as disability (Goodley 2014). Further, what is considered the standard, species-typical norm shifts over time and place, and in a time when neoliberal ideals are expanding into ever more spaces there is emerging a clear favouritism, as Goodley suggests, for the ability to be competitive, to be cognitively astute and to consume (2014, 22). With these 'neoliberal-able' standards in place, as we compete not only at school and work but also online and in our activist organising to perform at ever higher standards with ever increasing stakes, perhaps we can see the 'flesh-eating bacterium' of the individuating discourse, and its 'toxic waste – shame' producing increasing opportunities to feel and to identify as deviant or even as disabled.

As the ableist academic ground is normalised for staff and students it becomes increasingly difficult to level this ground. This results in disabled individuals being forced to either 'overcome' their disabilities or leave.[9] But further, this normalised ground risks figuring as 'impaired' increasing numbers of bodyminds that do not work in this 'standard' way, risking (further) debilitating them as they are forced to nonetheless to attempt to do so. Therefore, it seems to be becoming increasingly possible for individuals within the academy (and scholars excluded from it) to claim 'a physical or mental impairment that has a "substantial" and "long-term" negative effect on [their] ability to do *normal daily activities*' (http://www.legislation.gov.uk/ukpga/2010/15/contents, emphasis mine); but whether or not it is yet becoming socially or politically acceptable to claim such a position is much less clear.

Yet if we follow the autoimmune logic of this shameful story, and if we follow Davis to claim that all bodyminds are non-standard, we are able to render disability as an unstable (though not obsolete) category. Here, according to Davis, disability might indeed become a generalisable condition:

> It is too easy to say, 'We're all disabled'. But it is possible to say that we are all disabled by injustice and oppression of various kinds.

> We are all nonstandard [...]. What is universal in life, if there are universals, is the experience of the limitations of the body. Yet the fantasy of culture, democracy, capitalism, sexism, and racism, to name only a few ideologies, is the perfection of the body and its activities. (Davis 2006, 241)

That is, it is problematic to say 'We're all disabled' in a manner that demands entry to an identity category that confers protection on an oppressed group. Yet this identity model is often ineffective anyway in achieving its goal of equality and equity. Legal protections and 'reasonable adjustments' individualise disability, and while doing much to make individual lives more survivable, do little to challenge disabling neoliberal environments and their global effects (Davis 2002, 238; Puar 2017). If democracy, capitalism, sexism and racism all demand the perfection of the bodymind and its abilities then, Davis suggests, quoting Paul Gilroy, it is the recurrence of 'pain, disease, humiliation, grief, and care' that unites us (2002, 242). Therefore, perhaps by recognising that we are all 'disabled' – *and* privileged – in different ways by differing forms of injustice and oppression, we might locate the possibility for forging alliances with a politics of disability justice. This politics has the experiential knowledge necessary to challenge debilitating ableist assumptions and to find more careful, interdependent ways of working and learning through and with difference. Perhaps engaging with such knowledges will enable academics, scholars and learners to resist autoimmune defensive urges and survival strategies, and produce more sustainable practices for analysing and resisting global injustices.

Conclusion

In order to close, let's return to our anonymous academic and their suggestion to give lectureships to those amongst the hyper-able applicants who might most need the position due to precarity, 'age, race, ability, or health', and because they might be the *most able to think beyond these frameworks*. This suggestion makes some sense, for it intends to redress historical exclusions and perhaps, indeed, those with experience of systemic oppression might be best able to recognise and expose the frameworks that maintain these oppressions. Yet the assumption is that historical exclusions can be remedied simply by including representatives of these excluded groups. And yet in this case, each candidate interviewing for the position will have been forced already to prove themselves to be what Goodley (2014) calls 'neoliberal-able' – academic entrepreneurs, overcoming adversity in order to prove themselves ready to be 'exceptional', and to enter the neoliberal university. The admittance of *difference* with regard to many ableist norms, then, remains impossible. And further, by implying that those from marginalised groups are best placed to challenge normalised frameworks, the writer obscures the fact that this labour is *more*, not less onerous – and debilitating – for these individuals. Yet if we consider that the compulsory ableness of the academy is autoimmune, that its default defences – such as to work harder (to resist, to survive) – are turning, painfully, on and against the academic community as a whole, we might begin to locate already *within* the university the need, desire and commitment to explore alternative ways of working.

As I write, in February 2020, 74 UK universities are preparing to undertake strike action in order to resist the autoimmune defences of the neoliberal university, which, encouraged to maintain itself within a market economy through the use of precarious employment contracts, persistent gender and ethnic pay gaps, unmanageable workloads, real-terms pay cuts and the financialisation of pensions (UCU 2020), is debilitating its workforce and the student body. The risk of autoimmune paralysis, however, invites a weary, angry and resistant collective body to instigate an autoimmune opening as it votes to withdraw academic labour and looks for potential strategies to live differently. The withdrawal of normative academic labour, while primarily suggesting a desire for change in the management of the university, might also evidence a desire for alternative ways of producing academic work that resist the everyday autoimmune effects of self-enclosed individualism. As knowledge-exchange workshops are set up on picketlines for students to share lecture notes and thinking, as staff–student assemblies allow for the exchange of opinions and grievances, perspectives and experiences, and as reading groups and teach-outs give space and time to situating ourselves within a complex moment, new possibilities for working together might emerge. Such modes of working are never easy, or comfortable – they often give rise to conflict and disagreement – yet if accessibility and inclusion are centred in these moments, so that all might feel attended to and welcomed through overt inclusion strategies – including perhaps quiet spaces, and performance spaces, online spaces, crafting spaces and reflective spaces, spaces that allow for (differently) shared vulnerabilities of 'pain, disease, humiliation, grief, and care' (Davis 2002, 242) – perhaps methods for listening to and negotiating with differences in the ableist university might emerge.

What might it look like to translate such experiments in ways of working out of the temporality of strike action and into the everyday habits of the university? Might the timetabling of reflective practice sessions for staff and students allow for the pinpointing of problematic experiences and practices? Might timetabled spaces for exploring varied experiences of ableism allow for the sharing of survival strategies and an emergent potential for change? Might the development of research and pedagogy workshops allow for collective mentoring through difficulties and crises? While there are no certainties here, I have found that the timetabling of spaces that resist the prevalent demand for productivity and demonstrable 'outputs' invites ways of working that acknowledge that things do not and cannot always *work*; and that by acknowledging failure and difficulty, care and joy within interdependent forms of collective labour, the material, embodied, political and discursive character of knowledge production becomes discernible. Cripistemologies, I would insist, are *already* at work in the university and should we come to centre these, perhaps we might find with and within the autoimmune moment potential for *sustainable* transformative work to take place on both local and potentially more global scales.

But of course such collective work is not equally accessible, and therefore I would propose that within such a call for collective activity there remains a need for thinking with and within situated knowledges. For as the autoimmune paralysis of the university and university workers threatens, perhaps such a situated position is the only site from which to begin the work of looking, from wherever one might find oneself, for emerging ways to dismantle the demands for individual immunity that maintain normative assumptions regarding academic value. It is through my own experiences of ableism, of failure, shame and autoimmunity, that the motivation to engage in such work emerges. Yet it is clear to me that these experiences are not mine alone and that my own limited perspective might join with the experiences and knowledges of others. And so, by slowly and painstakingly navigating the autoimmunities of the self, and of collective work, I see a moment within which many are looking for alternative practices of care, protection and labour, and suggest that in this moment we might turn to those who centre racial and disability justice and radical accessibility in their thinking – those who write from their sickbeds, who work slowly, in crip time, dreamtime and crazy time (Piepzna-Samarasinha 2018; Sins Invalid 2019) – in order to resist the logic of (auto)immunity and render possible all the work that remains to be done.

Notes

1. Autoimmunity as a Derridean deconstructive neologism brings, however, a specificity that highlights the cruelty and even the terror of deconstructive actions – figured as a self-destructive defence of the self (Derrida and Borradori 2003), which is not so marked in other Derridean deconstructive terms – such as *différance*, the trace, etc.; it is for this reason that this term lends itself to analyses of illness and suffering in critical disability studies.
2. Clear examples of this tendency can be seen in the 'populist turn' in contemporary politics from Donald Trump's America and Jair Bolsonaro's Brazil to Brexit Britain, a turn that can be seen to result in some cases from austerity politics and the exclusions of disabled and migrant bodies from the *munus* (McRuer 2018; United Nations CRPD 2018).
3. The artist collective the Canaries state: 'Like the "canary in a coalmine", our autoimmune and other chronic health conditions warn of imbalances in the world at large' (wearecanaries.com n.d.).
4. Including Frank 1995; Cvetkovich 2012; Price 2011; Chen 2014; Patsavas 2014; Nishida 2016; Brady 2018; the Chronically Academic Network; and many more.
5. However, the focus on disability rights within neoliberal societies also autoimmunely maintains what Jaspir Puar (2017) calls the 'right to maim', as bodies, communities and populations who are excluded from the protection of legal rights come to be exploited and debilitated in the name of profit.
6. However, while we can say that unhealthy bodyminds tend to resist capitalist demands for productive labour, it is important to acknowledge that they do not escape capitalist capture by the medico-industrial complex – the pharmaceutical and wellbeing industries in particular.
7. Autoimmune diseases are understood to be triggered by environmental conditions, one of which is stress.
8. For example, since 12 March 2019 there has been an anti-racist occupation of Goldsmiths, University of London, with the stated aim of protesting the lack of anti-racist action in the management of the college. See https://tinyurl.com/GARAManifesto.
9. This 'overcoming' narrative is very familiar to those within disabled communities, where in order to do well disabled people are required to do so *in spite of* their disability; see Mitchell and Snyder 2000.

References

Ahmed, Sara. 'Against Students', *Feministkilljoys* (blog). 25 June 2015. Online. https://feministkilljoys.com/2015/06/25/against-students/ (accessed 25 June 2019).

Berlant, Lauren. 'Cruel Optimism'. In *Cruel Optimism*, 23–49. Durham, NC and London: Duke University Press, 2011.

Bhambra, Gurminder K., Gebrial, Dalia and Nişancıoğlu, Kerem, eds. *Decolonising the University*. London: Pluto Press, 2018.

Bothwell, Ellie. 'Work-Life Balance Survey 2018: Long Hours Take Their Toll on Academics', *Times Higher Education*, 8 February 2018. Online. https://www.timeshighereducation.com/features/work-life-balance-survey-2018-long-hours-take-their-toll-academics (accessed 25 June 2019).

Brady, Andrea. 'Bind me- I still can sing-' *Stillpoint Spaces* 2018. Online. https://stillpointmag.org/articles/bind-me-i-still-can-sing/ (accessed 27 May 2020).

Campbell, Fiona Kumari. 'Disability as Inherently Negative?: Legal Fictions and Battle Concerning the Definitions of "Disability"'. In *Disability with Attitude: Critical Issues 20 Years after International Year of Disabled Persons: Conference Proceedings: International Conference, 16–17th February 2001, Parramatta Campus, University of Western Sydney*.

Campbell, Fiona Kumari. *Contours of Ableism: The Production of Disability and Abledness*. Basingstoke and New York: Palgrave Macmillan, 2009.

Chen, Mel Y. 'Brain Fog: The Race for Cripistemology', *Journal of Literary and Cultural Disability Studies* 8/2 (2014): 171–84. Online. https://doi.org/10.3828/jlcds.2014.14 (accessed 27 May 2020).

Clare, Eli. *Brilliant Imperfection: Grappling with Cure*. Durham, NC: Duke University Press, 2017.

Cronin, A. 'Consumerism and Compulsory Individuality: Women, Will and Potential'. In *Thinking through Feminism*, edited by S. Ahmed, J. Kilby, C. Lury and M. McNeil, 273–87. London: Routledge, 2000.

Cvetkovich, Ann. *Depression: A Public Feeling*. Durham, NC: Duke University Press, 2012.

Davis, Lennard. *Bending Over Backwards. Disability, Dismodernism and Other Difficult Positions*. New York: New York University Press, 2002.

Davis, Lennard. 'Constructing Normalcy: The Bell Curve, the Novel, and the Invention of the Disabled body in the Nineteenth Century'. In *The Disability Studies Reader*, 2nd ed., 3–16. New York and London: Routledge, 2006.

Davis, Lennard. *The End of Normal: Identity in a Biocultural Era*. Ann Arbor, MI: University of Michigan Press, 2013.

Derrida, Jacques. *Rogues: Two Essays on Reason*. Translated by P.-A. Brault and M. Naas. Stanford: Stanford University Press, 2005.

Derrida, Jacques and Borradori, Giovanna. 'Autoimmunity: Real and Symbolic Suicides – A Dialogue with Jacques Derrida'. In *Philosophy in a Time of Terror: Dialogues with Jürgen Habermas and Jacques Derrida*, 85–136. Chicago: University of Chicago Press, 2003.

DiAngelo, Robin. 'White Fragility', *International Journal of Critical Pedagogy* 3/3 (2011): 54–70. Online. https://libjournal.uncg.edu/ijcp/article/view/249 (accessed 27 May 2020).

Dolmage, Jay Timothy. *Academic Ableism: Disability and Higher Education*. Ann Arbor: University of Michigan Press, 2017. Online. https://doi.org/10.3998/mpub.9708722 (accessed 19 May 2020).

Else, Holly. 'Academics "Face Higher Mental Health Risk" than Other Professions', *Times Higher Education*, 22 August 2017. Online. https://www.timeshighereducation.com/news/academics-face-higher-mental-health-risk-than-other-professions?fbclid=IwAR3lRAm4ZPB7rbukDkT99BpxqqvgNJSulcnY8xdlu0y9lEAuQx4RVGLN93Y (accessed 25 June 2019).

Erevelles, Nirmala. 'Understanding Curriculum as Normalizing Text: Disability Studies Meet Curriculum Theory', *Journal of Curriculum Studies* 37/4 (2005): 421–39. Online. https://doi.org/10.1080/0022027032000276970 (accessed 27 May 2020).

Erevelles, Nirmala. *Disability and Difference in Global Contexts: Enabling a Transformative Body Politic*. New York: Palgrave Macmillan, 2011. Online. https://doi.org/10.1057/9781137001184 (accessed 27 May 2020).

Erevelles, Nirmala and Minear, Andrea. 'Unspeakable Offenses: Untangling Race and Disability in Discourses of Intersectionality', *Journal of Literary and Cultural Disability Studies* 4/2 (2010): 127–45. Online. https://doi.org/10.3828/jlcds.2010.11 (accessed 29 May 2020).

Evans, Mary. *Killing Thinking: The Death of the University*. London: Continuum, 2005.

Fisher, Mark. 'Good for Nothing', *Occupied Times*, 19 March 2014. Online. https://theoccupiedtimes.org/?p=12841 (accessed 25 June 2019).

Fox, Oriana. 'Performance Art Can Change Your Life!: Shame Attacking and Parrhesia as Feminist Practices of Freedom'. Unpublished PhD diss. Goldsmiths, University of London, 2018.

Frank, Arthur W. *The Wounded Storyteller: Body, Illness, and Ethics*. Chicago: University of Chicago Press, 1995.

Fullagar, Simone. 'Foucauldian Theory'. In *Routledge International Handbook of Critical Mental Health*, edited by Bruce M.Z. Cohen, Chapter 4. Abingdon and New York: Routledge, 2018.

Gill, Rosalind. 'Breaking the Silence: The Hidden Injuries of Neo-Liberal Academia'. In *Secrecy and Silence in the Research Process: Feminist Reflections*, edited by Roisin Ryan-Flood and Rosalind Gill, 228–44. Abingdon and New York: Routledge, 2009.

Goodley, Dan. *Dis/ability Studies: Theorising Disablism and Ableism*. Abingdon and New York: Routledge, 2014.

Gov.uk. 'Definition of disability under the Equality Act 2010'. Online. https://www.gov.uk/definition-of-disability-under-equality-act-2010 (accessed 25 June 2019).

Guardian. 'I Struggle When Hiring Academics – Because the Candidates Are Too Good', *Guardian*, 1 June 2018. Online. https://www.theguardian.com/higher-education-network/2018/jun/01/academics-candidates-outstanding-application-recruitment (accessed 25 June 2019).

Johnson, Merri Lisa and McRuer, Robert. 'Cripistemologies: An Introduction', *Journal of Literary and Cultural Disability Studies* 8/2 (2014): 127–47. Online. https://doi.org/10.3828/jlcds.2014.12 (accessed 27 May 2020).

Kafer, Alison. *Feminist, Queer, Crip*. Bloomington: Indiana University Press, 2013.

Kalfa, Senia, Wilkinson, Adrian and Gollan, Paul J. 'The Academic Game: Compliance and Resistance in Universities', *Work, Employment and Society* 32/2 (2018): 274–91. Online. https://doi.org/10.1177/0950017017695043 (accessed 27 May 2020).

Lazard, Carolyn. 'How to be a Person in the Age of Autoimmunity', Project Row Houses, 29 March 2017. Online. https://projectrowhouses.org/blog/howtobeapersonintheageofautoimmunity (accessed 25 June 2019).

Lukin, Josh. 'Disability and Blackness'. In *The Disability Studies Reader*, 4th edition, ed. Lennard J. Davis, 308–15. New York: Routledge, 2013.

McRuer, Robert. *Crip Theory: Cultural Signs of Queerness and Disability*. New York: New York University Press, 2006.

McRuer, Robert. *Crip Times: Disability, Globalization, and Resistance*. New York: New York University Press, 2018.

Mitchell, David T. and Snyder, Sharon L. *Narrative Prosthesis: Disability and the Dependencies of Discourse*. Ann Arbor: University of Michigan Press 2000. Online. https://doi.org/10.3998/mpub.11523 (accessed 27 May 2020).

Moodley, Roy, Mujtaba, Falak and Kleiman, Sela. 'Critical Race Theory and Mental Health'. In *Routledge International Handbook of Critical Mental Health*, edited by Bruce M.Z. Cohen, Chapter 9. Abingdon and New York: Routledge, 2018.

Mountz, Alison et al. 'For Slow Scholarship: A Feminist Politics of Resistance through Collective Action in the Neoliberal University', *ACME: An International E-Journal for Critical Geographies* 14/4 (2015): 1235–59. Online. https://www.acme-journal.org/index.php/acme/article/view/1058 (accessed 27 May 2020).

Nakazawa, Donna Jackson. *The Autoimmune Epidemic*. New York: Touchstone, 2008.

Nishida, Akemi. 'Neoliberal Academia and a Critique from Disability Studies'. In *Occupying Disability: Critical Approaches to Community, Justice, and Decolonizing Disability*, edited by Pamela Block, Devva Kasnitz, Akemi Nishida and Nick Pollard, 145–58. Dordrecht: Springer, 2016.

Oliver, Michael. *Social Work with Disabled People*. Basingstoke: Macmillan, 1983.

O'Toole, Corbett. 'Disclosing Our Relationships to Disabilities: An Invitation for Disability Studies Scholars', *Disability Studies Quarterly* 33/2 (2013). Online. http://dx.doi.org/10.18061/dsq.v33i2 (accessed 27 May 2020).

Patsavas, Alyson. 'Recovering a Cripistemology of Pain Leaky Bodies, Connective Tissue, and Feeling Discourse', *Journal of Literary and Cultural Disability Studies* 8/2 (2014): 203–18. Online. https://doi.org/10.3828/jlcds.2014.16 (accessed 27 May 2020).

Pickens, Therí A. *New Body Politics: Narrating Arab and Black Identity in the Contemporary United States*. New York and Abingdon: Routledge, 2014.

Piepzna-Samarasinha, Leah Lakshmi. *Care Work: Dreaming Disability Justice*. Vancouver: Arsenal Pulp Press, 2018.

Preciado, Paul. *Testo Junkie*. New York: The Feminist Press, 2013.

Price, Margaret. *Mad at School: Rhetorics of Mental Disability and Academic Life*. Ann Arbor: University of Michigan Press, 2011. Online. https://doi.org/10.3998/mpub.1612837 (accessed 27 May 2020).

Price, Margaret and Kerschbaum, Stephanie L. 'Stories of Methodology: Interviewing Sideways, Crooked and Crip', *Canadian Journal of Disability Studies* 5/3 (2016). Online. https://doi.org/10.15353/cjds.v5i3.295 (accessed 27 May 2020).

Puar, Jasbir K. *The Right to Maim: Debility, Capacity, Disability*. Durham, NC: Duke University Press, 2017.

Radice, Hugo. 'How We Got Here: UK Higher Education Under Neoliberalism', *ACME: An International E-Journal for Critical Geographies* 12/2 (2013): 407–18. Online. https://acme-journal.org/index.php/acme/article/view/969 (accessed 27 May 2020).

Samuels, Ellen. *Fantasies of Identification: Disability, Gender, Race*. New York: NYU Press, 2014.

Siebers, Tobin. *Disability Theory*. Ann Arbor, MI: University of Michigan Press, 2008.

Sins Invalid. *Skin, Tooth, and Bone: The Basis of Movement is Our People: A Disability Primer*, 2nd ed., 2019. Online. https://www.sinsinvalid.org/news-1/2019/11/12/skin-tooth-and-bone-2nd-edition-available-now (accessed 28 May 2020).

Slaughter, Sheila and Rhoades, Gary. 'The Neo-Liberal University', *New Labor Forum* 6 (2000): 73–9.

Spade, Dean. *Normal Life: Administrative Violence, Critical Trans Politics, and the Limits of the Law*. Brooklyn: South End Press, 2011.

Timimi, Sami. 'Critical Cultural Theory'. In *Routledge International Handbook of Critical Mental Health*, edited by Bruce M.Z. Cohen, Chapter 6. Abingdon and New York: Routledge, 2018.

UCU (University and Colleges Union). 'HE Action Centre'. 2020. Online. https://www.ucu.org.uk/heaction (accessed 25 June 2019).

United Nations Convention on the Rights of Persons with Disabilities (CRPD). 2018. 'How Well is the UK Performing on Disability Rights?' UN Equality and Human Rights Commission Report. 18 January 2018. Online. https://www.equalityhumanrights.com/en/publication-download/how-well-uk-performing-disability-rights (accessed 25 June 2019).

Velasquez-Manoff, Moises. *An Epidemic of Absence: A New Way of Understanding Allergies and Autoimmune Diseases*. New York: Scribner, 2013.

Wendell, Susan. 'Unhealthy Disabled: Treating Chronic Illnesses as Disabilities', *Hypatia* 16/4 (2001): 17–33. Online. https://doi.org/10.1111/j.1527-2001.2001.tb00751.x (accessed 28 May 2020).

Wilson, Julie. *Neoliberalism*. Abingdon and New York: Routledge, 2018.

Washburn, J. *University, Inc. The Corporate Corruption of Higher Education*. New York: Basic Books, 2005.

wearecanaries.com. N.d. Online. http://wearecanaries.com/

7
'But you don't look disabled': Non-visible disabilities, disclosure and being an 'insider' in disability research and 'other' in the disability movement and academia

Elisabeth Griffiths

This chapter is a personal narrative of my getting to this point in my career, to 'here', as a disability law scholar and solicitor with a non-visible disability and a disabled woman working in academia. It is a self-reflection on my experience of the research process and an insider account of my position within that research. I had not anticipated that the well-established philosophy of the disability rights movement of 'nothing about us without us' would take on a personal meaning during my research. Framed within the field of autoethnography (Ellis 2004), I am inviting you, the reader, into my world as I have engaged in the research process while completing a professional doctorate in law. Autoethnography is a genre of qualitative, reflexive, autobiographical writing and research that uses the researcher as the subject (Haynes 2011, 135). In this chapter, I am writing about my personal experience of disability within academia. I am engaging with 'the self', myself and the interaction between my working life as an academic and my experience of an unseen or non-visible disability. As Ellis et al. (2011, 2) suggest, 'Autoethnographers recognize the innumerable ways personal experience influences the research process'. My own experience has certainly influenced the research process I have undertaken in the last few years and writing this chapter is a means of recognising that. In sharing this experience, I am joining forces with other academics who likewise believe their own experience and story is inextricably linked with how they do their research.

The fact that I am writing this chapter at all is a revelation to me. I had very little disability consciousness until I started my professional doctorate, despite living with a chronic illness since 2007. I was 'in the closet' (Garland-Thomson 2016) but, to borrow from Kleege (1999), studying for a doctorate has 'made me disabled'. Given the subject matter of my doctorate, it is important for me to acknowledge that there is an ongoing internal phenomenological dialogue in what I am writing (personal reflections alongside academic writing). This makes for disruptive reading, but the disruption is vital to challenge the understanding of disability in academia. 'Autoethnography, as method, attempts to disrupt the binary of science and art. Autoethnographers believe research can be rigorous, theoretical and analytical *and* emotional, therapeutic and inclusive of personal and social phenomenon' (Ellis et al. 2011, 8). This chapter is framed using this approach because I want to keep the conversation going about the experience of disability and chronic illness in academia – not merely to recognise its existence but to emphasise, through personal narrative, the effect it can have on those of us working in academia and to try to influence and disrupt current academic practice in some small way.

As Goodley suggests, 'the marked identity of a neoliberal citizen is a worker: willing, capable and able' (Goodley 2014, 52). For all of us, *capability* is a capacity to learn and develop and is often assessed on initial employment. *Ability* is contextual, temporal and often unclear. *Willingness*, which Goodley rightly puts first, is the neoliberal devolution of responsibility to the individual. *Willingness* is both what can drive individuals to overcome barriers of capability and ability, but unfortunately can also be used to criticise individuals when they cannot overcome those same (often structural) barriers. In the age of excellence in teaching, research and knowledge exchange in higher education, talking about chronic illness and disability has become increasingly challenging. It is often assumed that the 'willing, capable and able' worker can perform to an excellent standard in everything all of the time, but this creates a highly pressurised working environment and this frenetic pace of activity has somehow become normalised. For most, this can make for a stressful and difficult working day, particularly when the many, often clashing demands conflict. The non-visible nature of many chronic illnesses and disabilities can exacerbate this difficulty as it is not obvious to those we work with that sometimes, although *willing* and *capable*, we cannot always perform to those intense standards.

As soon as I embarked upon my research on disability using the law as my frame of reference, I realised that as an academic with a non-visible disability, doing disability research, a more open discussion about disability as experienced by academics was required. Much of what people experience around disability in academia is hidden for fear of stigma and the perception of not being able to 'keep up'. I want to feel welcomed and understood in academia, so that on the days when I cannot 'hyper-perform' then it is OK to say 'no more today', without it affecting my ambitions, prospects, collegiality or sense of self. I am also very aware that the profession I have come from, the law, is starting to have similar conversations about disability and in particular mental ill health. In recent years there has been anecdotal evidence about the difficulties faced by disabled people in the legal profession but there has been nothing with a rigorous evidence base. In January 2020, the first research report on disability in the legal profession was published (Foster and Hirst 2020). The authors report on the barriers experienced by disabled people across the legal profession. Their findings suggest that the legal profession is generally poorly equipped to anticipate reasonable adjustments; there is a poor understanding of how disability, impairments and health conditions impact on recruitment and career progression within law; there is a general reluctance to disclose an impairment or non-visible disability because of a fear of discrimination; and the fact that the legal profession continues to operate traditional career expectations and working patterns means that access and progression for disabled people can be difficult. The findings also suggest that a significant proportion of disabled people in the legal profession have experienced ill treatment, bullying or discrimination associated with their disability. Fear of discrimination at the recruitment stage has also been a key finding of my own research with disabled law students, who repeatedly tell me that they are not going to tell potential employers about their disability when they are applying for training contracts or pupillages to enter the profession. Alongside this new report, some writing is emerging on wellbeing in the legal profession of England and Wales (see Collier 2016) and concerns about poor mental health among lawyers are growing in number. Collier (2019) is continuing his research following on from the Junior Lawyers Division Resilience and Wellbeing Survey of 2019, which reports that 48 per cent of respondents experienced mental ill health (whether formally diagnosed or not) within the month leading up to the completion of the survey. This is an increase on the 38 per cent reported in 2018 and 26 per cent in 2017 (Law Society 2019). Therefore, as disabled professionals working within academia, we are not alone in our experiences.

How did I get to here? Where is 'here'?

I have been an academic and a lawyer for over 20 years. I teach and research employment law so the world of work and equality has always been important to me. During this time, I developed an autoimmune condition that triggered psoriatic arthritis, a form of arthritis affecting individuals with the skin condition psoriasis. Joints become inflamed, which causes pain, swelling and stiffness. Psoriatic arthritis is a chronic condition that waxes and wanes. What causes it is a matter of continuing research, although it is probably caused by a combination of genetic, immunological and environmental factors. Although psoriatic arthritis is a chronic long-term condition with no cure, there are a number of treatments to manage and control it. I have been on disease-modifying anti-rheumatic drugs since that diagnosis in 2007 in an attempt to slow down the biological processes that cause the persistent inflammation in an effort to control the development of the disease (for more information see the Psoriasis and Psoriatic Arthritis Alliance website, http://www.papaa.org/). In 2019 I developed a secondary autoimmune response known as Sjögren's syndrome, which at times makes writing at a computer for any length of time challenging because of the impact it has on my eyes. Therefore, my own 'disability' is now a collection of long-term chronic illnesses which I manage every day through medication and by taking periods of rest from work when I need to. Other than days off to manage pain and fatigue and occasional comments about how tired I look, my chronic illness was largely hidden from my work in academia until I started conducting research as part of my professional doctorate in law. My decision to undertake the doctorate was part of the change to cultures of *capability* in higher education. I began in 2016 as a result of the intensification and focus on research activity in my own place of work, which, like many post-1992 universities, began to transform its research profile. My doctorate is a phenomenological study, exploring the lived experience of disabled law students navigating their emerging graduate identities (Holmes 2015) and 'possible selves' (Markus and Nurius 1986) as they transition into the hyper-competitive world of the legal profession on graduation. This is inevitably sensitive research, but I had not anticipated that it would also become personal.

As an employment lawyer and a disability law scholar I have always focused on the legal definition of disability set out in section 6 of the Equality Act 2010. Disability is defined as a physical or mental impairment that has a substantial and long-term adverse effect on a person's ability to carry out normal day-to-day activities. The emphasis is on diagnosis of an impairment and its subsequent effect, in particular the effect that the impairment has on things that individuals do on a regular basis. Crucially for those with chronic illness, 'long-term' is defined as 12 months or more, so the effect of the impairment has to have lasted for at least a year. Fluctuation and recurrence can all be taken into account by the law. The deduced effect of the impairment is also critical, as most of us with any form of chronic illness would be so much worse without our daily dose of medication. The legal definition is sometimes criticised as being overly medicalised, but up to this point in my professional life it has always seemed appropriate. I am comfortable in myself as being acknowledged as having a disability within the eyes of the law; the law, after all, has been my frame of reference for much of my professional life. I understand my chronic illness to be a 'physical impairment' within the section 6 definition and I know what my rights are at work. The duty of reasonable adjustments set out in section 20 of the Equality Act 2010 also protects those rights and my continued ability to work. The duty of reasonable adjustments involves the employer taking any reasonable step, or combination of steps, necessary to remove a disadvantage experienced by the disabled person and which enable the disabled person to work. Arguably the duty also separates disability from other protected characteristics within the legal framework and it is therefore as much a part of the problem as it is a part of the solution.

The Equality Act 2010 brings all protected characteristics, such as sex, race, disability and religion, together into one piece of legislation, all separate 'silos' (Solanke 2011) but in theory equal before the law, no one more important than the other. However, some protected characteristics that may have an impact on one's ability to do a specific job at particular times, such as pregnancy, age or disability, are subject to special rules. Other protected characteristics, such as sex, race, sexual orientation and religion or belief, should have no impact on one's ability to do a particular job and ought to be ignored by the employer (Griffiths 2016, 162). Anti-discrimination law in England and Wales is designed largely to protect notions of formal equality, treating like cases alike and ignoring the personal characteristics of the individuals concerned. Disability, however, cannot be ignored and special rules have to be implemented: difference has to be acknowledged, which is often where the problems begin. The only way to benefit from a reasonable adjustment if you have a non-visible disability is disclosure, with all of the complexities of identifying as 'disabled'. Contrary to critics of the medical model on which the legal definition of disability is based, for me being 'disabled' within the legal definition is comfortable. I know where I stand, I know what protection I have as a disabled academic and I know my rights. My legal consciousness is alive and well (Ewick and Silbey 1998). Nevertheless, the discomfort I now feel as I explore further and deeper into my own disability consciousness is sometimes hard to acknowledge.

Disability is the only protected characteristic in the Equality Act 2010 subject to a reasonable adjustment duty, although there has been much academic debate about whether other characteristics would also benefit from such a duty (there are discussions about religion in particular: see Vickers 2010; Gibson 2013; Griffiths 2016). As a result of this unique treatment, those with a disability are sometimes viewed as being treated *more* favourably than others without a disability, or it can seem that there is some kind of positive discrimination at work. This can play out as a feeling of being separate, different, 'other', and when I am at my most vulnerable, asking for a reasonable adjustment makes me feel 'needy' – that I cannot function at work without a special chair or special software. Even that word 'special' sets me apart. Some people with disabilities do not even ask for the reasonable adjustments they are entitled to because they do not want to appear different. People routinely ask me about my keyboard and my 'special' mouse, so I always have to tell them why.

As my research has developed, I have begun to appreciate that the legal definition of disability plays just one part in this complex area, but it is a definition that I remain comfortable with. However, in developing a theoretical perspective for my professional doctorate I have come to appreciate that there is no one overarching definition, theory or model of disability: there are many, and this has led me to question my legal position as a person with a disability, my own position in the disability movement and my identity. Inevitably, however, *difference* has to be acknowledged. As a lawyer undertaking my doctorate, I have had to explore disability studies alongside the law, and as suggested by Kanter (2011, 406), 'Disability Studies offers an appropriate lens through which we can view the legal profession, and the meaning of difference within the legal system, and society'. Kanter goes on to say that Disability

Studies 'offers the law and legal education the opportunity to critically examine the role of "normalcy" within the law [...] it requires us to recognise, appreciate, and most importantly, value difference among us' (Kanter 2011, 406). Difference sets us apart, makes us 'other' within the legislation, within society and arguably within academia. For those of us with non-visible disabilities, the difference is intensified, but difference really does make a difference.

My 'coming out'

The immediate 'disclosure' process at work began quite soon after my diagnosis, but only to a very small number of people: close friends who also happened to be work colleagues. They understood when I had 'off' days, when I was truly fatigued as a result of my condition and when I needed to rest. To everyone else, it was 'business as usual'. Acknowledging my legal rights, I actively wanted to be dual-tracked in work for our capability procedures, knowing that when I needed days off because of my disability, they would not count towards any kind of performance or capability management. However, this was confidential between me and human resources: I understood my rights, after all. For a long time, this is as far as disclosure went.

As part of my doctoral research I presented a paper on disability and positionality in research at the 'Ableism in Academia' conference from which this book arose. This was not a law conference so I did not think anyone would know me and I felt 'safe' disclosing my disability to a room full of colleagues (strangers) from other higher education institutions, who were familiar with what I was going through. What I had not fully appreciated was that because this was a highly accessible conference, it was to be livestreamed over the internet. As a result of this livestreaming other people were able to see me, including a colleague from my own institution. Due to the power of social media, she saw me disclosing my disability in what was actually quite a public forum. This accidental encounter led to us doing a joint paper at our own institution's doctoral and faculty research conference in June 2018. Our paper was about sharing and disclosing our respective non-visible disabilities in our research but from two very different perspectives. I had been grappling with reflections on my own chronic illness and the impact it was having on my research and consequently my academic identity, while she, I discovered, had recently published an article about her own experience of anxiety and depression at a particular time in academia

(Campbell 2018). For her it was suddenly out there: everyone would now know she had suffered with bouts of anxiety and depression and had been off work for three months. Ironically, it had particularly come to the fore during her own research and professional doctorate. For me, it was still largely hidden.

After the faculty conference paper, what became clear in the feedback we were given was that very few people ever talk about disability, particularly the influence of their own disability in their research, and that we were suddenly viewed as 'brave' and 'courageous' for sharing. To be perfectly honest I do not feel 'brave' or 'courageous' and I am not really sure why I need to be. Bravery and courage, words synonymous with endurance and battle, suggest that I have a choice in accepting this sometimes daily encounter with pain and discomfort, that I have willingly entered the fray to tussle with the physical embodiment of my illness. This could not be further from the truth. It is not a battle or a struggle, it is just something I now have to tolerate. Just part of who I am. What really interests me, though, is what led to people referring to us as brave and courageous. Why do so few people talk about their chronic illness or disability, particularly when it is non-visible? There is a risk of course associated with disclosure. As already suggested, disability is 'other', different. The legal definition in particular forces us into that position because of the emphasis on the individual impairment and – to link back to being brave/courageous – implies that this is a personal tragedy that we have to endure and that somehow we are now lesser or part of a problem that needs to be fixed by an adjustment. I come back to a discussion on disability theory below, and explore why some of it is problematic for me, but for now, let us just say that in my naivety I had never really thought what impact this examination of disability could or would have on my *willing* and *capable* self. I had never thought of myself as 'other', or of the stigma associated with being 'other', but for now it is enough to acknowledge that my 'spoiled identity' (Goffman 1990/1963) was very much coming to the fore during the research process. Sometimes, though, I have to take a step back and think – really? Is this who I am now? As Brown and Leigh suggest, 'Illness and disability trajectories are often experienced as journeys of acceptance, particularly if these illnesses or disabilities occur later in life or appear suddenly' (Brown and Leigh 2018, 986–7). I have gradually started to realise as part of this research process that this is not just about my legal rights; it is also about how I have started to reconstruct my own identity as an academic with a disability, a disabled academic. This is the journey of acceptance I have begun.

Who am I now that this has happened?

Although I remain comfortable with the legal definition of disability and where I fit in that, as someone with a chronic illness I am not sure I am what society would consider to be a 'disabled person'. The legal definition confirms to me that a chronic illness is a disability. It is much harder to talk just in terms of 'illness' or 'disease'. But for my medication I would find life a lot harder and debilitating. The nature of my impairment is often varied, as is the effect of the impairment, which inevitably leads to a variety of legal and personal responses. Chronic illnesses are not fixed disabilities; rather we have good days when we might 'not be' or 'feel' disabled at all, and other days when we are very debilitated by our conditions. The various theories of disability do not necessarily account for this fluctuation and the position of chronic illness within the disability movement is often contested (see Barnes and Mercer 1996).

Unseen, hidden or non-visible disabilities, which are not readily seen or immediately obvious to others, also raise many issues about the presentation of self in everyday life (Goffman 1990/1959). For those of us with chronic illnesses our conditions can go largely unseen and this can present a problem for us within our workplaces and wider society. My own condition is not constant, which is the case with many chronic illnesses. It does fluctuate and 'flare', but it is always there, even if I can hide it some days. If I announce my condition, its invisibility becomes a concern – will people believe me? Am I actually disabled within the legal definition? What adjustments should I get, and do I really need them? Can I keep up on a daily basis in this hyper-challenging environment? Am I sick? Am I well? Am I disabled? Too many questions. Where do I go to find answers, and will the various disability theories help me position myself somewhere?

Two 'models' of disability prevail – the social model and the medical model. Both have been theorised, questioned, criticised and debated, and both have been expanded or rewritten to some extent. The British version of the social model of disability, first expressed by the Union of Physically Impaired against Segregation (UPIAS), stated, 'In our view, it is society which disables physically impaired people. Disability is something imposed on top of our impairments, by the way we are unnecessarily isolated and excluded from full participation in society' (UPIAS 1976, 3). This social model of disability was developed further by Oliver, who emphasised the need for a new way of looking at disability (Oliver 1983; 1990). The social model suggests that society over-medicalises disability, situating the problem firmly with the individual and the 'personal tragedy' of disability, rather than where it should lie, i.e. with society. This is an important definition – I do understand that – and crucially it sparked the development of the disability movement in the UK and political activism for disabled people. Society does disable, there is no denying that: I have seen it in practice on many occasions. But am I disabled within this definition? Probably not. I, personally, am not isolated or excluded. I am still *willing*, *capable* and, for the most part, *able* and I fully participate in society. Nevertheless, the medicalised impairment model on which the legal definition in the Equality Act 2010 is based does set me apart from colleagues because of the need for diagnosis of an impairment and subsequent requests for reasonable adjustments. But it is important to me, because without it I would not have been able to ask for the adjustments that I need to make my working life a possibility. In my own research with disabled students, all of whom unexpectedly presented with non-visible disabilities, I ask them: when they think of disability, what do they see? They all said 'someone with an obvious physical disability' or 'someone in a wheelchair'. They did not see themselves as having a disability even though when I went through the legal definition with them, they all acknowledged that they would fit squarely within it. Those same students would not see me as disabled, and although my chronic illness sets me apart in some ways, for the most part society does not even know that I have any impairment/disability at all. Whilst the social model would ignore my impairment, I cannot. The pain at times can be debilitating, the fatigue overwhelming and therefore my own lived experience is important. If all societal barriers were removed as advocated by the social model, my own physical impairment would still debilitate.

Goffman suggests disability is 'stigmatized' as a negative identity (Goffman 1990/1963). In his view, members of this group are assumed to be tainted or inferior in some way. This in turn prevents the individual from being included in society. In considering this stigmatised identity Loja et al. write that 'The concept of normality, embedded in the medical model, has been at the core of the othering process that has shaped the understanding of disability as a physical, moral, emotional, mental and spiritual deficit' (Loja et al. 2013, 198). I do experience this othering from time to time, particularly when asking for reasonable adjustments. Campbell states that 'inscribing certain bodies in terms of deficiency and essential inadequacy privileges a particular understanding of normalcy that is commensurate with the interests of dominant groups (and the assumed interests of subordinated groups)' (Campbell 2009, 11).

Therefore, this acknowledgement of normal and difference is problematic and contributes to the 'othering' of disability. Nevertheless, for those of us with non-visible disabilities this is not always the case. Controversially in some ways, we can choose who we are in front of others. Because we can 'pass', we can decide whether or not to assume this negative identity on the outside. I am not suggesting that this in any way helps, as we still have to decide whether or not to disclose our disability at some point. However, up until the point of disclosure we do not have to acknowledge this 'othering', except in our own minds.

I do appreciate why the medical model is problematic within the disability movement. Nevertheless, as an academic with a chronic illness that fits squarely within the medicalised legal definition of disability, I struggle to associate with the social model. I have to prefer Shakespeare's critical realist approach to disability. Shakespeare argues that '"social-modellists" would claim that so-called "medical-modellists" assume that "people are disabled by their bodies", whereas they say instead that "people are disabled by society, not by their bodies". I would argue that "people are disabled by society *and* by their bodies"' (Shakespeare 2014, 75). This is my authentic self. I have become disabled because of how people view me with my arthritis (once they know) and what I imagine people think of me with my arthritis (once they know). My body does, however, let me down on occasion, and work practices can be challenging. Being disabled by society only happened once knowledge of my chronic illness seeped out into the world. But my impairment or illness and the impact it has had on me has been my reality for years. As Williams suggests, 'endorsement of disability solely as social oppression is really only an option, and an erroneous one at that, for those spared the ravages of chronic illness' (Williams 1999, 812).

Thomas (1999; 2004) developed the social model to incorporate 'impairment effects' in an attempt to account for difficulties caused by medical conditions and impairments. In keeping with Thomas's relational interpretation of the social model of disability, my relationship with society changed once I disclosed my disability and my impairment does have an effect on me. Likewise, Shakespeare argues for an alternative approach to the social model, that of interaction between individual and structural factors (Shakespeare 2014, 74). Shakespeare acknowledges similarities between Thomas's relational approach and his own interactional approach. Both are relational in that disability is a 'relationship between intrinsic factors (impairment, personality, etc.) and extrinsic factors (environments, support systems, oppression etc.)' (Shakespeare 2014, 76). Nevertheless, I, like Shakespeare, disagree with Thomas's approach as it defines disability in terms of 'social oppression' (Thomas 1999, 60). Shakespeare suggests that 'to define disability entirely in terms of social oppression risks obscuring the positive dimension of social relations which enable people with impairment' and goes on to define 'disability as the outcome of the interaction between the individual and contextual factors, which includes impairment, personality, individual attitudes, environment, policy, and culture' (Shakespeare 2014, 77).

I have to reflect on the impact of all these theories on my own identity, professional and otherwise. The focus for me is not necessarily always on my own bodily impairment, although there are days when it lets me down and I feel the impact of non-normalcy on what I am doing. For me it is my emotional and mental self that imposes ableism on my own identity. I have come to see life in a different way and this has filtered through into my working life. I could argue that before the development of my chronic illness I felt I could do anything, and some days I still feel like that. Now, in my own mind, I know I am different in some way. Some days I cannot compete at the same pace. However, this difference does bring with it other advantages. Slowing down is important for all of us. Why do we constantly have to respond to this 'culture of perfectionism'? I am *willing* and *capable* – why isn't that enough? Many colleagues who do not have any form of disability or chronic illness struggle to keep up at times. Why has this become the new normal? Maybe it is down to those of us with a chronic illness or disability to challenge the mandatory demand for excellence in everything in academia. However, I do not feel socially oppressed. Once I disclosed, yes, my interactions changed, but some of that has been wholly positive and it has led to fruitful conversations in our faculty about disability and non-visible disabilities in particular, for staff and students alike.

It is important to affirm 'the diversity of bodies as a plus in a pluralist and inclusive society' (Loja et al. 2013, 200). In the struggle against ableism this recognition is crucial, and higher education institutions would do well to incorporate this diversity into their thinking on academic progression, teaching and learning strategies and employment policies. As Pinder writes, 'A successful employment policy needs to address the complexity and ambiguity of disabled people's experiences, as well as draw upon the common threads which underpin their struggle to compete economically in an ablist [sic] society' (Pinder 1996, 149). This is how I feel about academia. If we are to compete in the current version of higher education with its rival interests of excellence in teaching, research and knowledge exchange then higher education institutions must address the complexity and ambiguity of our experiences as disabled academics. It is also important that universities acknowledge how many of us there actually are. As Brown and Leigh ask, 'where are all the academics with disabilities, chronic illnesses or neurodiversity?' (Brown and Leigh 2018, 4). I only have to look at my own Twitter feed to work out that there are many of us, and of course that is just a small snapshot of the number of academics living with disability, chronic illness, mental ill health and neurodiversity. In Pinder's essay (1996) she writes about two people with arthritis: one, Peter, at the start of his diagnosis with rheumatoid arthritis, and the other, Lucy, with psoriatic (my own version of arthritis). In this study there is an acknowledgement of the discomfort that exists between not only disabled people and the able-bodied, or 'temporarily able-bodied (Zola 1989, 406), but also those who are disabled, the wider society and those who exist in the liminal space between these worlds – which I refer to below as my 'shade'.

The social model of disability as devised by Oliver (1983; 1990) has denied the impact of impairment. The disability movement that largely embodied this model fails to acknowledge the part that chronic illnesses play in disabling people. Chronic illness is still seen as 'medical' and therefore falls outside its province. I would suggest that the voices of the chronically ill, who 'weave in and out of disability' (Pinder 1996, 153), have been relatively muted in the disability movement. 'The contradictions inherent in relying primarily on a social model of disability to explain the difficulties the chronically ill and disabled people face at work cannot be ignored' and 'the experience of difference within difference needs to be acknowledged' (Pinder 1996, 153). Pinder suggests that feminists have already paved the way for this and the differences between women are crucial, just as the differences between disabled people are important. Of course, just as the disability movement lacks unity around a single definition, so does the feminist movement. However, feminist disability scholars have picked up the baton and are arguing for an all-encompassing and inclusive theory of disability. Feminist Liz Crow has criticised the social model for neglecting the individual experience of impairment: 'As individuals, most of us simply cannot pretend with any conviction that our impairments are irrelevant because they influence every aspect of our lives. We must find a way to integrate them into our whole experience and identity for the sake of our physical and emotional well-being, and, subsequently, for our capacity to work against disability' (Crow 1992).

The emphasis on difference brings us back to the legal definition and I would argue that difference has to be acknowledged as long as it does not suppress diversity within disability itself or reinforce false categorisation or hierarchies. Experience and voice have to be valued. As much as I want to 'pass' as 'normal' or 'able', as maybe I have not fully accepted my identity as a disabled academic, I do worry that in doing so I am denying an important role I could play in changing the way academia views disabled people. My own experience has been on the whole very supportive, and that is because of my great colleagues and my own head of department. I have, though, heard so many distressing stories. I cannot deny that my physical differentness is influencing the way I now see the world and I question the systems developing within higher education. When I realise that I cannot keep up, I worry about my position, but I still produce excellent work, I never fall behind, I push myself to present myself as *capable* and *able* to my students and colleagues – even though some days I would dearly love not to. If I do my job well, with no complaints, why do I feel inadequate some days? This is because of the pervasive culture of perfectionism in which we now operate.

The labour market of higher education emphasises what Pinder (1996, 152) refers to as 'productivity and performance'. We need to be always productive and always performing. I am productive and I do perform, but not always at the pace higher education demands. Past achievement seems to have no lasting currency. Achievement is no longer 'bankable'; it is now (almost instantly) reframed as the new baseline for which more or different achievement is urgently required. You see it everywhere – schooling, assessment, the job market, workplaces.

Why does any of this matter?

Doing my professional doctorate has made me more aware of my own position in the research process, as a disability law scholar and a disabled academic doing disability research. Relating to, or imagining, the likely experiences, concerns and claims of the participant group in my research – disabled law students – can be beneficial when using interpretative phenomenological analysis, but it does not require the researcher to have 'insider' status. Nevertheless, the research has required me to negotiate access to insider accounts and relate to and reflect on the experiences of the participants (Smith et al. 2009). My research has cast a spotlight on my disability and my disability is influencing my research and my position within it. My experience as a disabled academic in the competitive world of higher education has led me to question the ableism within academia but also within the professional employment we are preparing or 'training' our students for. We count our students in and count them out, and assume they are on a linear trajectory to professional graduate employment. However, this is not always the case for the disabled student.

As a disability researcher with a non-visible disability, I am also presented with an ethical dilemma – whether or not I should reveal my own disability to my research participants. Disclosing my disability to students in the institution where I work is revealing a part of my life that I might prefer to keep private. My legal training demands empathy but impartiality. My disability and my place of work also being the site of my research give me 'double' insider access, and the challenges of my position in my own research are compounded by my own identity as an academic, as a lawyer, as an academic with a disability, as a disabled lawyer – the list could go on. I have faced a number of dilemmas I had not anticipated when I started this doctorate, but there is no doubt that my interest in this research has stemmed from my own ill health. While exploring my 'position' in my research I have been forced to explore the nature of being an insider in research. Mercer (2007) explores the various concepts of 'insiderness' and I am using her work to explore my own questions about conducting insider research at my place of work with students who are part of my teaching cohort, while also reflecting on my position as a 'disabled' researcher and disability law scholar. My position has become an essential part of my research and the internal dialogue continues. Do I have more empathy or less? Do I understand the group better or not? Is my data going to be richer or not? I have access, the setting is familiar, I can build rapport, I have a shared frame of reference in the law and disability. However, I do not want to 'contaminate' my data and my non-visible disability means I can remain silent about my own experience of disability.

Alongside the acknowledged 'insiderness' of my professional status as a lawyer, my power as an academic and my visible signifiers of position, mine is also a 'secret' insiderness in that after much discussion and deliberation, I have chosen not to disclose my disability during the research process. I am, after all, 'temporarily able' and I am not ready to 'out' myself in this way in the interviews I am undertaking as part of my research. This doctoral research is not about 'me' and I do not need to disclose and, as I am still questioning how much disability is a part of my own identity, I do not want to delve into my own position with my research participants. I do, however, fully acknowledge the influence I have had on my research and I would suggest the research has become richer because of it.

Where does this get me?

Recently, I have come to identify myself as being part of Frank's (2004) 'remission society', which brings its own discomfort. I am declared medically 'in remission' as my chronic illnesses are largely 'under control' because of the medication I take. I have fewer obvious flares; my pain can be lesser. Most people think that individuals are either well *or* sick. 'Sickness and wellness shift definitively as to which is foreground and which is background at any given moment' (Frank 2004, 163). In the remission society, 'the foreground and background of sickness and health constantly shade into each other' (Frank 2004, 163). This is Sontag's 'kingdom of the sick':

> Illness is the night-side of life, a more onerous citizenship. Everyone who is born holds dual citizenship, in the kingdom of the well and the kingdom of the sick. Although we all prefer to use only the good passport, sooner or later each of us is obliged, at least for a spell, to identify ourselves as citizens of that other place. (Sontag 1978, 3)

This 'shade' has become part of my identity. Some days I inhabit the 'kingdom of the sick', but unlike Sontag's suggestion, I never get to fully leave this domain. Because of the stigma associated with illness and disability that we have yet to overcome, sometimes it is easier just to lie. I can exist in the world of the well because of medication and so I can 'pass' as 'normal' and 'able', even if only temporarily on some days. As Goffman suggests, the rewards of being or appearing 'normal' are such that most of us who are in such a position will choose to do so at some point and conform to ableist views of the world and what it is to be 'normal'. However, in remaining silent for so long and in this context, I am not facilitating the need for change in academia about how disabled academics are viewed and how much our presence and our research matters.

It is fair to say all of this has led me to see things differently. This autoethnographic narrative has been used to explore my own position in my research as part of the research process but also my own identity. I have transitioned from a practice-based lawyer to a qualitative researcher and the influence of my own personal phenomenon of a hidden or non-visible disability cannot be ignored. Much as I exist in the shaded area between health and sickness, so too do I exist in the shaded area between insider and outsider status in my research, thus reinforcing the continuum. However, this transition is still in a state of flux and I certainly do not have all the answers but I am now content to contribute to the conversation.

Returning to Goodley, 'the functioning neo-liberal self is an able-bodied and minded one. This is a self that is widely desired. Such visions of selfhood threaten to neutralise alternative ways of becoming' (Goodley 2014, 28). In one sense, I have 'become' someone else in doing this research. I am *willing, capable* and *able* – just not always at the same pace or always at the same time. I have decided there is nothing wrong with that. Academia needs to acknowledge this difference, which is crucial in the functioning of our legal rights in the workplace as academics with disabilities (visible or otherwise). It is crucial to acknowledge how much we contribute to academic life and how we see ourselves in wider society. Nevertheless, acknowledging and respecting this difference is important for our own wellbeing and our voice and experience must be heard. I would strongly argue that this should be the new 'normal'. After all, aren't we all exploring alternative ways of becoming? Aren't we all constructing or reconstructing our identities as our position in the world changes as we age, as we develop illness, as we are promoted, as we retire, as we take on new challenges?

Acknowledgements

I am grateful for the support of my colleagues at Northumbria Law School in writing this piece, for their comments and suggestions but above all their encouragement. Thanks must go in particular to Professor Elaine Hall, Dr Elaine Gregersen, Professor Chris Ashford (my supervisor) and Professor Ray Arthur for their backing, encouragement and reassurance that writing this would turn out to be OK.

References

Barnes, Colin and Mercer, Geoffrey. *Exploring the Divide. Illness and Disability*. Leeds: Disability Press, 1996.

Brown, Nicole and Leigh, Jennifer. 'Ableism in Academia: Where are the Disabled and Ill Academics?' *Disability and Society* 33/6 (2018): 985–9. Online. https://doi.org/10.1080/09687599.2018.1455627 (accessed 19 May 2020).

Campbell, Elaine. 'Reconstructing My Identity: An Exploration of Depression and Anxiety in Academia', *Journal of Organizational Ethnography* 7/3 (2018): 235–46. Online. http://doi.org/10.1108/JOE-10-2017-0045 (accessed 28 May 2020).

Campbell, Fiona Kumari. *Contours of Ableism: The Production of Disability and Abledness*. Basingstoke and New York: Palgrave Macmillan, 2009.

Collier, Richard. 'Wellbeing in the Legal Profession: Reflections on Recent Developments (Or, What Do We Talk About, When We Talk About Wellbeing?)', *International Journal of the Legal Profession* 23/1 (2016): 41–60. Online. http://dx.doi.org/10.1080/09695958.2015.1113970 (accessed 28 May 2020).

Collier, Richard. 'Surviving or Thriving? Researching Wellbeing and Mental Health in the Legal Profession'. 13 May 2019. Online. https://www.lawsociety.org.uk/news/blog/surviving-or-thriving-researching-legal-profession-wellbeing-and-mental-health/ (accessed 25 June 2019).

Crow, Liz. 'Renewing the Social Model of Disability', *Coalition News*, July 1992. Greater Manchester Coalition of Disabled People.

Ellis, Carolyn. *The Ethnographic I: A Methodological Novel About Autoethnography*. Walnut Creek, CA: AltaMira Press, 2004.

Ellis, Carolyn, Adams, Tony E., Bochner, Arthur P. 'Autoethnography: An Overview', *Forum: Qualitative Social Research* 12/1 (2011): 1–12. Online. http://dx.doi.org/10.17169/fqs-12.1.1589 (accessed 28 May 2020).

Ewick, Patricia and Silbey, Susan S. *The Common Place of Law, Stories from Everyday Life*. Chicago: University of Chicago Press, 1998.

Foster, Debbie and Hirst, Natasha. 'Legally Disabled? The Career Experiences of Disabled People Working in the Legal Profession'. 2020. Online. http://legallydisabled.com/research-reports/ and http://legallydisabled.com/ (accessed 28 May 2020). The research is supported by The Lawyers with Disabilities Division of the Law Society, the independent professional society for solicitors, and funded by the National Lottery, through Disability DRILL (Disability Research into Independent Living and Learning).

Frank, Arthur W. 'The Remission Society'. In *The Sociology of Health and Illness, Critical Perspectives*, edited by Peter Conrad. New York: Worth Publishers, 2004.

Garland-Thomson, Rosemarie. 'Becoming Disabled', *New York Times*, 19 August 2016. Online. https://www.nytimes.com/2016/08/21/opinion/sunday/becoming-disabled.html (accessed 28 May 2020).

Gibson, Matthew. 'The God "Dilution"? Religion, Discrimination and the Case for Reasonable Accommodation', *Cambridge Law Journal* 72/3 (2013): 578–616. Online. https://doi.org/10.1017/S0008197313000718 (accessed 28 May 2020).

Goffman, Erving. *The Presentation of Self in Everyday Life*. London: Penguin Books, 1990, originally 1959.

Goffman, Erving. *Stigma: Notes on the Management of Spoiled Identity*. London: Penguin Books, 1990, originally 1963.

Goodley, Dan. *Dis/ability Studies: Theorising Disablism and Ableism*. Abingdon and New York: Routledge, 2014.

Griffiths, Elisabeth. 'The "Reasonable Accommodation" of Religion: Is This a Better Way of Advancing Equality in Cases of Religious Discrimination?' *International Journal of Discrimination and the Law* 1/2-3 (2016): 161–76. Online. https://doi.org/10.1177/1358229116655652 (accessed 28 May 2020).

Haynes, Kathryn. 'Tensions in (Re)Presenting the Self in Reflexive Autoethnographical Research', *Qualitative Research in Organizations and Management: An International Journal* 6/2 (2011): 134–49. Online. https://doi.org/10.1108/17465641111159125 (accessed 28 May 2020).

Holmes, Leonard M. 'Becoming a Graduate: The Warranting of an Emergent Identity', *Education and Training* 57/2 (2015): 219–38. Online. https://doi.org/10.1108/ET-08-2013-0100 (accessed 28 May 2020).

Kanter, Arlene S. 'The Law: What's Disability Studies Got to Do With It *or* an Introduction to Disability Legal Studies', *Columbia Human Rights Law Review* 42/2 (2011): 403–79.

Kleege, Georgina. *Sight Unseen*. New Haven, CT: Yale University Press, 1999.

Law Society. *Resilience and Wellbeing Survey Report 2019*. Junior Lawyers Division. April 2019. London: The Law Society.

Loja, Ema, Costa, Maria E., Hughes, Bill and Menezes, Isabel. 'Disability, Embodiment and Ableism: Stories of Resistance', *Disability and Society* 28/2 (2013): 190–203. Online. https://doi.org/10.1080/09687599.2012.705057 (accessed 27 May 2020).

Markus, Hazel and Nurius, Paula. 'Possible Selves', *American Psychologist* 41/9 (1986): 954–69.

Mercer, Justine. 'The Challenges of Insider Research in Educational Institutions: Wielding a Double-Edged Sword and Resolving Delicate Dilemmas', *Oxford Review of Education* 33/1 (2007): 1–17. Online. https://doi.org/10.1080/03054980601094651 (accessed 28 May 2020).

Oliver, Michael. *Social Work with Disabled People*. Basingstoke: Macmillan, 1983.

Oliver, Michael. *The Politics of Disablement*. Basingstoke: Macmillan, 1990.

Pinder, Ruth. 'Sick but Fit or Fit but Sick'. In *Exploring the Divide. Illness and Disability*, edited by Colin Barnes and Geoffrey Mercer, 135–56. Leeds: Disability Press, 1996.

Shakespeare, Tom. *Disability Rights and Wrongs Revisited*. Abingdon and New York: Routledge, 2014.

Smith, Jonathan, Flowers, Paul and Larkin, Michael. *Interpretative Phenomenological Analysis: Theory, Method and Research*. London: Sage, 2009.

Solanke, Iyiola. 'Infusing the Silos in the Equality Act 2010 with Synergy', *Industrial Law Journal* 40/4 (2011): 336–58. Online. https://doi.org/10.1093/indlaw/dwr024 (accessed 28 May 2020).

Sontag, Susan. *Illness as Metaphor and AIDS and its Metaphors*. London: Penguin Classics, 2009. *Illness as Metaphor* originally 1978.

Thomas, Carol. *Female Forms: Experiencing and Understanding Disability*. Buckingham: Open University Press, 1999.

Thomas, Carol. 'Developing the Social Relational in the Social Model of Disability: A Theoretical Agenda'. In *Implementing the Social Model of Disability: Theory and Research*, edited by Colin Barnes and Geoffrey Mercer, 32–47. Leeds: Disability Press, 2004.

UPIAS. *Fundamental Principles of Disability*. London: UPIAS, 1976.

Vickers, Lucy. 'Religious Discrimination in the Workplace: An Emerging Hierarchy?' *Ecclesiastical Law Journal* 12/3 (2010): 280–303. Online. https://doi.org/10.1017/S0956618X10000414 (accessed 28 May 2020).

Williams, Simon J. 'Is Anybody There? Critical Realism, Chronic Illness and the Disability Debate', *Sociology of Health and Illness* 21/6 (1999): 797–819. Online. https://doi.org/10.1111/1467-9566.00184 (accessed 28 May 2020).

Zola, I. K. *Report on the American Association for the Advancement of Science Workshop on the Demography of Scientists and Engineers with Disabilities*. Washington, DC: American Association for the Advancement of Science, 1989.

8
Invisible disability, unacknowledged diversity

Carla Finesilver, Jennifer Leigh and Nicole Brown

It might seem odd to start with the assertion that bodies are invisible when they are plainly in sight. We all have bodies: meaty, fleshy, breathing bodies that take us through the world. And yet much of the time many people are not aware of their bodies; for the most part, if they are working well, we can ignore them. They disappear from our awareness. Drew Leder (1990) described this as 'the absent body. The idea is that unless we are injured, sick, in pain or – at a lesser level – hungry, cold or needing the toilet we pay little or no attention to the inner workings of our bodies. We might be aware of what they look like, particularly in the current cultural climate with so much attention given to body shape, diet, clothes and the like, but this is more concerned with the external appearance than a conscious awareness of our bodies as part of us. If they work 'as they are meant to', then unless our profession is such that we use them for our craft – as dancers or athletes, say – they are mostly absent from our awareness. Some might argue that even for dancers or athletes it is the pain of such work that calls them to attention (Thomas and Tarr 2009). Leder was a phenomenological philosopher, and as such he was interested in human experiences. He, like Maurice Merleau-Ponty (2002), believed that in order to incorporate the totality of someone's experience, we needed to include the information that arose from the body. Such an approach might be called 'embodied'. However, it is worth noting that the term 'embodied' is somewhat contested (Sheets-Johnstone 2015). One approach, taken in this chapter, is that to be embodied is about bringing conscious awareness to the feelings, sensations, thoughts, images and emotions that arise from the body (Leigh 2012). As such, it is both an ongoing process and a state of being (Leigh 2019). Such awareness is not limited (as Leder postulates) to dancers, athletes and the like, but is available to anyone who chooses to pay attention to their body, and the feelings, sensations, thoughts, images and emotions that arise from it. Such attention is not limited to the able-bodied and the 'well' but is accessible to anyone, with any body. However, consciously drawing attention to our bodies in this way is, for most of us, a choice. Whatever the state of our bodies, we can choose to pay attention to them or not. This kind of work is hard, and can be process work (Fogel 2009). It is tiring to be self-aware and conscious of one's body in this way, even while it is valuable, aiding reflexivity and creativity (Leigh and Bailey 2013). However, if a person is in chronic pain, or disabled by their body not working as it 'should', such awareness, as Leder points out, is no longer a choice but instead a constant, chronic, unavoidable reality. For those of us who live with chronic pain or disability, our bodies are continually present and reminding us of their presence – they are dys-appearing.

A profession like academia, which is competitive, cerebral (Leigh 2019) and – according to some (e.g. Bloch 2012) – devoid of emotion, is not conducive to embodied awareness of our bodies. Although we all 'do in academia in our own way', there are inherent tensions between the collegial and the individual, and between an embodied awareness of our bodies and the fixed structures of teaching, learning and researching. The academy values the mind, the intellect and the work of its inhabitants, in all but a few disciplines to the exclusion of their bodies. Exceptions might be in fields such as drama, dance or performance art, where practice as research is an accepted and valued contribution to knowledge (Thomson 2003). However, even within practice as research, the exegesis or written, intellectual element is an essential part of an output (Trimingham 2002). The practice is not enough on its own, and there is still a requirement for academics to foreground the cerebral rather than the embodied perspective (May 2015).

The very structure of academic work makes our bodies invisible and unimportant. In order to produce written research outputs we sit at desks, type on computers and are asked to put in many hours of work in order to meet externally driven targets (Fitzgerald et al. 2012). Hidden labour behind such work – which might involve our bodies (for example, the thinking, dreaming and moving that might underlie the creative process of writing) – is just that: hidden (Malcolm and Zukas 2009).

Other aspects of academic work, such as meetings, require us to sit, to hear, to maintain attention and to speak out; we also have to transport ourselves from office to meeting. Likewise, with teaching, we are often constrained to teach inside lecture halls or seminar rooms full of tables and chairs, up stairs or in remote parts of labyrinthine buildings, where we sit or stand in the designated part of the room (e.g. within range of the microphone). The time and space of academia constrains us, and encourages us to ignore our bodies, and any sensations, feelings, thoughts, images or emotions that we might be having (Herring and Standish 2019), and instead to focus only on the cerebral in our thoughts and outputs. However, those academics who have a disability or chronic illness are faced with a reality in which the body makes its presence known and felt. Being an academic takes effort. Living with a disability or chronic illness also takes effort (Livneh and Antonak 1997) and impacts on quality of life (Megari 2013). Being consciously self-aware takes effort. How much more effort, in both a physical and emotional sense, does it take to be an academic with a disability or chronic illness navigating through academia with the necessary self-awareness?

Understanding disability

Although the invisibility of the body in academia on its own is problematic, the lived experience of disability in academia is complicated further as wider understanding of the disabled body is often limited. Typically, disability is understood as a physical or mental impairment that has a substantial and long-term negative effect on individuals' ability to take part in everyday activities, and may entail accessibility issues that require accommodations. The social model of disability (Oliver 1983) considers disability from the standpoint of the pervasive barriers in society that exclude disabled people. As Oliver himself stated (2013), this social model of disability was meant to develop understanding among non-disabled medical and care professionals and to highlight the fact that every person individually, and indeed society as a whole, can take steps to prevent discrimination against the disabled. As such, the social model was intended as a teaching tool to raise awareness, which it has done. However, the social model does not enable individuals to understand the individuality of experiences. It was never meant to completely replace or overrule the individual model, which had prevailed until the 1980s. While it emphasises society's role in creating the 'disability' label, the focus remains on the dichotomy of disabled versus non-disabled.

One reason the social model of disability became as popular as it did is the societal tendency to impose categories on human diversity and to categorise individuals. Consequently, in academia, as in society more generally, disability is expected to take on particular forms. Examples of disability that are commonly simplified into easily understood binaries include: having a mobility impairment, equated to being completely unable to walk, and publicly signified by using a wheelchair; or having a visual impairment, equated to being completely blind, and publicly signified by using a white stick and/or a guide dog. And therein lies the problem, as accessibility issues, while increasingly considered in our environments, are often still conceived of as binary. In an abled-normative society, the absence of obvious visible identifiers such as a wheelchair results in an automatic assumption of non-disability. Impairments that are not externally visible at a glance, or visible but mistaken for temporary injuries, are not part of the general consciousness, unless the individuals concerned choose to actively and repeatedly publicise them. In this sense, public consciousness frames disability as a rare, tragic, non-normal experience that an individual must overcome (Goffman 1990/1963). In this understanding, as discussed in detail below, a person can either walk up stairs or cannot; there is no space in between. Within this, there is also the implied assumption that if the person can walk up the stairs, then they should. To decide not to take the stairs when there is the (perceived/assumed) physical possibility of doing so incurs negative judgement from others. In our society exercise has positive connotations, and with this and the environmental emphasis on saving energy, to (appear to) choose not to take the stairs and instead use a lift is difficult for able-bodied people to understand in any other framework than laziness.

Irrespective of whether individuals identify with and subscribe to the medical, the individual or the social model of disability, the premise of these approaches is the disabled body as the dis-abled, abnormal, weak body that a person is afflicted with. What if, however, a disabled person does not wish to be addressed in person-first language, but sees their disability as an inextricable part of who they are? This is the premise of crip theory (McRuer 2006). 'Cripping' the body means establishing the disabled body not as defunct or defect, but as a complete entity of 'becoming, reflection and production' (Goodley 2013, 638). We find such a multi-factor model of disability useful, where an individual's particular capabilities and characteristics are considered in interaction with the various systems and environments they move through. After all, in reality, disability is not always black or white, but consists of shades of grey. There are diagnostic grey areas and fuzzy boundaries, overlaps and individual differences. Disability may well be understood in terms of the limitations brought upon individuals through societal barriers, but it is at the same time a personal experience. In our abled-normative society, there is as yet particularly poor understanding of the existential spaces within and between disabilities and chronic illnesses, with pain conditions notably problematic. On the one hand, these conditions result in individuals feeling and being disabled (Deegan 2010); on the other hand, the conditions fluctuate, are often invisible and unproven, contested and doubted, as is the case for conditions that are medically unexplained in general (Kirmayer et al. 2004; Nettleton 2006). In everyday life, this means that there are those of us who use walking aids such as a cane or crutches in particular situations or on some occasions but not others. Where this is the case, we will be asked how we got injured (or how we injured ourselves *again*, if the person recalls previously seeing us with mobility aids). A much nastier version of this is experienced by ambulant wheelchair users who dare to take a few steps in public, or by those who use disabled parking spaces but then walk to the supermarket to do the shopping. Furthermore, even where difference from the abled norm is acknowledged, it is often assumed by others to be constant. If a person has limitations, it is assumed that these limitations will broadly be the same all the time. This is somewhat understandable as our brains like predictable patterns of simple dichotomies: right and wrong, true and false, disabled and non-disabled.

What is needed is a clear move away from the thought processes of 'I cannot see that, therefore it is not real or true' towards a more empathetic stance of mutual kindness, tolerance and acceptance. For disability to be understood in society generally, and more particularly in academia, it is therefore necessary to reframe the parameters for what disability is and means for the individual (see Goffman 1986/1974). Instead of considering the disabled body as non-normative, non-normal, deviant and defunct (Goffman 1990/1963), its fluctuation and variability and thus the fluidity of the disabled experience need to be emphasised (Deegan 2001). Additionally, a new frame (Goffman 1986/1974) needs to incorporate the potential invisibility of disability.

Invisibility and fluctuation

As we see it, there are two key issues relating to having a chronic illness as an invisible disability within an abled-normative educational environment. These are *invisibility* and *fluctuation*.

Firstly, unlike with an 'obvious' physical disability, it can be hard for others to see and to recognise that a person has additional challenges in negotiating everyday work and life. In our society, there has recently been a growing voice and presence of those who have an invisible condition, calling out those who would question whether or not an individual has a disability – whether they have a right to a blue badge, to use a disabled toilet or other accommodations. Initiatives such as the purple 'not all disabilities are visible' campaign (https://wearepurple.org.uk/not-all-disabilities-are-visible/) have deliberately set out to raise the profile of such conditions and insert them into the conservation. More controversial initiatives such as the sunflower lanyard (see hiddendisabilitiesstore.com), which was rolled out across airports and companies in the UK in 2019, have been designed so that those with an invisible condition can be recognised and supported. These have had a mixed reception from those who might use them as potentially they could visually mark out people based on only one aspect of their identity. However helpful or concerning these schemes may be, they are not generally meant for day-to-day use within a workplace such as academia. They might help us navigate busy train stations, supermarkets or airports, but can they be of use to us as we go about teaching and research?

The second key issue, fluctuation, is similar in that it encompasses the idea that disability and illness is not static and constant. Conditions can fluctuate, so that one day an individual might need to use a wheelchair, on another they may manage with crutches or a stick, and the next week they may need no physical supports to stand or walk. This fluctuating nature of chronic conditions has been recognised in guidance documents on how the Care Act should be implemented (see for example Action for ME et al. 2014). On an individual level, this can be frustrating – not knowing from one day to the next how we might be affected. For others working or living around people with such conditions this can be confusing – e.g. why does a person need to use mobility aids one day, but not on others? Are they making it up? And what does it mean for workplace accessibility arrangements if they are only needed part of the time?

In the particular context of academia, many of our day-to-day tasks and duties can be impacted by invisibility and fluctuations. Our timetables of teaching, research deadlines, committee meetings and the like are often rigid, and have little give in them to accommodate fluctuations of health, pain or energy. We may find ourselves expected to travel across or between campuses, sit in unforgiving chairs, carry heavy loads of paper, books or materials for our students, and having to estimate how possible this will be on a given day. The physical strength needed to command a lecture hall or teaching space for hours may 'cost' us more energy or exert a higher price on our health some days than others. Without visible reminders of disability, we may find ourselves repeatedly scheduled in rooms without adequate accessibility arrangements (although, as can be seen in Fiona Kumari Campbell's chapter in this volume, physical, visible disability is no guarantee of appropriate or adequate access) or feeling as though we have to explain or justify ourselves continuously to colleagues and/or students. These two issues can play out in several ways:

- Overestimation: If a person has an invisible illness or condition, and appears to be abled, they may be expected to cope with all tasks without appropriate accommodation of needs or differences.
- Underestimation: Conversely, when a person 'outs' themself as having a disabling condition, colleagues may perceive them to be 'too disabled' to cope with tasks that are well within their capabilities. Both of these can be exacerbated with a fluctuating condition, in which tasks may be too much on some occasions and very achievable on others.
- Lack of flexibility: Academic timetables and systems are often unable to cope with fluctuations in capacity and need, and how specific accommodations might be required at different times, with little warning.
- Disability as an exclusively 'student' issue: While there is an increasing amount of scholarship around the support of students, there is little on the presence or support of staff with disabilities or chronic illnesses.

Some universities have disability support services for students that provide advice and equipment, with little similar provision available to staff. In this dichotomy of support there is evidence for the idea that endemic ableism impregnates academia, in the unspoken assumption that staff are not disabled and do not need such services. Indeed, the popular discourse suggests that disabled people are assumed to be not working, 'on benefits' or scroungers (Turner 2012), and, as experienced by Kirstein Rummery (see her chapter in this volume), as incapable of the intellectual work necessary to hold down a job in academia.

What this feels like: Using narrative to explore invisibility and fluctuations

In order to share and illustrate what this might feel like to individual academics, we have chosen to include fictionalised reflective extracts from real-life experiences of ableism specifically due to invisible and/or fluctuating conditions. One of these accounts was the basis for an article in the *Guardian*'s 'Academics Anonymous' series and was used to draw attention to and stimulate debate around invisible disability and cognitive dysfunction in academia. It has been included here, along with some of the comments, in order to demonstrate the reactions of academics to those who disclose or make visible their differences. The inclusion of these vignettes draws on fiction as research practice (Leavy 2016) and autoethnographic methods (Ellis and Bochner 2000) and serves to highlight the emotional and social as well as physical aspects of the experience. We are explicitly using them in order to evoke the reality faced and lived by people who have invisible disabilities or chronic illness in academia. Whilst individually each instance of ableism described might not be considered heinous or an intentionally ableist action, the build-up of such microaggressions (Ahmed 2012) takes a toll on the individual emotionally, and in the case of those with chronic illness or disability, often also physically, impacting on their participation in academic activity (Harris 2017).

Stairs: Calculating accessibility

> I recently attended an academic event which was spread over four floors of a building with no lifts. My medical condition is not externally visible, although I often use a cane or crutches. I am usually physically able to go both up and down stairs, but often at significant cost. In this case it was acutely painful at the time, and the cumulative effect of the 16 flights in one day rendered me housebound for the following two days, with over a week for pain and mobility levels to return to their usual level. (I only skipped two of the meal/tea breaks, and by skipping all of them I could have reduced the sets of stairs to 'only' ten. If you wonder why I did not do this, consider how much useful networking goes on during the unstructured, social parts of conferences.) Throughout the day I observed various other attendees struggling up and

down, or deciding to miss out on sessions that required doing this. Meanwhile, nearby I overheard two of my colleagues talking about the 'lovely' building, and how they hoped we would use it again! It was this that actually bothered me the most, and impelled me to share my experience.

I am not suggesting that the able-bodied organisers and staff did not care that their choice of venue was physically detrimental to colleagues (and excluding of others who were not able to manage stairs at all); I think it was just out of the realm of their own current physical experience, and so not a factor in their thought processes. It is not difficult to think of many reasons why both those who do and do not consider themselves disabled might struggle significantly with stairs – musculo-skeletal pain, a fatigue condition, balance issues, breathlessness or a temporary injury. However, accessibility is often considered purely in the either/or, tick-box terms of wheelchair accessibility, and here, in the absence of a wheelchair user speaking up, it was assumed not to be an issue. This is not helped by the fact that those of us affected will often put up with significant pain or stress before complaining and risking being seen as 'difficult' by colleagues, or annoying those who will make decisions on future events (and thus, indirectly, who can attend them) – although it is totally understandable. And those who are not physically present may, due to abled norms, be assumed to have other reasons for not attending (if they are remembered at all). I believe these things need to be talked about, although – and perhaps because – it can be uncomfortable for all concerned.

This account demonstrates some of the internal calculations being done by individuals with chronic illness, disabilities or an injury. For example, when we look at flights of stairs we have to include:

- Pain: How much will this hurt now? How long will the (increase in) pain last? How will this affect me today? How much will it hurt later? What will the physical cost be of climbing these stairs, and how will it affect the quality of what I have to do next?
- Energy: How much energy do I have right now? If I can rest, how long will it take to recharge? If I over-exert today, will I have the opportunity to recuperate tomorrow? What will the

energetic cost be of climbing these stairs, and how will it affect the quantity of other things I can do today?
- Time: Will it make me late to locate and wait for the lift (if there is one)? What will I miss? Will I be late and cause a disturbance? If I need to travel to a venue, how much longer will the journey take if I only use step-free stations? What will the time cost be of climbing (or not climbing) these stairs?

These kinds of effects are cumulative, so it is not just important whether there are stairs, it is important how many there are. Similarly, even if there are lifts, if the distance between buildings or rooms is large (including the distance to the toilets, etc.), there will be similar cost-benefit analyses constantly running. Many people have the good fortune to go through life rarely running these kinds of calculations about everyday activities: their body is absent from these considerations; however, academics who are aiming to organise accessible events need to be conscious that some individuals do not have this luxury.

In addition to the physical, energetic and time costs that we have to weigh up, there are interpersonal aspects to consider when we think about whether to take each set of stairs, or move to another room or location. Some of these internal calculations also include: What informal but important conversations, information or opportunities will be missed if I leave to take the lift while the rest of the group walks? In a culture where individual responsibility for our environment is heightening, what will people think of me if I appear to be an able-bodied person choosing to take the lift rather than doing the 'right' and 'healthy' thing of taking the stairs? Will my colleagues think that I am unfit, weak or lazy, and judge me for it? Do I need to disclose my invisible condition? Every time? If I take the stairs one day but not another, will others think that I am faking or exaggerating the effects of my condition?

Cognit... I can't remember the word...

Difficulties with environmental aspects of the workplace are physical issues. However, invisible disabilities and chronic conditions do not only affect the physical body. They can also affect cognitive function. Examples of the kinds of conditions that can affect cognitive function include brain injury (BrainLine 2018), fibromyalgia (Shiel 2017), multiple sclerosis (Multiple Sclerosis Trust 2018), chemotherapy treatment (Cancer Research UK 2017), the menopause (Biggers and Marcin 2017) and other conditions associated with ageing, such as forms of dementia. Difficulties in cognition may carry even more stigma within academia than other work environments, as it is such a cerebral profession. If we cannot think, are we truly academics? In another fictionalised autoethnographic reflective extract, we share a story of an individual affected by such issues.

> I have a chronic and disabling condition. It's comparable to sudden-onset acquired brain injury, and it took me over a year to figure out what was going on. I struggled to process information, I had difficulty following a conversation if more than one person was talking, I had panic attacks – I got lost driving down a straight road that I had travelled many times. I didn't know where I was. I couldn't think, couldn't retain information; it felt as though I was in a lonely, isolating fog. Sometimes I could see people talking, or hear the noises that they were making, but I didn't follow what the words were. I couldn't understand what was going on. I lost myself. I wasn't this way before: I was driven, an over-achiever and perfectionist, known for my photographic memory and academic ability. My brain fog came suddenly without warning, and for that year was a constant, pervasive presence. For others it is more variable, as though you can get glimpses of sunshine and normality before it descends once more.
>
> For that year I couldn't teach. I could hardly write. If I'm honest, looking back, every paper that I wrote in that time was rejected by multiple journals. I couldn't be creative and clear, because my brain felt like it was smothered in toxic fumes. Normal everyday tasks took longer than they used to. Marking became a marathon of effort with 2,000-word essays taking over an hour to get through. I had bone-crushing fatigue, collapsing into bed at 6 pm. My family were concerned that I had depression; maybe I did, as a result of living in a body and in a life so far removed from the one I had before. I thought I would lose my job, and was terrified to disclose what was happening, but knew that I needed help. I was referred to occupational health, and they gave me a reduced workload while I had tests and appointments with hospital consultants. My manager supported me, but I felt that my team were frustrated that I wasn't pulling my weight. I didn't look any different – why did they have to cover my work? I focused on surviving. I was silent in meetings. I did not put my hand up for tasks or roles that might

enhance my career progression; I was looked over and dismissed as opportunities were handed out. I had no energy or capacity to stand up for myself. I just tried to survive. Things started to ease when my consultant began medication, and now as long as I keep taking the drugs every day I can function. Maybe not where I was before this began, but I can function.

As I surfaced from that time, I took stock and began to notice the attitudes around me. They weren't good. I was told, point blank, that I had to make up for the work I hadn't done, which I now know goes against the Disability Discrimination Act. I had to prove myself again; I wasn't taken seriously as a researcher any more.

If you saw me now, you'd not know there was anything wrong with me. I truly have an invisible condition. Even if I am having a bad day or miss a dose of my drugs, you might presume that I was tired, or maybe hungover. But I know that I am not ever going to recover from this. I might get better treatment, I might learn new tricks to help accommodate my capacity, but my condition is progressive. I meet both the Equality Act and the Disability Act[1] definitions of someone who has a disability. I worry I am not seen as an ambitious, valuable scholar. I worry my disability will stop me achieving. I worry my desire to prove myself in this field is impacting negatively on my health. (Academics Anonymous 2017; Courtesy of Guardian News and Media Ltd)

As academics, are we understanding enough of stories such as this? Cognitive dysfunction might occur, as discussed, for a variety of reasons and have a later life onset. In a session delivered on academic ableism in a higher education institution this story was shared, and one reaction was vocalised loudly – 'They are just making it up to get out of work!' While this opinion might seem more reminiscent of tabloid newspapers than educated academics, unfortunately it seems that in today's neoliberal culture of overwork (Davies and Bansel 2005) we are less and less understanding towards others with different needs. This can be seen in the comments sections of anonymous blogs such as that in the *Guardian* column 'Academics Anonymous' (*Guardian* n.d.), where more experiences of living with illness, disability and mental health have been shared. The responses can be vitriolic and heart-breaking by turn. Some, taken from the piece from which the above extract is drawn, are quoted below:

Work as an academic probably just isn't for you.

Long hours are non-negotiable. Academic life is a profession, not a job, and you work the hours needed to get it done. Anyone who tries to do it 9–5 will find it very hard to progress and will thoroughly piss off their colleagues.

A lecturer at my university once told me to my face I had no business being there because I was partially sighted. I wish I'd reported him. He tried to ruin my future because he simply didn't like disabled people, I would have dearly loved to hang him out to dry because that's what he tried to do to me.

I would strongly advise minimising the effects of any disability to both staff and managers and, if need be, not being honest about the reasons for any effects a long-term condition or disability might have on working life. (Academics Anonymous 2017. Courtesy of Guardian News and Media Ltd)

These comments were made by academics or those interested in the world of academia, and they strongly suggest that if an individual is struggling with their cognitive functions, they have no place in the academic world. There was little compassion, little empathy for the nature of the injury – described as similar to sudden-onset brain injury. We may assume that had the narrative suggested a different cause – such as a chronic illness, cancer treatment or menopause – the responses would be little different. Indeed, the many anonymous blogs concerned with aspects of mental health, disability, invisible disability and ableism in this series and others suggest that this account and the reactions to it are typical. If this is the academic society that we live in, do we want to? Our options are to leave, or to change the environment and culture in which we work.

Dys-appearing bodies: Discussion and conclusion

Academia is often accused of not being diverse (Stewart and Valian 2018) or representative enough (Sian 2019). Meanwhile, we know that across the sector fewer people are disclosing disability or chronic illness than within the general working population (according to data from the Higher Education Statistics Agency). We cannot know whether this is due to academics choosing not to disclose (Brown et al. 2018) or because they are driven out of the profession or discriminated against when attempting to enter it. We do know that even where they have disclosed, they are under-represented in leadership and senior positions, and over-represented in junior, part-time and precarious temporary positions.

If we are abled, then paying attention to our body and noticing the sensations and information that come from it is a choice. If we have a chronic condition or disability, that choice may not be open to us. Instead, pain or inability forces our bodies into the forefront of our experience (Leder 1990). Chronic pain is tiring (AbleTo 2018). Dealing with disability is tiring (Mackelden 2019). Academia, particularly within its current managerialised and metric-driven context, is tiring (Gill 2009). Academics living with chronic illness or a disability are being forced to confront their dys-appearing body at every turn, within an environment and culture that is not welcoming to difference or diversity. Their brains have to constantly run pain/energy/activity calculations alongside the work they are actually doing, so part of their cognitive ability is taken up with this even while they teach, read, research and write. If they are to attend an event, lecture or conference, they need to spend additional time organising, checking and re-checking accessibility arrangements for the travel, for the event itself, for meals. These academics have to weigh up the risks of choosing to explain and educate others on their conditions or not. This additional labour is not part of the academic load for everyone, but it is for disabled academics, and particularly those with an invisible and/or fluctuating condition.

In this chapter we have argued that working in academia has a hidden cost for persons who have an invisible disability or chronic condition. This might be emotionally draining, entailing dealing with ableism and microaggressions on a daily basis. It might be physically draining, with the demands placed on a hurting or fatigued body such as navigating across campus or up stairs, and the cognitive demands described above. It might be a cost to work–life balance – as the time taken to organise accessibility and to do ordinary tasks such as marking or writing take substantially longer than for others. These costs can have implications for the individuals involved, and also for the institutions that employ them and the sector more widely. If, in our commitment to the Equality Act (and any future legislation against disability discrimination), we want to do more than pay lip service to the law, we need to start valuing different perspectives. We need to bring to the foreground that those who dismiss initiatives aimed at redressing the balance as 'PC nonsense' (or similar disparaging terms) are contributing to the systematic exclusion of potential fellow contributors to knowledge. We need to recognise that being inclusive is also about being empathetic, compassionate humans who have consideration for others. If we want to promote opportunity for our students and staff and celebrate the diversity we find in our campuses and workplaces, some small changes could help create a more inclusive academic environment.

If we take as a starting assumption the fact that there will be diversity in any group, that there will be individuals with many different needs that may not be obvious to others and that might change over time or circumstances, we can build in accessibility. This is encompassed for students in the idea of universal design for learning (Bracken and Novak 2019), and could be extended to a universal design for research, teaching and learning, so also accommodating staff. In turn, this would allow students to encounter and learn from diverse role models, which is an important part of encouraging diversity and equality (Diversity Role Models 2020) – and that diversity must include disability, visible and invisible. Simple aspects of this include looking at institutional branding and print materials and considering accessibility (Featherstone 2015), as well as considering accessibility in all events hosted by an institution as a matter of practice, with guidelines for organisers to follow (see Brown et al. 2018 for suggestions), and having a clear policy on equality, diversity and inclusion matters, backed up by a high-level strategy.

On a more individual and cultural basis, if we as academics see that one of our number is not participating in an activity (e.g. shifting chairs, volunteering to take minutes) and it is not obvious why not, we should assume they have a good reason. It should not be necessary to provide a verbal sick note or to explain every decision. Similarly, while it is appreciated when colleagues do remember impairments or support needs, it is also important not to assume that because an individual has been observed doing something in the past, they necessarily can today. Even more importantly, we should not assume the converse – that because someone could not do something on a previous occasion, it is and will always be impossible. We should trust that individuals (staff or students) know best how to 'do academia' in the ways that work best for them – however different those are from the ways of their colleagues. We should not assume that others work or study in the ways that we do, and need to trust their judgement and knowledge of their own body, mind and condition.

Ableism is discrimination in favour of able-bodied people, people who are not ill, who do not have a disability, who are neurotypical. Ableism is the discrimination and social prejudice against people who fall outside those normal boundaries. Ableism characterises such people as defined by their disabilities and sees them as inferior; unfortunately, it is endemic within the culture and fabric of academia. It is up to all of us to challenge this, to acknowledge our human complexities and fluctuations, including the invisible parts of the iceberg of experience, to celebrate the vivid diversity already present in the academy, while striving for more, and to help make change.

Notes

1 The Equality Act 2010 was put in place to protect people from discrimination in the workplace and in wider society. It replaced multiple previous anti-discrimination laws (including the Disability Discrimination Act 1995) with a single Act. 'Disability' is currently defined as 'a physical or mental impairment that has a "substantial" and "long-term" negative effect on your ability to do normal daily activities' (Government Equalities Office 2011).

References

AbleTo. 'Why Chronic Pain Causes Fatigue And Depression'. 2018. Online. https://www.ableto.com/resources/why-chronic-pain-causes-fatigue-and-depression/ (accessed 29 September 2019).
Academics Anonymous. 'If I Tell My University About My Disability Will I Be Seen as the Weakest Link?', *Guardian*, 8 December 2017. Online. https://www.theguardian.com/higher-education-network/2017/dec/08/if-i-tell-my-university-about-my-disability-will-i-be-seen-as-a-weak-link (accessed 29 September 2019).
Action for ME, Arthritis Research UK, Crohn's and Colitis UK, M.E. Association, MS Society, NAT (National Aids Trust), National Rheumatoid Arthritis Society and Parkinson's UK. 'Implementing the Care Act for People with Long-Term Fluctuating Conditions', 2014. Online. https://www.nat.org.uk/sites/default/files/implementing-the-care-act.pdf (accessed 24 September 2019).
Ahmed, Sarah. *On Being Included: Racism and Diversity in Institutional Life*. Durham, NC: Duke University Press, 2012.
Biggers, Alana and Marcin, Ashley. 'What Causes Menopause Brain Fog and How Is It Treated?' 22 December 2017. Online. https://www.healthline.com/health/menopause/menopause-brain-fog (accessed 29 September 2019).
Bloch, Charlotte. *Passion and Paranoia: Emotions and the Culture of Emotion in Academia*. Farnham: Ashgate. 2012.
Bracken, Sean and Novak, Katie, eds. *Transforming Higher Educationt Through Universal Design For Learning: An International Perspective*. Abingdon and New York: Routledge, 2019. Online. (accessed 28 May 2020).
BrainLine. *Traumatic brain injury is....* 2018. Online. https://www.brainline.org/article/traumatic-brain-injury-is (accessed 22 June 2020).
Brown, Nicole, Thompson, Paul and Leigh, Jennifer S. 'Making Academia More Accessible', *Journal of Perspectives in Applied Academic Practice* 6/2 (2018): 82–90. Online. https://doi.org/10.14297/jpaap.v6i2.348 (accessed 19 May 2020).
Cancer Research UK. 'Chemo brain'. 2017. Online. https://www.cancerresearchuk.org/about-cancer/cancer-in-general/treatment/chemotherapy/side-effects/chemo-brain (accessed 29 September 2019).
Davies, Bronwyn and Bansel, Peter. 'The Time Of Their Lives? Academic Workers In Neoliberal Time(S)', *Health Sociology Review* 14/1 (2005): 47–58. Online. https://doi.org/10.5172/hesr.14.1.47 (accessed 19 May 2020).

Deegan, Mary Jo. 'Counting Steps: The Phenomenology of Walking with Variable Mobility', *Disability Studies Quarterly* 20/3 (2001): 232–42.

Deegan, Mary Jo. '"Feeling Normal" and "Feeling Disabled"'. In *Disability as a Fluid State* (Research in Social Science and Disability, vol. 5), edited by Sharon N. Barnartt, 25–48. Bingley: Emerald Group, 2010. Online. https://doi.org/10.1108/S1479-3547(2010)0000005004 (accessed 25 May 2020).

Diversity Role Models. 'Embedding Inclusion and Empathy in the Next Generation'. 2020. Online. https://www.diversityrolemodels.org/ (accessed 25 May 2020).

Ellis, Carolyn and Bochner, Arthur. 'Autoethnography, Personal Narrative, Reflexivity: Researcher as Subject'. In *Handbook of Qualitative Research*, 2nd ed., edited by N.K. Denzin and Y.S. Lincoln, 733–68. London: Sage, 2000.

Featherstone, Lisa. 'How Can You Make Resources Accessible For Those With Disabilities?' 13 July 2015. Online. https://www.jisc.ac.uk/blog/how-can-you-make-resources-accessible-for-those-with-disabilities-13-jul-2015 (accessed 29 September 2019).

Fitzgerald, Tanya, White, Julie and Gunter, Helen. *Hard Labour? Academic Work and the Changing Landscape of Higher Education*. Bingley: Emerald Group, 2012.

Fogel, Alan. *The Psychophysiology of Self-Awareness*. London: Norton, 2009.

Gill, Rosalind.'Breaking the Silence: The Hidden Injuries of Neo-Liberal Academia'. In *Secrecy and Silence in the Research Process: Feminist Reflections*, edited by Roisin Ryan-Flood and Rosalind Gill, 228–44. Abingdon and New York: Routledge, 2009.

Goffman, Erving. *Frame Analysis: An Essay on the Organization of Experience*. Boston, MA: Northeastern University Press, 1986, originally 1974.

Goffman, Erving. *Stigma: Notes on the Management of Spoiled Identity*. London: Penguin Books, 1990, originally 1963.

Goodley, Dan. 'Dis/entangling Critical Disability Studies', *Disability and Society* 28/5 (2013): 631–44. Online. https://doi.org/10.1080/09687599.2012.717884 (accessed 27 May 2020).

Government Equalities Office. 'Disability: Equality Act 2010 – Guidance on Matters to be Taken into Account in Determining Questions Relating to the Definition of Disability'. 2011. Online. https://www.gov.uk/government/uploads/system/uploads/attachment_data/file/570382/Equality_Act_2010-disability_definition.pdf (accessed 29 May 2020).

Guardian. N.d. *Academics Anonymous*. Online. https://www.theguardian.com/education/series/academics-anonymous (accessed 29 September 2019).

Harris, Lynsie. 'Exploring The Effect of Disability Microaggressions on Sense of Belonging and Participation in College Classrooms'. Logan, UT: School of Psychology, Utah State University, 2017.

Herring, Catherine and Standish, Paul. 'Displacing the One: Dislocated Thinking in Higher Education'. In *Conversations on Embodiment: Teaching, Practice and Research*, edited by Jennifer Leigh, 71–83. Abingdon and New York: Routledge, 2019.

Kirmayer, Laurence J., Groleau, Danielle, Looper, Karl J. and Dao, Melissa D. 'Explaining Medically Unexplained Symptoms', *Canadian Journal of Psychiatry* 49/10 (2004): 663–72. Online. https://doi.org/10.1177/070674370404901003 (accessed 27 May 2020).

Leavy, Patricia. *Fiction as Research Practice: Short Stories, Novellas, and Novels*. Abingdon and New York: Routledge, 2016, originally 2013.

Leder, Drew. *The Absent Body*. Chicago: University of Chicago Press, 1990.

Leigh, Jennifer. 'Somatic Movement and Education: A Phenomenological Study of Young Children's Perceptions, Expressions and Reflections of Embodiment through Movement'. PhD. diss., University of Birmingham, 2012.

Leigh, Jennifer, ed. Conversations on Embodiment across Higher Education: Research, Teaching and Practice. Abingdon and New York: Routledge, 2019.

Leigh, Jennifer. 'Embodied Practice and Acdemic Identity'. In *Conversations on Embodiment across Higher Education: Research, Teaching and Practice*, edited by Jennifer Leigh, 151–70. Abingdon and New York: Routledge, 2019.

Leigh, Jennifer and Bailey, Richard. 'Reflection, Reflective Practice and Embodied Reflective Practice', *Body, Movement and Dance in Psychotherapy* 8/3 (2013): 160–71. Online. https://doi.org/10.1080/17432979.2013.797498 (accessed 29 May 2020).

Livneh, Hanoch and Antonak, Richard. *Psychosocial Adaption to Chronic Illness and Disability*. Gaithersburg, MD: Aspen, 1997.

Mackelden, Amy. 'Being Disabled Is Exhausting', 2 February 2019. Online. https://clarissaexplainsfa.com/blog/2019/2/1/being-disabled-is-exhausting (accessed 29 September 2019).

McRuer, Robert. *Crip Theory: Cultural Signs of Queerness and Disability*. New York: New York University Press, 2006.

Malcolm, Janice and Zukas, Miriam. 'Making a Mess of Academic Work: Experience, Purpose and Identity', *Teaching in Higher Education* 14/5 (2009): 495–506. Online. https://doi.org/10.1080/13562510903186659 (accessed 29 May 2020).

May, Shaun. *Rethinking Practice as Research and the Cognitive Turn*. Basingstoke: Palgrave Macmillan, 2015.

Megari, Kalliopi. 'Quality of Life in Chronic Disease Patients', *Health Psychology Research* 1/3 (2013): e27. Online. https://doi.org/10.4081/hpr.2013.e27 (accessed 29 May 2020).

Merleau-Ponty, Maurice. *Phenomenology of Perception*. Abingdon and New York: Routledge, 2002.

Multiple Sclerosis Trust. 'Thinking and Memory Problems'. May 2018. Online. https://www.mstrust.org.uk/life-ms/wellbeing/thinking-and-memory-problems (accessed 29 September 2019).

Nettleton, Sarah. '" I Just Want Permission to be Ill": Towards a Sociology of Medically Unexplained Symptoms', *Social Science and Medicine* 62/5 (2006): 1167–78. Online. https://doi.org/10.1016/j.socscimed.2005.07.030 (accessed 29 May 2020).

Oliver, Michael. *Social Work with Disabled People*. Basingstoke: Macmillan, 1983.

Oliver, Michael. 'The Social Model of Disability: Thirty Years On', *Disability and Society* 28/7 (2013): 1024–26. Online. https://doi.org/10.1080/09687599.2013.818773 (accessed 25 May 2020).

Sheets-Johnstone, Maxine. 'Embodiment on Trial: A Phenomenological Investigation', *Continental Philosophy Review* 48/1 (2015): 23–39. Online. https://doi.org/10.1007/s11007-014-9315-z (accessed 29 May 2020).

Shiel, William. 'Medical Definition of Fibro Fog'. 24 January 2017. Online. https://www.medicinenet.com/script/main/art.asp?articlekey=125458 (accessed 29 September 2019).

Sian, Katy. 'Extent of Institutional Racism in British Universities Revealed Through Hidden Stories'. 27 June 2019. Online. http://theconversation.com/extent-of-institutional-racism-in-british-universities-revealed-through-hidden-stories-118097 (accessed 29 September 2019).

Stewart, Abigail J. and Valian, Virginia. *An Inclusive Academy: Achieving Diversity and Excellence*. Cambridge, MA: MIT Press, 2018.

Thomas, Helen and Tarr, Jennifer. 'Dancers' Experiences of Pain and Injury: Positive and Negative Effects', *Journal for Dance Medicine and Science* 13/2 (2009): 51–9.

Thomson, Peter. 'Practice as Research', *Studies in Theatre and Performance* 22/3 (2003): 159–80.

Trimingham, Melissa. 'A Methodology for Practice as Research', *Studies in Theatre Performance* 22/1 (2002): 54–60.

Turner, David M. 'Superhumans or Scroungers? Disability Past and Present', *History and Policy*, 6 August 2012. Online. http://www.historyandpolicy.org/opinion-articles/articles/superhumans-or-scroungers-disability-past-and-present (accessed 29 September 2019).

9
Imposter

Jennifer A. Rode

In 'Imposter', Rode provides a powerful stream of consciousness from the point of view of someone whose **different** *body and mind influence her academic work. Her poetic enquiry discusses how disability challenges productivity and produces self-doubt. 'Imposter' acknowledges the inherent ableism of the academies conception of merit and yet remains defiant to contribute scholarship.*

There is a book inside me
It is not written
Instead I sleep
The pages are cloaked in fog

I know the argument I will write
The literature I will cover
I know my contribution
But, don't we all say that?

Am I too afraid or too ill to write?
Is the fog too thick to see?
Or is it an excuse?
Or perhaps I am too addled.

Is the clarity in my mind a dream?
Is the disability an excuse?
Is my prose lacking?
Because I am.

Are the pages empty, because I am a coward?
Are the manuscripts returned,
Because it is my prose that's thick

And not the fog?
Am I deluded,
Thinking I can write?
Is ableism an excuse I use?

My resumé has gaps
But I write

My resumé has gaps
And I have migraines
Days I can't move my hand

My resumé has gaps
Days I can't see enough to read become weeks
And I spend time in the hospital
Or in too much pain to focus

My resumé has gaps
    While I remain at home alone
        Struggling to regain enough balance to walk
        Silent on social media lest I am negative
        Invisible

But you see the gaps.
Low Productivity.
Decreasing H-index.
Grant money drying up.

Academia is greyhound dog racing
Fastest around the track
Youth and speed
Promote the best
Hotdogs from the worst

Broken
I limp around the track
And still I write
Between the gaps

And I peer through doors where I can not go
And I crawl up stairs to teach
And I get stranded in airports waiting

Blood and sweat and tears
As I suffer what they cannot see
As I suffer what they do not understand
As I suffer their prejudices and assumptions
As I suffer so many indignities
My disability is so inconvenient
And the lines of hotdog casings feel so clean

And still I write.

10
Internalised ableism: Of the political and the personal

Jennifer Leigh and Nicole Brown

In the popular imagination academia is perceived as a privileged working environment, with high-status occupations, long holidays, and little pressure and accountability. Yet this is not how academics describe the work they do and the environment they work in. Academics are bound by personal values and social norms, which they internalise through their moral commitment to the academy (Scott 1971). Therefore academic identity, working in academia and the specific characteristics and personality traits of academics can be seen as manifestations of internalisation processes (Parsons 1970/1964). The role of work in relation to identity is well documented (Wrzesniewski and Dutton 2001; Witt et al. 2002; Kirpal 2004a; 2004b; Walsh and Gordon 2008; Haslam et al. 2000). Work is not merely a means to be productive, it also influences and moulds us, so that we find our selves in and through work (Gini 1998). Within the context of higher education, work identity and the interrelationship between work and identity are commonly explored in the context of professional identity (Trede et al. 2012) or in terms of belonging to a community (Smith et al. 2010; Billett and Somerville 2004). Becoming or being academic in contemporary higher education is an active process of reconciling, or indeed refusing to reconcile, autonomy, authenticity and values with the success criteria audit of the neoliberal university (Archer 2008a; 2008b; Henkel 2005).

The personal, private

Our argument in this chapter is that the political and personal intersect in a mutually interconnected relationship so that the political impacts the personal, that the public influences the private and vice versa, and that these tensions are played out within the body. Therefore, taking a stand as a disabled or chronically ill academic is a political as well as a personal act and can have physical consequences. Exploring lived experiences as a basis for understanding the social has a long tradition (Van Manen 1990; Ellis and Flaherty 1992). Personal stories and narratives, autobiographies and autoethnographies are perhaps less commonly accepted as a 'scientific' method and sometimes dismissed as too narcissistic or self-centred (Holt 2003; Salzman 2002; Sparkes 2002). And yet, if employed systematically and rigorously, the personal narratives (*auto*) within autoethnographies are merely a starting point for the analytical research (*graphy*) on culture (*ethno*) (Ellis and Bochner 2000). In other words, the emphasis on the self is not a narcissistic or self-indulgent fixation: it is a lens through which the social is explored in order to provide better understanding of cultural phenomena. The personal stories are therefore necessary in order to provide the context for socio-cultural interpretations. With this in mind, the following section offers confessional-emotive writing (Chang 2016, 145ff.), which will allow us to contextualise the concerns of being ill in the current climate of neoliberal academia. These extracts draw from a reflective journal of an academic written in the years after becoming chronically ill.

Coming to terms, 2015

> So I'm feeling very emotional. The ramifications and consequences of being ill seem to be looming larger than ever.
>
> It feels like I am having to prove myself three times over to make up for being ill. As though I am being punished for being ill. As though living it is not enough.
>
> What's the line between bullying/discrimination? Being treated differently? Made to feel as though I wanted to be ill?

They call it 'brain fog' – for me it was a complete inability to process. I could hear but not understand what people were saying. I was disorientated, confused. This made me anxious.

It was only when I began to feel better – when I started on the correct medication – that I realised that not only was my brain fogged, but my body also.

My research is about embodiment, about being in the body, and not only could I not think, but I could not feel into my own body. Moving was painful. Exhausting. Where once it had been a source of energy.

The invisible illness/disability aspect of this is so pertinent too. Am I protected? Who protects me? I am fighting to do my job to live my life and every thought is a struggle. But other people can't see it. I don't feel like 'me'.

But they don't know who 'me' is. They assume/think I don't know what. I'm slacking? I want to be like this? It's an excuse? That I'm trying to get out of teaching to do research?

I was told to concentrate on what I could do – research, writing. I could do this – slowly. But not creatively. No original thoughts. Yet when I did this it was seen as an easy option?

I remember applying for conferences – but it was vetoed because it would upset the team if I went to a conference when I wasn't teaching.

Complete lack of understanding.

Thing is, it's only now, when I am feeling so much more like myself, that I can conceptualise it and write, more, express what it was.

But I'm not in it any more.

That said, I'm not yet out of it either.

Am I disabled?

I have a disabling condition.

Where does that sit with a marginalised status?

Or not?

It is hard to have a voice if my mind is not processing my body isn't working.

I need to move tomorrow to prepare.

To protect.

Am I subject to more scrutiny than my peers? It feels that way.

New normal, 2016

I used to feel an expert in my own body and my ability to read others. Now I don't. This brain/body fog that inhabits and pains me obscures my sense of myself and my confidence is shaken when it comes to anyone else. I don't inhabit or represent what I believe and I feel I 'should'. How can I help anyone else or educate them when they only have to look at me to see how I am lacking?

This inability/unwillingness to accept how I am as a new normal does seem to be driven by the need to produce, to drive around, when in fact in my body I am crying out to do nothing but rest and breathe and heal. I need to heal so much. Then I resent this academy that keeps pushing me to injure myself. I feel broken but I don't know if they can see or if they care.

Broken academy, 2017

I want to acknowledge the structural issues such as overwork or casualisation that are endemic in the academy. Recently I found myself delivering a session to postgraduate research students at my university on 'balancing research, teaching and life'. I was struck by the irony of this, as my co-facilitator and I had been exchanging emails about the session at 11 pm and 5 am in the previous days, and I arrived for the session itself hot and out of breath, having run from nursery drop-off to meeting after meeting to get there. How can we preach the need for wellbeing when we model anything but? When we are driven to do anything but? Is this an environment I would want my daughter to be in? I'd want her to have her eyes wide open. Why do I think of it as a win when a PhD student tells me that they are looking for a career outside academia?

Being perfect, 2019

Today I taught for 5 hours. I was in a room full of people who needed and expected me to show them how to teach, while also expecting the day to be a waste of time, and not wanting to be there. I sometimes feel like I am a performing monkey. I have to be upbeat, I have to have energy, I have to be engaged, I have to be *good*. I have to be the teacher they dream of being. I have to deliver the right message. Teaching is *fun*. Teaching is *worthwhile*. Last week I was teaching a different full-day course and I was so aware of the cost it had on me. I hadn't been practising, I didn't feel strong in my body and I was hyper-aware of how hard it was even to stand. My pores were tired, I wasn't able to hold the energy in the room without leaning or sitting, and yet the room layout was such that I couldn't sit and be seen by everyone. When I would normally perch on a table the table tipped up. I wasn't on my own. I don't think anyone else 'noticed' and the feedback we had was good. But I knew that to get through this week and next, teaching for five hours at a stretch day after day, I needed to be more in my body. This means that for the last four days I have got up at 6 am to practise, to be more in my body, to feel whether today I am stiff (always) or off balance, or where I need to be gentle with myself. And yet I end today with iron behind my eyes clamping them down because I know that I can't rest and recover and recuperate ready for tomorrow, instead I have to sit and write and think and *be creative* because this manuscript is due in. I cannot take the time I need and it is costing me. My teeth hurt, I am so tired. I don't have it in me to put in the hours in the evening, at the weekend, that I need to do to get it all done. Others would. Others do. But I can't. I am only one day into this teaching load. The pressure is relentless. And still, in the classes, I am continually putting in more content, asking my students, my would-be teachers, to consider the needs of their students, to consider their own needs as teachers, to be aware of the pressures of overwork and hyper-productivity. I asked them to think about what it means to be a good teacher, while modelling being one, engaging with them, conducting the class, as one said, as an adaptive stand-up comedian. She didn't mean that I had a comedy routine, but that I had to adapt and change what I did to fit the needs of the room. Which is what a good teacher does. But a good teacher doesn't flake out or fade out when her students are talking. I did. A good teacher isn't counting the minutes until the class ends so she can get on with something else, something that counts more. I did. And should a good teacher be a role model? I think so. But I did not tell them my story even after a conversation around disclosing aspects of your identity as a teacher and acting as a role model. At the end of the day we talked about the things every teacher should know. I said 'don't be a dick'. It covers a lot. And they said 'a shitty session doesn't mean you're a shitty teacher'. I feel shitty right now, what does that count for?

Seen from the outside, 2019

Good job on handling the late student and demonstrating professionalism.

I expected to fall asleep in 5 minutes but it was very interesting.

Really well-led talk, managed to keep attention for a long period of time.

I loved the fact that you refer to what you did earlier in the workshop as an example of group management.

I really enjoyed this … Pace of the lesson was great and was an excellent example of the kind of teaching I'd like to do.

Neoliberal academia as a workplace

Within the context of the neoliberal academy, overwork and being a high achiever are valued. Academics are high achievers and have matching expectations of themselves. Such ways of working are not inclusive to those of us who are unable or unwilling to work at this level or pace. Female academics particularly seem to make sacrifices for their work, and fatigue, burnout and ill health seem common (Currie et al. 2000; Gore 1999; Kolodny 1998). Through having high expectations, it is possible for academics to strive for more knowledge, produce better research articles and contribute to the academic community, and thus to feel validated in their identity and their work. However, the line between having high expectations or setting high standards and being a perfectionist is thin.

Models of perfectionism are diverse. Following the traditions of Freud, for example, researchers see perfectionism as a uniform and unitary concept so that a person is or is not a perfectionist. A second school of thought revolves around Hamachek's (1978) understanding of perfectionism as multidimensional and multifarious. The discrepancy here lies within the disciplinary views of perfectionism as clinical and a stable trait versus seeing it as fluid and changeable. By interpreting perfectionism as multifarious and multidimensional, Hamachek made it possible to hone in on particular elements, such as frequency of perfectionist thoughts or domain specificism (i.e. people may be perfectionists in one area of their lives and not in others: Matte and Lafontaine 2012). This allows for deeper engagement with specific elements and components of perfectionism, which in turn helps forge and understand definitions of the concept. Generally, perfectionism is understood as setting and pursuing unsuitably high and unreasonable standards along with a disproportionate focus on achieving these unfeasible standards and self-evaluation that is overcritical (Frost et al. 1990). This definition forms the basis of the current biopsychosocial understanding of perfectionism, which combines perfectionist strivings with perfectionist concerns and other-oriented perfectionism:

> PS [perfectionist strivings] refers to the propensity to set excessively high personal standards that are often unrealistic in nature and to demand nothing less than perfection from the self. [...] PC [perfectionist concerns] includes extraordinarily critical appraisals of one's own behaviour, chronic harsh self-scrutiny, excessive preoccupations with others' evaluations, expectations and criticism, and an inability to gain satisfaction even when one is successful in an endeavor. [...] OOP [other-oriented perfectionism] measures the extent to which individuals rigidly demand perfection from others in an exacting and entitled way and are being highly critical of others. (Sirois and Molnar 2016, 8–9)

Within academia, conversations relating to imposter syndrome, overwork and workaholism (Fassel 2000) emphasise an unhealthy openness towards having high expectations, being pedantic and potentially having low self-esteem because the high standards set are not met. In this context, perfectionism and perfectionist traits might be the prime determinant for being successful in academia, and they are generally seen as a positive characteristic. Existing research into perfectionism in connection with health and wellbeing highlights that such perfectionist traits play a significant role in psychological disorders (e.g. Flett and Hewitt 2002; Frost and DiBartolo 2002) and thus impact wellbeing (e.g. Bieling et al. 2004; Stoeber and Otto 2006).

The body in academia

There is little space for the body within neoliberal academia. While interest in embodiment within higher education is growing (see for example Leigh 2019a), the push towards managerialism and productivity means that working environments in universities have been described as being devoid of emotional and physical presence (Bloch 2012). The cerebral rather than the physical, emotional or sensory aspects of learning, teaching and research are often privileged. Emotion work is becoming more visible (see for example Brown and Collins 2018). However, traditional teaching spaces and practices are the norm in most higher education institutions due to constraints on resources and space. One of the consequences of this is the perceived impact on the wellbeing of those within universities – both staff and students are reporting more instances of mental health problems and disability (Gill 2010). This often results in an institutional emphasis on wellbeing. Wellbeing in academia is a somewhat slippery concept. It is often measured quantitatively, with the imperative to be 'well' or 'happy' (Ahmed 2010) seen as an outcome.

In a chapter considering the impact of embodied practices on academics' own sense of wellbeing, Jennifer Leigh considered that a personal sense of wellbeing is not the same as an institutional definition of wellbeing, which is more likely to equate to productivity:

> In the neoliberal drive to control employees, create productive labourers and ideal consumers, wellbeing has become another measurable commodity and tool of governance. Dominant discourses of wellbeing (institutional, governmental, health) articulate neoliberal individualism and responsibilisation for wellbeing. In other words they say that wellbeing is an individual responsibility, putting the emphasis on individual decisions,

behavior, and choices and do not take into account structural determinants like wealth or class.

Research has shown that embodied practices can act as a counterbalance to the dominant Cartesian mind/body disconnect, which views the body as a machine or tool in which to carry the intellect or mind around. Embodied practices could also raise the 'set-point' of wellbeing for an individual (Dodge et al. 2012), so that they have a better balance between their psychological, social and physical resources and the challenges that they face. As a consequence some embodied practices, or techniques derived from embodied practices (such as mindfulness) have been co-opted by employers and universities to form part of 'wellbeing' programmes designed to reduce the structural problems in the sector with overwork, stress and burnout to individual responsibilities around developing resilience and the ability to 'manage time' (Gill and Donaghue 2015). These co-opted techniques often 'focus on various forms of self-management' (ibid., 97) and do not incorporate the aforementioned philosophies of self-acceptance that characterise embodied practices. Instead, they appear to be utilised in relating wellbeing to the imperative to be a 'good' productive neoliberal worker. (Leigh 2019b, 225–6)

In this context, Leigh was using the term 'embodied practice' to describe any activity where the intention was to increase conscious self-awareness of the thoughts, emotions, visual images, sensations and proprioceptions of the mind and body (Leigh and Bailey 2013). Such practices include yoga, martial arts and dance, and could be more internal, such as meditation. In the study, Leigh found that the academics all equated their own practice with an increased sense of wellbeing, regardless of whether they had a chronic illness or disability or not. It is generally accepted that an active lifestyle helps to establish positive health habits and contributes to wellbeing, so this is not unexpected; however, many of the academics interviewed had chronic illnesses, injuries or disabilities. Embodied practices are inclusive in that when the intention is on increasing conscious self-awareness, there is no requirement for physicality. This is important, and differentiates them from physical activities. The distinction is not clear cut, of course, as some embodied practices are also physical, and some physical practices that might be embodied for some people are not for others. One example here could be running – which can be practised meditatively with an intention to increase self-awareness, or as an opportunity to disengage and listen to loud music. Wellbeing is not just the absence of illness, but an active and ongoing pursuit of something (Blei 2017). Some individuals living with disability or chronic illness may not experience the absence of illness or pain, but that does not mean that they have no wellbeing (Hedva 2016).

The politics of being ill in academia

The role of society and cultural environment within the context of and understanding of illness and illness narratives is well documented (e.g. Kleinman 1982; 1986; 1992; 1995; Good 1992; Ware 1992; 1998; 1999) in medical anthropological and sociological discourses, and increasingly within the medical realm (Hadler and Greenhalgh 2005). Within these conceptualisations, illness is seen as constructed at three different levels, as it is embedded with cultural meaning, but also defined at an experiential level and shaped by medical discourse (Conrad and Barker 2010). Illness symptoms that individuals experience are felt as sensations, but also experienced at an emotional, embodied level as learnt responses to conventions (Trigg 1970). In this sense, illness symptoms are physical manifestations of societal ills and cultural influences (Kleinman 1986) or a lived experience placed within a society or culture (Ware 1998). Through the expressive body's (Williams and Bendelow 1998) manifestation of pain, individuals' experiences are validated and become 'real'. The physical pain can be explained more easily to oneself and to others, and as such represents a protective mechanism that allows individuals to avoid dealing with the underlying emotional issues. In effect, the bodily expression of pain is in lieu of the individual's verbalisation of pain (Guignard 2013). How individuals report and respond to pain is shaped by cultural and societal conventions (Kotarba 1983). Indeed, the entire illness experience is a social experience that impacts and is impacted by individuals and their relationships to others (Kleinman 1995). Any illness experience therefore needs to be seen in the context of the social. In the personal narrative quoted above, we can see the journey taken as individual pain (and loneliness and frustration) is pitted against the reactions perceived by those around the writer. This illustrates the struggle and turmoil felt when living with chronic illness and pain, and how, within the context of academia – a cerebral (Leigh 2019b) and unforgiving (Bloch 2012) environment – internalised ideals of what is expected exacerbate the intensity of the emotions experienced. We can see the tension between perfectionism and the reality of stress, pressure and overwork played out in the body and the emotions.

As we have seen earlier in this chapter, academics have integrated the external values of the neoliberal academy to such an extent that they represent a new behaviour and new personal values. In a society that prides itself on the final outcomes and end products of labour rather than the process or labour itself, work has become necessary to find one's identity. As a consequence, individuals identify themselves and are identified by the work they do (Gini 1998), and when unable to complete this work to the perfectionist standards they set themselves, they are set up into a spiral of rumination that in turn causes both physical and psychological ill health (Joireman et al. 2002). In academia, work identification is so strongly linked to personal identity that individuals will continue to 'live up to values, even when they are not being monitored' (Tyler 1999, 19) because they are forfeiting their personal rewards for the benefit of the organisation and the collective (Van Knippenberg 2000), which in turn reduces the need for managerial interventions (Haslam et al. 2000). It is at this level that individuals will perform activities without external controls and without seeking to impress others (Kelman 1958). Academics' moral commitment to the academy leads to their internalisation of academia's values of performance and productivity.

But at what point does this become political? The autoethnographic extracts emphasise the tension between the public and private self – the sharp contrast between the internalised 'feeling shitty' and the external view of the ideal teacher, the personal journey and need for acceptance and healing and the anxiety of how one is perceived and the realities of facing bullying. These demonstrate how neoliberal values are continually reinforced through academics' fear of isolation or pronounced change in status (Scott 1971). In the extract 'Broken Academy, 2017', rather than modelling a work–life balance to these aspiring academics, we were instead embodying the overwork, stress and fatigue that appear to be endemic, along with the expectation that academic work does not stop when the office day ends (Acker and Armenti 2004). As teachers, we modelled these traits to our students, embodying them in our behaviours and our flesh even as our mouths repeat rote-learned speech regarding balance and wellbeing. We were giving in to the idea of performativity within academia (Pereira 2016). Whilst feeling the constraints and pressures of the measured university and overwork (Acker and Armenti 2004; Gill 2010; Pereira 2016), some also felt the impact of ill health and injury as disrupting forces. It seemed that there are both elements of justification and rationalisation as academics tried to make sense of the sometimes opposing demands of their practice and work while remaining open to the benefits and ideals of both. This view of being comparatively less productive or unproductive is ingrained in academics' psyche. On the one hand, the comparisons help individuals identify areas for improvement and further development in order to compete against others within the academic environment of precarious contracts and to succeed in their scholarly work of developing original contributions to knowledge. On the other hand, for people with high expectations and perfectionist tendencies such comparisons lead to feelings of inadequacy or falling short and, ultimately, feelings of failure (Lovin 2018).

The increase in status academics may potentially experience when they are productive and successfully contribute to the knowledge society is offset against the cost of experiencing personal failure instead of achieving higher status, thereby further reinforcing unreasonable standards (Scott 1971). Being ill compounds matters further. In order to manage bodily symptoms most effectively, chronically ill, disabled and neurodiverse academics embrace the flexibility part-time work offers. However, the flexibility that is so hailed results in academics being able to engage fully, which in turn precludes specific positions or roles and thus leads to feeling and being excluded from certain career prospects.

Disability as a personal and political act in academia

In a previous article (Brown and Leigh 2018) we wrote that ticking the 'I am disabled' box is a statement and commitment. We could also have asked whether declaring a disability is *always* a political act. By underwriting a disability, the academic has to be confident and comfortable with identifying as a disabled person. This might change from moment to moment, as can be seen in the extract above headed 'Being perfect, 2019'. Illness and disability trajectories are often experienced as journeys of acceptance, particularly if these illnesses or disabilities occur later in life or appear suddenly. We can begin to see how declaring a disability can become a political act and what it might take for us to come to that point. Whether we are acting as teachers, leaders or researchers, it is not uncommon for academics to draw attention to unfairness and inequity. It is part of our role within society to educate and to share knowledge, and to be aware of the situations of those around us, to amplify voices that cannot be heard. Just as it is necessary for women to be visible in STEM, and for people of colour to be visible at all levels in academia, it is necessary for those with disabilities to be visible. By declaring a disability, we can act as role models for our students, showing them that education and research are possibilities for them, that they have a place within higher education. We can participate in networks, councils and committees, speaking up about inclusion and accessibility issues so that these are less of an afterthought and instead are built into every aspect of university life. We can live the mantra 'nothing about us without us' by ensuring that academics with chronic illnesses and disabilities are present and visible and participate in all aspects of academic work and life.

And yet the structural inequalities built into academia are vast. Within a culture of overwork, it is hard for an able-bodied, well, neurotypical academic to thrive and feel supported, as goalposts for success are constantly moving (Shipley 2018). What then for a chronically ill, disabled or neurodiverse academic? Ableism, both external and internalised, means that admitting a chronic illness or disability may be equivalent to confessing to a failing, to laying oneself open to prejudice, ignorance and discrimination, as experienced in the first autoethnographic extract. If we out ourselves to act as a role model and shed light on an invisible condition, we are also becoming visible by raising our heads above the parapet and potentially becoming a target. While an individual journey towards acceptance of their condition can be a long one, the moral sense of unfairness can be felt before or as soon as one falls out of the category of 'abled' or 'well'. What do we do when we feel a moral imperative to stand up and act as a role model, and yet are not ready to do so on a personal level? There is a cost to choosing to make a declaration. If we declare ourselves, and our conditions, this can affect the way others see us. In the context of fluctuating invisible conditions (see chapter 8 in this volume), there may be a variation in how each aspect of disability or illness is experienced, which can in turn lead to internalised judgements – as seen above, under 'Coming to terms, 2015' – of whether one is 'disabled enough' to claim that status. It is possible to experience a feeling of having to justify yourself, to declare your own condition or disability, to explain your presence or interest in such activist work. We should not have to declare or explain ourselves, and yet the real or imagined whispers – 'why is she here? What's wrong with her? She doesn't look disabled…' – can colour our authority as activists. Being 'out' might often mean engaging in emotional labour (Gaeta 2019; Hochschild 1983) in that you are expected or asked to act in a capacity that supports or advises others, purely because of your own experience. Often this type of work is unpaid or under-paid. You are expected to be a point of disclosure for others. Without adequate training and support yourself, this work can be tiring and draining, and could have consequences for your own condition.

In addition, there are the perceived and potentially real judgements from the outside when you claim a disabled status. If your condition is not visible, is there an expectation that you explain, educate and share personal medical information in order to justify your claim? There is emotional labour (Hochschild 1983) associated with every aspect of this, even contemplating it.

Political engagement and activism are a way of life for many people. Social media such as Facebook have increased political engagement for some (Conroy et al. 2012), and higher education is seen as one of the most important ways to raise political engagement within the population (Hillygus 2005). Political engagement can take many forms, and activism is one of those. For many academics, particularly those working in the social sciences, engagement in research and teaching provides the basis for understanding lived experiences and exploring how to ameliorate situations for individuals or society as a whole. Academic work in this sense can be understood as a form of activism (Chomsky 1969), an action that goes beyond conventional politics, typically being more energetic, passionate, innovative and committed. Political activism may be seen as incompatible with the rationality of research and scholarly engagement (Martin 2009), and yet academics see their work as a stepping stone towards understanding and improving the social world they study. Kirstein Rummery describes her journey of navigating political engagement and activism from a feminist, disabilities studies perspective (see chapter 11 in this volume). However, the intersection of the political and the personal is not one-directional. Given an emotive topic such as ableism, where there is a moral imperative to do 'the right thing' as well as comply with legislation and legal duties to work and behave in a manner that does not discriminate against those who have 'protective characteristics', political activity and compulsions impinge on personal, lived experience.

It is one thing to be an activist, to take a stand and to 'get political' about ableism or any other topic. Many would agree that ensuring that there is an inclusive policy to protect staff or students, and working actively to improve conditions, is a 'good' thing. However, there are potentially personal consequences for us if we start to identify as disabled in our place of work, in our writing, teaching or research. Choosing to disclose, or to become an activist, can have implications for the individual, thrusting them into a position of visibility as contrast with the invisibility of many such conditions. Taking a stand, being open and activist in endeavours, means balancing being a 'killjoy' (Ahmed 2017) and challenging injustice with fitting in, going and getting along in order to have and make a career (Murray 2018). If we choose not to disclose, to act up as a role model, then instead we are 'passing' – a path not always open to women, people of colour or those with a physical, visible disability (Tatum 2014). Choosing to pass, if we can, is an individual, personal choice. As we have argued here, that choice may in turn be affected by our desire to be political.

References

Acker, Sandra and Armenti, Carmen. 'Sleepless in Academia', *Gender and Education* 16/1 (2004): 3–24. Online. https://doi.org/10.1080/0954025032000170309 (accessed 29 May 2020).

Ahmed, Sara. *The Promise of Happiness*. Durham, NC: Duke University Press, 2010.

Ahmed, Sara. *Living a Feminist Life*. Durham, NC: Duke University Press, 2017.

Archer, Louise. 'The New Neoliberal Subjects? Young/Er Academics' Constructions of Professional Identity', *Journal of Education Policy* 23/3 (2008a): 265–85. Online. https://doi.org/10.1080/02680930701754047 (accessed 29 May 2020).

Archer, Louise. 'Younger Academics' Constructions of "Authenticity", "Success" and Professional Identity', *Studies in Higher Education* 33/4 (2008b): 385–403. Online. https://doi.org/10.1080/03075070802211729 (accessed 29 May 2020).

Bieling, Peter J., Israeli, Anne L. and Antony, Martin M. 'Is Perfectionism Good, Bad, or Both? Examining Models of the Perfectionism Construct', *Personality and Individual Differences* 36/6 (2004): 1373–85. Online. https://doi.org/10.1016/S0191-8869(03)00235-6 (accessed 29 May 2020).

Billett, Stephen and Somerville, Margaret. 'Transformations at Work: Identity and Learning', *Studies in Continuing Education* 26/2 (2004): 309–26. Online. https://doi.org/10.1080/158037042000225272 (accessed 29 May 2020).

Blei, D. 'The False Promises of Wellness Culture', *Daily JSTOR*, 4 January 2017. Online. https://daily.jstor.org/the-false-promises-of-wellness-culture (accessed 22 June 2020).

Bloch, Charlotte. *Passion and Paranoia: Emotions and the Culture of Emotion in Academia*. Farnham: Ashgate, 2012.

Brown, Nicole and Collins, Jo. 'Using LEGO® to Understand Emotion Work in Doctoral Education', *International Journal of Management and Applied Research* 5/4 (2018): 193–209. Online. (accessed 29 May 2020).

Brown, Nicole and Leigh, Jennifer. 'Ableism in Academia: Where are the Disabled and Ill Academics?' *Disability and Society* 33/6 (2018): 985–9. Online. https://doi.org/10.1080/09687599.2018.1455627 (accessed 19 May 2020).

Chang, Heewon. *Autoethnography as Method*. Abingdon and New York: Routledge, 2016, originally 2008.

Chomsky, Noam. *American Power and the New Mandarins*. New York: Pantheon Books, 1969.

Conrad, Peter and Barker, Kristin K. 'The Social Construction of Illness: Key Insights and Policy Implications', *Journal of Health and Social Behavior* 51/1 (2010): S67–79. Online. https://doi.org/10.1177/0022146510383495 (accessed 19 May 2020).

Conroy, Meredith, Feezell, Jessica and Guerrero, Mario. 'Facebook and Political Engagement: A Study of Online Political Group Membership and Offline Political Engagement', *Computers in Human Behaviour* 28/5 (2012): 1535–4. Online. https://doi.org/10.1016/j.chb.2012.03.012 (accessed 29 May 2020).

Currie, Jan, Harris, Patricia and Thiele, Bev. 'Sacrifices in Greedy Universities: Are they Gendered?' *Gender and Education* 12/3 (2000): 269–91. Online. https://doi.org/10.1080/713668305 (accessed 29 May 2020).

Dodge, Rachel, Daly, Annette, Huyton, Jan and Sanders, Lalage. 'The Challenge of Defining Wellbeing', *International Journal of Wellbeing* 2/3 (2012): 222–35. Online. https://doi.org/10.5502/ijw.v2i3.4 (accessed 29 May 2020).

Ellis, Carolyn and Bochner, Arthur. 'Autoethnography, Personal Narrative, Reflexivity: Researcher as Subject'. In *Handbook of Qualitative Research*, 2nd ed., edited by N.K. Denzin and Y.S. Lincoln, 733–68. London: Sage, 2000.

Ellis, Carolyn and Flaherty, Michael. *Investigating Subjectivity: Research on Lived Experience*. London: Sage, 1992.

Fassel, Diane. *Working Ourselves to Death: The High Cost of Workaholism and the Rewards of Recovery*. Lincoln, NE: iUniverse.com, 2000.

Flett, Gordon L. and Hewitt, Paul L., eds. *Perfectionism: Theory, Research, and Treatment*. Washington, DC: American Psychological Association, 2002.

Frost, Randy O. and DiBartolo, Patricia M. 'Perfectionism, Anxiety, and Obsessive-Compulsive Disorder'. In *Perfectionism: Theory, Research, and Treatment*, edited by Gordon L. Flett and Paul L. Hewitt, 341–71. Washington, DC: American Psychological Association, 2002.

Frost, Randy O., Marten, Patricia A., Lahart, Cathleen and Rosenblate, Robin. 'The Dimensions of Perfectionism', *Cognitive Therapy and Research* 14/5 (1990): 449–68. Online. https://doi.org/10.1007/BF01172967 (accessed 29 May 2020).

Gaeta, Amy. 'Cripping Emotional Labor: A Field Guide'. Disability Visibility Project. 3 June 2019. Online. https://disabilityvisibilityproject.com/2019/06/03/cripping-emotional-labor-a-field-guide/?fbclid=IwAR1PUFSWPnJof5v1_Tyr3WTszLv3GRb6_JXBCKxt7CjHLGctPSK-DApyE5q0 (accessed 25/09/2019).

Gill, Rosalind. 'Breaking the Silence: The Hidden Injuries of Neo-Liberal Academia'. In *Secrecy and Silence in the Research Process: Feminist Reflections*, edited by Roisin Ryan-Flood and Rosalind Gill, 228–44. Abingdon and New York: Routledge, 2010.

Gill, Rosalind and Donaghue, Ngaire. 'Resilience, Apps and Reluctant Individualism: Technologies of Self in the Neoliberal Academy', *Women's Studies International Forum* 54/January-February (2015): 91–9. Online. https://doi.org/10.1016/j.wsif.2015.06.016 (accessed 29 May 2020).

Gini, Al. 'Work, Identity and Self: How We Are Formed By The Work We Do', *Journal of Business Ethics* 17/7 (1998): 707–14. Online. https://doi.org/10.1023/A:1017967009252 (accessed 29 May 2020).

Good, Byron J. 'A Body in Pain – The Making of a World of Chronic Pain.' In *Pain as Human Experience: An Anthropological Perspective*, edited by Mary-Jo DelVeccio Good, Paul Brodwin, Byron J. Good and Arthur Kleinman, 29–48. Berkeley: University of California Press, 1992.

Gore, J. 'Unsettling Academic/Feminist Identity'. In *Everyday Knowledge and Uncommon Truths: Women of the Academy*, edited by L. Christian-Smith and K. Kellor, 17–23. Boulder, CO: Westview Press, 1999.

Guignard, S. 'Fibromyalgia: A Daring New Look', *Clinical and Experimental Rheumatology* 31/79 (2013): 3–5.

Hadler, N. M. and Greenhalgh, S. 'Labeling Woefulness: The Social Construction of Fibromyalgia', *Spine* 30/1 (2005): 1–4.

Hamachek, Don E. 'Psychodynamics of Normal and Neurotic Perfectionism', *Psychology: A Journal of Human Behavior* 15/1 (1978): 27–33.

Haslam, S. Alexander, Powell, Clare and Turner, John. 'Social Identity, Self-Categorization, and Work Motivation: Rethinking the Contribution of the Group to Positive and Sustainable Organisational Outcomes', *Applied Psychology* 49/3 (2000): 319–39. Online. https://doi.org/10.1111/1464-0597.00018 (accessed 29 May 2020).

Hedva, Johanna. 'Sick Woman Theory'. 2016. Online. http://www.maskmagazine.com/not-again/struggle/sick-woman-theory (accessed 29 May 2020).

Henkel, Mary. 'Academic Identity and Autonomy Revisited'. In *Governing Knowledge: A Study of Continuity and Change in Higher Education. A Festschrift in Honour of Maurice Kogan*, edited by Ivar Bleiklie and Mary Henkel, Chapter 10. Dordrecht: Springer, 2005.

Hillygus, D. 'The MISSING LINK: Exploring the Relationship Between Higher Education and Political Engagement', *Political Behaviour* 27/1 (2005): 25–47. Online. https://doi.org/10.1007/s11109-005-3075-8 (accessed 29 May 2020).

Hochschild, Arlie. *The Managed Heart: The Commercialization of Human Feeling*. Berkeley: University of California Press, 1983.

Holt, Nicholas L. 'Representation, Legitimation, and Autoethnography: An Autoethnographic Writing Story', *International Journal of Qualitative Methods* 2/1 (2003): 18–28. Online. https://doi.org/10.1177/160940690300200102 (accessed 29 May 2020).

Joireman, Jeffrey, Parrott III, Les and Hammersla, Joy. 'Empathy and the Self-Absorption Paradox: Support for the Distinction between Self-Rumination and Self-Reflection', *Self and Identity* 1/1 (2002): 53–65. Online. https://doi.org/10.1080/152988602317232803 (accessed 29 May 2020).

Kelman, Herbert C. 'Compliance, Identification, and Internalization: Three Processes of Attitude Change'. *Journal of Conflict Resolution*, 2/1 (1958): 51–60. Online. https://doi.org/10.1177/002200275800200106 (accessed 29 May 2020).

Kirpal, Simone. 'Work Identities of Nurses. Between Caring and Efficiency Demands', *Career Development International* 9/3 (2004a): 274–304. Online. https://doi.org/10.1108/13620430410535850 (accessed 29 May 2020).

Kirpal, Simone. 'Researching Work Identities in a European Context', *Career Development Journal* 9/3 (2004b): 199–221. Online. https://doi.org/10.1108/13620430410535823 (accessed 29 May 2020).

Kleinman, Arthur. 'Neurasthenia and Depression: A Study of Somatization and Culture in China', *Culture, Medicine and Psychiatry* 6/2 (1982): 117–90. Online. https://doi.org/10.1007/BF00051427 (accessed 29 May 2020).

Kleinman, Arthur. *Social Origins of Distress and Disease: Neurasthenia, Depression, and Pain in Modern China*. New Haven, CT: Yale University Press, 1986.

Kleinman, Arthur. 'Pain and Resistance: The Delegitimation and Relegitimation of Local Worlds'. In *Pain as Human Experience: An Anthropological Perspective*, edited by Mary-Jo DelVeccio Good, Paul Brodwin, Byron J. Good and Arthur Kleinman, 169–97. Berkeley: University of California Press, 1992.

Kleinman, Arthur. *Writing at the Margin*. Berkeley: University of California Press, 1995.

Kolodny, Annette. *Failing the Future: A Dean Looks at Higher Education in the Twenty-First Century*. Durham, NC: Duke University Press, 1998.

Kotarba, Joseph A. *Chronic Pain: Its Social Dimensions (Sociological Observations)*. London: Sage, 1983.

Leigh, Jennifer. 'An Embodied Approach in a Cognitive Discipline'. In *Time and Space in the Neoliberal University*, edited by Maddie Breeze, Yvette Taylor and Cristina Costa. Cham, Switzerland: Palgrave Macmillan 2019a.

Leigh, Jennifer, ed. *Conversations on Embodiment: Teaching, Practice and Research*. Abingdon and New York: Routledge, 2019b.

Leigh, Jennifer and Bailey, Richard. 'Reflection, Reflective Practice and Embodied Reflective Practice', *Body, Movement and Dance in Psychotherapy* 8/3 (2013): 160–71. Online. https://doi.org/10.1080/17432979.2013.797498 (accessed 29 May 2020).

Lovin, C. Laura. 'Feelings of Change: Alternative Feminist Professional Trajectories'. In *Feeling Academic in the Neoliberal University: Feminist Flights, Fights and Failures*, edited by Yvette Taylor and Kinneret Lahad, 137–62. Palgrave Studies in Gender and Education. Cham, Switzerland: Palgrave Macmillan, 2018. Online. https://doi.org/10.1007/978-3-319-64224-6_7 (accessed 19 May 2020).

Martin, Randy. 'Academic Activism', *PMLA* 124/3 (2009): 838–46. Online. https://doi.org/10.1632/pmla.2009.124.3.838 (accessed 29 May 2020).

Matte, Melody and Lafontaine, Marie-France. 'Assessment of Romantic Perfectionism: Psychometric Properties of the Romantic Relationship Perfectionism Scale', *Measurement and Evaluation in Counseling and Development* 45/2 (2012): 113–32. Online. https://doi.org/10.1177/0748175611429303 (accessed 30 May 2020).

Murray, Órla M. 'Feel the Fear and Killjoy Anyway: Being a Challenging Feminist Presence in Precarious Academia'. In *Feeling Academic in the Neoliberal University: Feminist Flights, Fights and Failures*, edited by Yvette Taylor and Kinneret Lahad, 163–89. Palgrave Studies in Gender and Education. Cham, Switzerland: Palgrave Macmillan, 2018. Online. https://doi.org/10.1007/978-3-319-64224-6_8 (accessed 19 May 2020).

Parsons, Talcott. *Social Structure and Personality*. New York: The Free Press, 1970, originally 1964.

Pereira, Maria do Mar. 'Struggling Within and Beyond the Performative University: Articulating Activism and Work in "Academia Without Walls"', *Women's Studies International Forum* 54/January-February (2016): 100–10. Online. https://doi.org/10.1016/j.wsif.2015.06.008 (accessed 30 May 2020).

Salzman, Philip C. 'On Reflexivity', *American Anthropologist* 104/3 (2002): 805–11. Online. https://doi.org/10.1525/aa.2002.104.3.805 (accessed 30 May 2020).

Scott, John F. *Internalization of Norms: A Sociological Theory of Moral Commitment*. Englewood Cliffs, NJ: Prentice-Hall, 1971.

Shipley, Heather. 'Failure to Launch? Feminist Endeavors as a Partial Academic'. In *Feeling Academic in the Neoliberal University: Feminist Flights, Fights and Failures*, edited by Yvette Taylor and Kinneret Lahad, 17–32. Palgrave Studies in Gender and Education. Cham, Switzerland: Palgrave Macmillan, 2018. Online. https://doi.org/10.1007/978-3-319-64224-6_2 (accessed 19 May 2020).

Sirois, Fuschia M. and Molnar, Danielle S., eds. *Perfectionism, Health, and Well-being*. Cham, Switzerland: Springer International Publishing, 2016. Online. https://doi.org/10.1007/978-3-319-18582-8 (accessed 30 May 2020).

Smith, Tracey, Salo, Petri and Grootenboer, Peter. 'Staying Alive in Academia: Collective Praxis at Work', *Pedagogy, Culture and Society* 18/1 (2010): 55–66. Online. https://doi.org/10.1080/14681360903556830 (accessed 30 May 2020).

Sparkes, Andrew C. 'Autoethnography: Self-indulgence or Something More'. In *Ethnographically Speaking: Autoethnography, Literature, and Aesthetics*, edited by Arthur Bochner and Carolyn Ellis, 209–32. Walnut Creek, CA: AltaMira Press, 2002.

Stoeber, Joachim and Otto, Kathleen. 'Positive Conceptions of Perfectionism: Approaches, Evidence, Challenges', *Personality and Social Psychology Review*, 10/4 (2006): 295–319. Online. https://doi.org/10.1207/s15327957pspr1004_2 (accessed 30 May 2020).

Tatum, Erin. 'Ableism Online: Virtually Passing While Disabled'. 21 April 2014. Online. https://everydayfeminism.com/2014/04/ableism-online/ (accessed 27 September 2019).

Trede, Franziska, Macklin, Rob and Bridges, Donna. 'Professional Identity Development: A Review of the Higher Education Literature', *Studies in Higher Education* 37/3 (2012): 365–84. Online. https://doi.org/10.1080/03075079.2010.521237 (accessed 30 May 2020).

Trigg, Roger. *Pain and Emotion*. Oxford: Clarendon Press, 1970.

Tyler, T.R. 'Why People Co-operate with Organizations: An Identity-Based Perspective'. In *Research in Organizational Behaviour*, vol. 21, edited by B.M. Staw and R. Sutton, 201–46. Greenwich, CT: JAI Press, 1999.

Van Knippenberg, Daan. 'Work Motivation and Performance: A Social Identity Perspective', *Applied Psychology*, 49/3 (2000): 357–71. Online. https://doi.org/10.1111/1464-0597.00020 (accessed 30 May 2020).

Van Manen, Max. *Researching Lived Experience: Human Science for an Action Sensitive Pedagogy*. New York: State University of New York Press, 1990.

Walsh, Kate and Gordon, Judith R. 'Creating an Individual Work Identity', *Human Resource Management Review* 18/1 (2008): 46–61. Online. https://doi.org/10.1016/j.hrmr.2007.09.001 (accessed 30 May 2020).

Ware, Norma C. 'Suffering and the Social Construction of Illness: The Delegitimation of Illness Experience in Chronic Fatigue Syndrome', *Medical Anthropology Quarterly* 6/4 (1992): 347–61. Online. https://doi.org/10.1525/maq.1992.6.4.02a00030 (accessed 30 May 2020).

Ware, Norma C. 'Sociosomatics and Illness Course in Chronic Fatigue Syndrome', *Psychosomatic Medicine* 60/4 (1998): 394–401.

Ware, Norma C. 'Toward a Model of Social Course in Chronic Illness: The Example of Chronic Fatigue Syndrome', *Culture, Medicine and Psychiatry* 23/3 (1999): 303–31. Online. https://doi.org/10.1023/A:1005577823045 (accessed 30 May 2020).

Williams, Simon J. and Bendelow, Gillian. *The Lived Body: Sociological Themes, Embodied Issues*. London and New York: Routledge, 1998.

Witt, L.A., Patti, A.L. and Farmer, W.L. 'Organisational Politics and Work Identity as Predictors of Organisational Commitment', *Journal of Applied Psychology* 32/3 (2002): 486–99. Online. https://doi.org/10.1111/j.1559-1816.2002.tb00226.x (accessed 30 May 2020).

Wrzesniewski, Amy and Dutton, Jane E. 'Crafting a Job: Revisioning Employees' as Active Crafters of their Work', *Academy of Management Review* 26/2 (2001): 179–201. Online. https://doi.org/10.5465/amr.2001.4378011 (accessed 30 May 2020).

11
From the personal to the political: Ableism, activism and academia

Kirstein Rummery

Content warning: mentions rape and sexual assault

Both feminist and disability studies scholars have written about the need for the academy and activism to work closely together, to produce theoretical and empirical understandings and to challenge social barriers facing women and disabled people (Pétursdóttir 2017; Stone and Priestley 1996). As feminist and disability researchers we consciously aim to be activist scholars to a greater or lesser extent. This informs our research and teaching practice, our empirical approaches, our epistemologies, our choice of topics to research and teach and our methodological approaches. Many of us seek to engage with the wider non-academic world, to ensure our work has policy and practice relevance and impact.

However, it is a very different thing to step outside the relatively protected and rarefied world of the academy and attempt to engage with the world of political activism. There have been very few studies that incorporate political activism and look at the 'velvet triangle' (Holli 2008) between the academy, activism and political participation. This chapter is a reflection on the findings of a participant ethnographic study of the 2017 general election in the UK. I ran for Parliament as a disabled and feminist activist while maintaining my role as an academic. I encountered both resistance and support from all three sectors, and in this chapter, I explore the empirical challenges faced by academic activists working in more than one sector. I draw on both feminist and disability studies theory to explain the findings, and examine policies and practices that could help support more effective activist engagement and partnership working across the academic/activist divide. Drawing on the evidence from political science and social policy, I argue for significant changes in working practices to support women and disabled people in political engagement. Finally, I reflect on what this means for feminist and disability activism within the academy.

Reflections on my position

Intellectually, my feminism came from my experience as an undergraduate. I was raped by an ex-boyfriend, and I was studying law at the time. I was very aware of the theoretical and legal barriers facing women who experience rape, and I very quickly became aware of the real-life practical issues as well. When I made a complaint to my university, I was told that the perpetrator had 'suffered enough' by being questioned and there was no point taking more formal action against him. When I tried to report it to the police, I was told in no uncertain terms that because I had been drinking at the time of the attack, he was my ex and I had willingly opened the door of my dorm to him, there was absolutely no case to be made. The fact that it was violent and non-consensual, even that it was admitted as such by the perpetrator, was irrelevant. The only theoretical approach to the world that made sense and did not blame me was feminism. So, like many women, I experienced the reality of women's oppression before I found a language and theoretical base to explain it. The personal became political: I moved from being an activist to being an academic.

From a disability perspective, I came to it from the other direction. I carried out postgraduate research into feminism and disability because, drawn to writers such as Oliver, Barnes and Morris, I found interesting and under-explored connections between the structural oppression facing women and that facing disabled people. In particular, I was interested in the relative lack of attention paid to disability issues within feminism, and to feminist issues within disability studies – an issue which, thanks to writers such as Morris, is no longer the case. Then I was in a car accident and broke my pelvis, had an autistic son, developed psoriatic arthritis and then fibromyalgia, and also complex post-traumatic stress disorder. Within the space of a few short years my interest in disability studies went from being theoretical to real lived experience. The political became personal: I moved from being an academic to being an activist.

In both roles I have always had a foot in both camps, but have been at heart driven by my academic role. I have used my research findings to support third-sector stakeholders and to inform policy and practice, as well as campaigning as an individual citizen on issues, but still drawing on my academic knowledge. This project took me to a very different area of activism: running for elected office as a political activist, placing the corporeal reality of myself as a disabled feminist into the material reality of political campaigning. It enabled me to reflect on the key similarities and differences between ableism and activism within and outwith the academy.

Background

Activism, politics and the academy

For many academics, the act of being an academic is in itself political. Chomsky argued that the academy has a political responsibility as a result of its privileged status:

> For a privileged minority, Western democracy provides the leisure, the facilities, and the training to seek the truth behind the veil of misrepresentation, ideology and class interest through which the events of current history are presented to us. (Chomsky 1969, 324)

However, for many others, it is not enough to exercise that privilege within the relative safety of academia. While activists can be found within many disciplines, the separation of the two roles is often actively encouraged (Flood et al. 2013). In disciplines where rationality, objectivity and the scientific method are particularly valued, the very nature of political or activist engagement appears to be antithetical to academic enquiry (Martin 2009). However, most social science disciplines have engaged with the idea that positionality has its merits, and encourage researchers to engage emotionally and politically with the matter of their research (Maxey 1999).

Both feminism and disability rights scholarship go further than acceptance of political engagement. They actively encourage academics to embrace both being activists and engaging in intellectual enquiry, and for each role to inform the other. Indeed, an ongoing critique of women's studies is that it is too overtly political (Sommers 1994). Eschle and Maiguashca point out that creating space for feminism within the academy is in itself a political act, and that most feminists within the academy do more:

> Feminists have established their own sites of knowledge production that aim to bridge the gap between universities and the feminist movement, ranging from consciousness-raising groups to autonomous women's colleges, and from women's libraries to women's studies and latterly gender studies programmes in universities. (Eschle and Maiguashca 2006, 120)

Disability studies goes further, and claims that scholars who do not engage in activism to support disabled people or actively fight oppression are simply adding to their oppression. Research should actively seek to improve material circumstances (Oliver 1992). Stone and Priestley go so far as to call non-disabled researchers 'parasites' unless they embrace an emancipatory and non-objective research paradigm, calling academics to understand that:

> the political standpoint of the researcher is tied to political action in challenging oppression and facilitating the self-empowerment of disabled people. The researcher engages in processes of emancipation, rather than merely monitoring them from sympathetic sidelines. (Stone and Priestley 1996, 6)

Therefore, as an academic who embraces both feminism and disability studies as my key theoretical perspectives, the onus is on me to incorporate activism into my research: to not just observe and write about the social world in which women and disabled people are oppressed, but to actively engage in tackling that oppression. In order to do that in the field of women's and disabled people's political participation, it was not enough for me to understand from a theoretical perspective how ableism and sexism shaped the experience of academic activists: I had to immerse myself ethnographically in that world as both a means of enquiry and a political act.

Barriers to political participation for women and disabled people

Although in the UK there are no formal barriers to women's political participation, there are clearly structural barriers that come into play. As of June 2020, 220 (out of 650) Members of Parliament are women in the House of Commons, the elected chamber in the UK. When choosing candidates to run for election, the incumbent always has an advantage, having already proved they can win an election: on current proportions of UK parliamentarians, that means that 66 per cent of the incumbents standing for re-election are likely to be men. Moreover, unless political parties take proactive measures to increase female party membership generally, and to put female candidates up for election in winnable seats, this proportion will remain static, as structural reasons favour male candidates. Candidates are often chosen from elite networks within the party, with a history and track record of working or volunteering for the party (Close and Kelbel 2019). These elite networks tend to favour privately educated men and those who attended elite higher education institutions, which mitigates against non-middle-class women, black and ethnic minority (BAME) women and disabled women. Moreover, as Shames (2015) and others point out, informal mentoring often plays a huge role in political success, but working women politicians often do not have resources spare to undertake that mentoring for the potential next generation of political women.

Socio-cultural barriers, such as seeing leadership as a 'male' quality, mean that female candidates face implicit selection bias (Alexander 2012). Moreover, political campaigning and working as an elected representative are jobs that tend to lead to high numbers of working hours, being away from home for lengthy periods, late nights and other working conditions that are not conducive to balancing family and work commitments. This impacts far more directly on mothers than on fathers, both practically and culturally, and for low-income women who cannot afford childcare or mothers of disabled children for whom there may not be appropriate childcare available, this makes campaigning inaccessible. These barriers also apply to women with caring responsibilities involving disabled adults, although these receive less attention than childcare.

Barriers to political participation for disabled people

As of June 2020 there are only five MPs in the House of Commons who self-identify as disabled, a rate of 0.8 per cent compared to around 17 per cent of the general population, and 50 per cent of the over-65s. The same elite networks who provide the male political class also provide an able-bodied political class: disabled people are excluded from higher education, particularly from elite institutions. Able-bodied people are 40 per cent more likely than disabled people to go to university. Disabled activism and the disability rights movement have grown exponentially since challenges to segregated residential care and the rise of the social model of disability (Campbell and Oliver 1996), and this has translated into what Young calls the 'plural activities of civic associations' (Young 2002, 153). Disabled people volunteer, self-organise and are politically engaged around specific issues such as benefits, social care, housing, transport and other areas that affect their lives. However, this civic engagement has not translated into participation in mainstream politics in the same way that feminist activism has.

There are structural reasons for this relative lack of participation. As well as exclusion from elite institutions and networks, disabled people are far less likely than able-bodied people to be working in elite professions with clear links to party political engagement such as journalism, law and higher education. European research has found a clear link between income and political participation, with higher-income groups being far more likely to engage than lower-income groups (Priestley et al. 2016). Disabled people are far more likely to be living in poverty and experiencing social exclusion in terms of employment, education, relative income and material deprivation than able-bodied people: they are thus less likely to have access to, or the resources to support, political participation. As Postle and Beresford (2007) point out, disabled people did not magically acquire the resources to self-organise: for 'user' movements to be able to engage effectively with policymakers and service providers took a lot of capacity building and a significant change in culture on the part of those in power. In addition, services and support for disabled people are largely focused on either the private sphere (e.g. social care support for personal care needs) or employment. There are very few services that are specifically to support disabled people to participate in civic and political activities.

In many ways disabled people face similar cultural barriers to women: they are not seen as natural leaders and so face implicit selection bias when seeking to run for office. Guldvik et al. point out that:

> At an individual level, political participation depends in part on the candidate's resources and her/his motivation. Disabled people have to varying degrees resources such as education, income, organizational affiliation, and social capital. In addition, the motivation to participate politically also varies amongst disabled people. The motivation is related to the degree representatives gain recognition and respect in their role as elected representatives. (Guldvik et al. 2013, 80)

Political campaigning requires a great deal of physical stamina, with late nights and working away from home being the norm during election periods. This can make it inaccessible to disabled people, whose impairment(s) may contribute to the lack of social and structural support in raising barriers to participation. Guldvik et al. (2013) found that issues such as the physical and cultural environment in government did not support disabled elected representatives being able to act independently and with influence: as a result they were seen as less effective politically than able-bodied colleagues and less likely to be reselected as political candidates. These socio-cultural barriers are of course in place before disabled people even reach the stage of serving as political representatives, and can act as comprehensive barriers to political participation.

Intersectionality and activism

In trying to make sense of my own experiences as a disabled woman, it is clear that we need to pay attention to the intersectionality of disability and gender. While the term 'intersectionality' was coined by Crenshaw (1989) to refer to the dual discrimination faced by BAME women, an understanding of the 'double burden' of being a disabled woman has underpinned scholarship in feminist and disability studies (Lloyd 2001; Morris 1992). Disabled women face far more than just the 'double burden' of disability and femaleness when becoming activists, and when seeking to make the transition from activism to political participation.

Firstly, the structural oppression of lack of resources, and lack of access to elite spaces, acts as a compound barrier for disabled women. Disabled women are at risk of poverty because of lack of access to material resources, social care and support to participate in public life generally. Moreover, in engaging in civic activism in disability rights – which recognises the structural oppression faced by those with impairments, but not necessarily faced by women – disabled women can encounter sexism or gender blindness within their own activist organisations. Issues include a lack of recognition of the additional risks disabled women face in engaging in public life. Disabled women are at significant risk of sexualised violence and domestic abuse, lack of understanding and support for complex caring and parenting responsibilities, and a lack of awareness of feminist political issues. See, for example, disabled organisations' campaigns to support 'sex work' and prostitution as a way of enabling disabled men to access women's bodies with little thought of the harm and violence to women inherent in that approach. Disabled women who are active feminists also face ableism within the feminist movement: for example, by focusing on childcare as a structural oppression, feminist organisations often leave out access to social care and support; by focusing on the gendered nature of informal caring, feminist organisations often ignore disabled women's disempowering experiences of being reliant on informal care, and of their own experiences of giving care.

Secondly, disabled women also face more than the 'double burden' of socio-cultural expectations arising from being disabled and female. They are seen as passive, as recipients rather than givers of care, as both sexualised and not sexualised enough for not conforming to ableist and sexist standards of appearance and bodily autonomy. They are definitely not seen as active, charismatic leaders in the male able-bodied model.

Autoethnography

Autoethnography is an approach to research and writing that seeks to describe and systematically analyse personal experience in order to understand cultural experience. This approach challenges canonical ways of doing research and representing others and treats research as a political, socially just and socially conscious act. A researcher uses tenets of autobiography and ethnography to do and write autoethnography. Thus, as a method, autoethnography is both process and product (Ellis et al. 2010).

In seeking to establish the legitimacy of feminist approaches to social science research, Gilligan (1982) found that women's experiences were often ignored or downplayed as they did not easily fit deductive, rational approaches to empirical enquiry. As a result, different approaches to feminist social enquiry have been developed which place an onus on the researcher not just to centre the experiences of women, but also to reflectively position the researcher within the research process. At the same time there are strong arguments for those engaging in feminist research to seek not just to observe, record and explain the experiences of women in academic terms, but to treat the research process itself as a political act. As Ackerly and True remind us:

> many feminist researchers share a 'sense of accountability to the women's movement' conceived as a changing and contested discourse […] They seek to do research that is explicitly of value to women and that could result in actions that are beneficial to women. (Ackerly and True 2010, 465)

Similar challenges are articulated within disability studies. As part of a growing political consciousness, disabled people have rejected being the 'objects' of rational empiricism, seeing it as part of the social oppression they face (Oliver 1992). The history of the relationship between scientific research and the oppression of disabled people is a long and troubled one, including segregation, eugenics and systematic human rights abuses (Stone and Priestley 1996). Moreover, social science enquiry, even that which steps away from the rationalist paradigm, has tended to place researchers in a powerful position vis-à-vis the researched, placing disabled people firmly in the latter category. Non-disabled researchers who are not part of an anti-oppressive political movement are seen as part of the problem, not the solution to disabled people's oppression.

> Disabled people have come to see research as a violation of their experience, as irrelevant to their needs and as failing to improve their material circumstances and quality of life. (Oliver 1992, 105)

Moreover, both feminist and disability studies point out the dangers of empirical detachment from the process of research. They argue that researchers must reflexively locate themselves in the research process, reflecting on their influence and positionality (Burman 2006), and that research is an embodied experience (Longhurst 2011). Perhaps because disability studies has, until fairly recently, sought to shift attention away from the body towards the social construction of disability, there is less of a history of autoethnography as an embodied approach to research. However, it has been used to explore the disabled experience by disabled researchers in creative ways (Baurhoo 2017). There is, arguably, no more thorough way to be reflexive than to turn the research focus on yourself, to subject your own life and actions to scrutiny. Before presenting findings, I will briefly outline how I employed autoethnography.

I had been selected to run as a candidate for election to the UK Parliament by the Women's Equality Party. In order to gain the 'insider's perspective' of the issues facing women and disabled people as they take part in political activity, particularly when running for election, I kept a fieldwork diary over the course of my campaign, writing up my fieldnotes at the end of each day whilst the observations were fresh in my mind. I also gathered data through photographs, social media engagement, newspaper articles, communications such as emails and WhatsApp discussions and other related data. After the campaign was over, I undertook inductive thematic analysis on my data, testing the reliability and validity of emerging themes with some of my campaign team. It was not possible to obtain informed consent from everyone I encountered: indeed, this would have run contrary to the approach to ethnography endorsed by Bulmer (1982), which stresses that to gain insight into social worlds it is necessary to be a covert rather than overt observer.

It is beyond doubt that those I was observing would have changed their behaviour had they known they were taking part in a research project rather than purely an election campaign. In situations where covert observation is used, there is a particular onus on the researcher to protect the identities of those involved, so all have been given aliases, identifying characteristics have been changed and my fieldwork notes have a coded date stamp. For the purposes of this chapter, I have focused on the findings related to the resistance and support I encountered from the three corners of the 'velvet triangle' of the academy, activists and other candidates/parties and the public.

Resistance and support from the academy

I encountered both individual and structural resistance from the academy. I declared my intention to run as a candidate, and when I explained to senior management that I was intending to write it up as an ethnographic study they were supportive. However, this soon changed. I gave an interview to a local newspaper discussing why I was running, and I made the point that 25 years after my experience of sexual assault on campus, women in universities were still experiencing the same thing. The local paper ran this particularly lurid heading: 'My election bid is driven by campus sex attack'. I was accused of bringing the institution into disrepute, which is gross misconduct, despite it being very clear that I was not responsible for the phrasing or the way the article was written. This was, understandably, very distressing. Although it was not followed up as a formal complaint, it was referred to in a later unconnected formal disciplinary action against me as evidence of a 'pattern of behaviour' that justified a formal sanction. However, the following extract from my fieldwork notes shows that this newspaper article was not necessarily harmful to my political campaign:

> At the end of the hustings [Mr C, candidate for party C] approached me and said 'Well done on that headline in the [local paper]. We'd love to get free publicity like that.' (Datestamp 14.6)

This was 'free publicity' I was at best ambivalent about. On the one hand, it was a deliberately sexualised manipulation of my story, one that got me into trouble at work. On the other hand, it was also a way of reaching an audience that I would not have been able to with any other kind of story. Notably, most of the interview was actually about my care for my disabled son, which did not feature in the article at all.

Resistance and support from activists

This is the finding that was the most surprising to me. I received very little support from women's groups, despite having previously been active in many. One group, on whose board I had served for many years, refused to invite me to an equalities hustings they were organising. Another, whom a fellow political party member was working for, went so far as to make a formal complaint about me:

> Emotional lecture on domestic abuse today, coincided with the Manchester bombing. As 'host' I gave an introductory speech saying I wasn't canvassing but we should remember that an attack on young women and girls attending a pop concert was a form of violence against women and girls, just like domestic abuse. Afterwards a woman from [Scottish Women Against Rape] approached me and said 'That *was* canvassing and it was out of order.' I apologised. Got home to email from WEP Head Office that official complaint had been made by the organisation. Told Head Office what I had actually said, backed up by fellow WEP members at the lecture. Told 'no, it doesn't sound like canvassing to me either but feelings are running high so please apologise in writing'. (Datestamp 11.5)

This was in sharp contrast to the support I received from the disability sector. I asked a fellow activist from a local carers' organisation to come and introduce me at my launch campaign:

> Discussed with [Ms P] from [Caring Stirling] what she would say at my launch. She said she and the organisation were thrilled I was running for office and highlighting social care as an issue of equality for women, as no-one else presented it like that. She also said that due to restrictions she could not appear in public to endorse me as her organisation would break the terms of their funding. We agreed that she would do a 'vox pop' interview with me off camera, and invite her workers to attend my launch as a compromise. Her support meant a lot. (Datestamp 1.1)

I had hoped to apply to the 'Access to Elected Office' fund for help with equipment and personal assistance during my campaign, but it transpired that this fund was not available to candidates running for general elections, only Scottish Parliament elections. However, the disability organisation who ran that fund were very helpful and supportive, offering to put me in touch with former candidates from different political parties who had previously been successful, and to try to find equipment for me. There were no negative reactions from disability or carers' organisations, only unmitigated support. This was in sharp contrast to the negative reactions and lack of support from women's organisations.

Resistance and support from the public and political sector

Being honest about my personal experiences of sexual violence enabled me to connect to other survivors:

> After hustings, several women approach me in tears and say they are so pleased I spoke out about rape because they had experienced it too and no other party seemed to be taking it seriously. As I turned to shake hands with my opponent [Ms W, Candidate for party D], she surprisingly gave me a hug and said 'Me too. Thank you.' (Datestamp 12.5)

I found repeatedly that the personal, emotional connection with potential voters that came after I shared my experiences of being a rape survivor, carer, disabled person or someone with mental health issues was a very powerful one for both me and them. One audience member emailed me after listening to me on local radio:

> Email from [Mrs T] has really touched me. 'I am so glad you are speaking up about your experiences. If people in public do this more, it can end the stigma of mental health. I think this is so important.' (Datestamp 9.5)

I also received support from the public for being a 'visibly' disabled candidate. One participant in a hustings for learning-disabled people made this point:

> 'I like that you are disabled. More disabled people should be MPs. MPs don't understand how hard we have to fight for jobs, for transport, just to be heard. If they did they would help us more.' (Datestamp 10.1)

This was in contrast to the sexist attacks I received both online and in person:

> At hustings for learning-disabled people, and my opposition clearly doesn't really understand the question about benefits and mobility cars. When I speak I emphasise that austerity is hitting disabled people very hard, and this removes their independence and makes it harder for them to work, putting pressure on carers. [Mr S, Candidate for Party A] interrupts me and says loudly 'It's time for you to shut up now, the women have spoken long enough.' I was pretty shocked at this, as were the audience. His fellow male candidate [Mr C, Candidate for Party C] laughed and appealed to the (mainly male) audience: 'Women, eh?' (Datestamp 10.1)

I did encounter ableism from the general public. Several people asked me during hustings and canvassing if I would 'be able to manage' the work of an MP with crutches. I gave an interview to a national newspaper, in which I described why, as a professor and as a political candidate, I needed a PA to keep me organised because of the 'brain fog' that goes along with fibromyalgia and PTSD, which received the following online comment:

> Em. I don't wish to be unkind but do voters want their Bills scrutinised by someone with **intellectual deficits this severe?!** Absolutely, Parliament should be made accessible, but MPs are public servants and have to have the capacity to serve the public properly. (http://www.thenational.scot/politics/15295758.Here_s_why_you_don_t_see_more_disabled_MPs__explains_candidate/#comments-anchor, accessed 16 June 2020)

I am fairly sure as a professor I had already demonstrated in that article that I did not have 'intellectual deficits'.

This questioning of my abilities was also a tactic used by my political opponents. During one hustings, a question was raised about the funding and delivery of social care, to which I gave quite a detailed answer. Mr S, Candidate for party A, then got up and shouted: 'No-one knows what to do about social care, not even the so-called professor.' I am still not sure if this was ableism or sexism, but it was certainly an attempt to demean my status and expertise. Later in that same hustings a member of the audience asked us to speak up, as she was having difficulty hearing us:

> Mr C [candidate for party C] said we should all stand up so we could be seen and heard better. I, obviously, can't stand up. All three male candidates stood, and Ms W [candidate for party D] says, 'No, that's not fair to Kirstein,' and remains seated. I am now very conscious that the two female candidates look weaker than the men because they are sitting down. (Datestamp 12.1)

I encountered numerous incidences of this, as well as inaccessible venues with steps, where I was made to feel I was being difficult, or sat somewhere away from other candidates. Some audience members noted this and commented to me afterwards that it was done deliberately and was unfair. It is interesting that the only other female candidate often showed solidarity with me – by moving, commenting or helping – and the male candidates never did.

Discussion

Intersectionality, ableism and sexism

There is no doubt in my mind, based on the analysis of my findings, that every stage of the political process demonstrates clear evidence of both ableism and sexism. From the moment someone decides to make the transition from grassroots and/or academic activist to engaging in political action as a member of a political party campaigning for election, there are substantial physical, social and attitudinal barriers to be overcome, and these are not insubstantial.

The ableism I faced in political life was much more overt than I had faced in academia and activism. This was not from my own political party, who were very willing to support me and use their limited resources to try to overcome some of the barriers I faced as a disabled candidate. However, the women's movement, the other political parties and the public demonstrated clearly that the able-bodied political candidate was the norm, and everyone else was somehow diminished, flawed and not as desirable (Campbell and Oliver 1996). To a certain extent, working in the academy, with an institutional framework intended to protect me against disability discrimination, had left me ill prepared for the level of overt ableism I faced outside that relatively protected environment. I had encountered what Campbell and Oliver (1996) call 'microaggressions'. This included expectations of performance that did not account for my impairment, such as a failure to take my impairment into account during formal processes. However, I had also encountered a lot of goodwill to make 'reasonable adjustments' for my impairment – for example, excusing me from certain tasks that were not core to my job, supporting me to work flexibly and funding extra support for travel. I had also encountered a willingness to make 'reasonable adjustments' in my activist life: for example, moving meetings to more accessible venues, enabling PA support and taking into account the inaccessibility of public transport for me. However, that willingness was markedly absent within the sphere of political campaigning. I was not able to access funding for equipment that would have enabled me to carry out the canvassing work that is crucial to a political campaign. Organisers of hustings, debates, events and media coverage were not willing to accommodate my needs, often citing the 'fairness' aspect of possibly giving me an unfair advantage. Yet from my perspective at least it was levelling the playing field and removing the unfair advantage that able-bodied candidates had. There was also a difference between attitudes towards my physical impairment, where people were sometimes more willing to make adjustments and less willing to tolerate overt ableism from others, and the cognitive/mental health elements of my impairment, where it was more acceptable to call into account my capacity and refuse to make adjustments for me. The stigma surrounding mental health issues compared to physical impairments was particularly noticeable.

I was more prepared for the overt sexism I encountered on the campaign trail. This, again, was not from my own party, but it was very clear from other political parties and the public. I encountered abuse on social media, comments and questions about my appearance, questions about my children (which were never directed at male candidates), mild threats, efforts to silence me by complaining to my employer and several other tactics well known to feminists with a public presence in political life. My own 'red lines' on this involved my family: any attempt to involve them, identify them, stalk them or use them triggered an instant involvement of whatever formal protection I could invoke. For everything else I developed a thick skin and tried to ignore it. The level of abuse was relatively mild – in fact, I had encountered far more worrying abuse from men's rights activists in the course of my academic job than I did during political campaigning.

Here I am going to reflect on two elements of intersectionality that acted in my favour and offered me some protection: class and race. As a well-educated woman and despite the taunts, I am not a 'so-called' professor. I have been a professor on merit – i.e. based on my international reputation for the quality and significance of my research – for over ten years, so I was well placed in the campaign. My knowledge was respected: often more so than that of my fellow candidates from other political parties, even from supporters of those parties. I could more than hold my own in debates, hustings and media appearances because I had a wealth of knowledge and experience of engaging publicly with students, stakeholders, practitioners and policymakers. My education and my middle-class background and, in the context of a Scottish election, sounding like a posh Englishwoman gave me a status and confidence that to some extent mitigated the ableism and sexism I encountered.

It was also clear when compared to my sister candidates in the Women's Equality Party and other parties that I enjoyed a great deal of protection due to my race. As a white woman I did not encounter the overt racism (sometimes very violent) directed at black women campaigning politically during the general election. I was not perceived to have Jewish heritage, so I did not encounter any overt anti-Semitism either (again, not a protection always offered to Jewish women campaigning politically).

Structural and individual challenges

I certainly encountered both structural and individual challenges that tie in with what the literature tells us about the sexism and ableism faced by political candidates. When I discovered I would not be eligible for funding under the 'Access to Elected Office' scheme, I asked my political party for funding for a PA. They needed to check with the Electoral Commission whether or not this counted as 'allowable expenses' under campaigning laws. It transpired that the Women's Equality Party were the first to ask if childcare was an allowable expense, and the first to ask if personal assistance for a disabled candidate was an allowable expense. This indicates either that other political parties in the UK are supporting candidates with childcare and personal support needs and not declaring the expenditure, which is unlikely given the severe penalties for breaking campaigning laws, or they are not supporting candidates directly in this way.

There is no equivalent to the 'Access to Elected Office' fund for people with parenting and caring commitments, who are overwhelmingly women. Moreover, it became clear to me that the incumbent does not have an advantage just in terms of being selected by their party, but also during campaigning. For them, running for office is part of their day job, for which they are still drawing a salary: they can engage in it full-time with all the support that comes with a job. This also applies to other candidates with political roles, for example, elected councillors. For the other candidates, campaigning needs to be fitted in alongside other commitments: in my case working full-time, being a parent and carer, managing my own impairments and having the resources to deal with the micro- and macroaggressions of ableism and sexism in the workplace and in activist life.

Many of the barriers to engagement with political activism faced by disabled women begin way before the 'end' of engaging directly with political campaigning. There is no structural support for those who are not candidates for elected office, for example canvassers, campaigners, workers and volunteers. Activism is resource heavy and it favours those who have the structural and individual supports in place: these are overwhelmingly middle-class, well-connected, able-bodied women. I acquired my impairments relatively late in life (in my late twenties), by which time I had already had several years of a privileged middle-class upbringing, private schooling and a degree from an elite Russell Group university. I had begun to establish my academic career and reputation, and I could draw on these advantages as my impairments and the resulting social, environmental and attitudinal barriers that I faced grew worse. Indeed, when I developed serious mobility problems from psoriatic arthritis and fibromyalgia, and mental health issues from PTSD, I was already a professor with a reputation for activism and engagement with the women's and disability sector, and had been for five years.

On activism within the academy

Here I will reflect on what this journey means for academic activism within the academy, rather than crossing the velvet triangle to political activism. Firstly, most of us within the academy do not see our own privilege and our protected status. While we do encounter microaggressions connected with social divisions, particularly along the lines of gender, race and disability, they are nowhere near the level of the macroaggressions that we encounter in political life. While being passed over for promotion or feeling bullied and harassed may make our jobs more difficult than those of our more privileged colleagues, it is rare for an academic to receive death and rape threats from their colleagues or managers. When such macroaggressions happen, we are relatively protected by our institutions: there are policies and procedures, as well as legal safeguards, available to help us. That is not to say that these macroaggressions are not real and painful, nor that they do not have a material impact on our lives – not least in terms of our income, mental health, physical safety and wellbeing. But – even though the onus is on us to invoke those protections – there are some protections and mitigations in place within the academy.

This is simply not the case for women and disabled political activists. Although they have some legal protections, they are often isolated and have to develop a far higher level of personal resilience to cope with the abuse and violence that they attract simply by being a woman (and a disabled person) in a public space. I would argue that this places a responsibility on academic activists to be brave and resilient and to take advantage of this protection, not just on behalf of themselves, but also for their sister activists without such protections. We academics should be calling out the public abuse of female politicians, and ableism in politics, every time we encounter it. We should also be turning our theoretical and empirical resources to documenting and explaining this abuse far more than we do. This has less of an impact on us than calling out the abuse and ableism we experience ourselves: collective action and sisterhood against ableism and sexism is both powerful and necessary for our survival.

Secondly, the skills and protections that we use as academics are not the same as those that political activists need, and being a good academic activist does not necessarily make you a good political activist. While politicians need to be able to understand complex data, and communicate and persuade effectively, they also have to demonstrate charismatic leadership and the ability to network within their own political party, to gain access to elite spaces where a much wider range of skills other than intellectual ability are valued. Some of us have those skills and abilities, but others simply do not. We are better allies to political activists if we use our protected elite spaces wisely. This project demonstrated to me that I am more effective in supporting social change as a good activist academic than as a poor politician. Moreover, the skills that make someone a good politician probably mitigate against them being a good academic: you cannot, by definition, be impartial or cautious about your theoretical and empirical claims as a politician, and as a responsible academic, you probably should be.

Conclusions

On reflection, the ableism and sexism faced by disabled women as they enter political campaigning reflects the ableism and sexism they encounter in everyday life. Substantial barriers exist for us in accessing elite spaces from which political candidates are drawn; and those barriers inhibit access to political parties and political spaces generally. Activism within the academy and within non-party political organisations is not risk-free or resource-neutral for those of us who engage in it: but it does not come with the much higher risks and resource demands of political activism.

The answer to the question 'why are there not more disabled women in politics?' is, then, because there are not more disabled women in public life generally, and because political organisations do not make enough effort to tackle structural ableism and sexism. Those of us with the resources can overcome the barriers to political engagement. Those of us with the protection of class, education and race have more capacity to overcome the ableism and sexism we face in public life. One key to improving political life and disabled women's chances and experiences of engaging with it would be to ensure that those resources are much more widely available. Access to adequate unconditional income, to proper care and support services, to high-quality affordable or free childcare, and to aids and equipment without having to go through endless obstacles and fighting would transform disabled women's lives. It would enable them to participate fully in political life and I would argue that politics would be vastly improved.

Acknowledgement

Thank you to Julia Lawrence for the provision of expert disability-related assistance.

References

Ackerly, Brooke and True, Jacqui. *Doing Feminist Research in Political and Social Science*. Basingstoke: Palgrave Macmillan, 2010.

Alexander, Amy C. 'Change in Women's Descriptive Representation and the Belief in Women's Ability to Govern: A Virtuous Cycle', *Politics and Gender* 8/4 (2012): 437–64. Online. https://doi.org/10.1017/S1743923X12000487 (accessed 30 May 2020).

Baurhoo, Neerusha G. 'An Autoethnographic Exploration of Disability Discourses: Transforming Science Education and Research for Students with Learning Disabilities', *Educational Research for Social Change* 6/2 (2017): 115–32. Online. http://dx.doi.org/10.17159/2221-4070/2017/v6i2a8 (accessed 30 May 2020).

Bulmer, Martin, ed. *Social Research Ethics: An Examination of the Merits of Covert Participation Observation*. New York: Holmes and Meier, 1982.

Burman, Erica. 'Engendering Development: Some Methodological Perspectives On Child Labour', *Forum: Qualitative Social Research* 7/1 (2006) Art. 1. Online. http://dx.doi.org/10.17169/fqs-7.1.69 (accessed 30 May 2020).

Campbell, Jane and Oliver, Mike. *Disability Politics: Understanding Our Past, Changing Our Future*. London: Routledge, 1996.

Chomsky, Noam. *American Power and the New Mandarins*. New York: Pantheon Books, 1969.

Close, Caroline and Kelbel, Camille. 'Whose Primaries? Grassroots' Views on Candidate Selection Procedures', *Acta Polit* 54 (2019): 268–94. Online. https://doi.org/10.1057/s41269-018-0086-0 (accessed 30 May 2020).

Crenshaw, Kimberle. 'Demarginalizing the Intersection of Race and Sex: A Black Feminist Critique of Antidiscrimination Doctrine, Feminist Theory and Antiracist Politics', *University of Chicago Legal Forum* 1 Art 8 (1989).

Ellis, Carolyn, Adams, Tony E. and Bochner, Arthur P. 'Autoethnography: An Overview'. *Forum: Qualitative Social Research* 12/1 (2010) Art. 10. Online. http://nbn-resolving.de/urn:nbn:de:0114-fqs1101108 (accessed 30 May 2020).

Eschle, Catherine and Maiguashca, Bice. 'Bridging the Academic/Activist Divide', *Millennium: Journal of International Studies* 35/1 (2006): 119–37. Online. https://doi.org/10.1177/03058298060350011101 (accessed 30 May 2020).

Flood, Michael G., Martin, Brian and Dreher, Tanja. 'Combining Academia and Activism: Common Obstacles and Useful Tools', *Australian Universities Review* 55/1 (2013): 17–26.

Gilligan, Carol. *In A Different Voice*. Cambridge, MA: Harvard University Press, 1982.

Guldvik, Ingrid, Askheim, Ole P. and Johansen, Vegard. 'Political Citizenship and Local Political Participation for Disabled People', *Citizenship Studies* 17/1 (2013): 76–91. Online. https://doi.org/10.1080/13621025.2013.764219 (accessed 30 May 2020).

Holli, Anne Maria. 'Feminist Triangles: A Conceptual Analysis', *Representation* 44/2 (2008): 169–85. Online. https://doi.org/10.1080/00344890802080407 (accessed 30 May 2020).

Lloyd, Margaret. 'The Politics of Disability and Feminism: Discord or Synthesis?' *Sociology* 35/3 (2001): 715–28. Online. https://doi.org/10.1017/S0038038501000360 (accessed 30 May 2020).

Longhurst, Robyn. 'Becoming Smaller: Autobiographical Spaces of Weight Loss', *Antipode* 44/3 (2011): 871–88. Online. https://doi.org/10.1111/j.1467-8330.2011.00895.x (accessed 30 May 2020).

Martin, Randy. 'Academic Activism', *PMLA* 124/3 (2009): 838–46. Online. https://doi.org/10.1632/pmla.2009.124.3.838 (accessed 29 May 2020).

Maxey, Ian. 'Beyond Boundaries: Activism, Academia, Reflexivity and Research', *Area* 31/3 (1999): 199–208. Online. https://doi.org/10.1111/j.1475-4762.1999.tb00084.x (accessed 30 May 2020).

Morris, Jenny. 'Personal and Political: A Feminist Perspective on Researching Physical Disability', *Disability, Handicap and Society* 7/2 (1992): 157–66. Online. https://doi.org/10.1080/02674649266780181 (accessed 30 May 2020).

Oliver, Mike. 'Changing the Social Relations of Research Production?' *Disability, Handicap and Society* 7/2 (1992): 101–14. Online. https://doi.org/10.1080/02674649266780141 (accessed 30 May 2020).

Pétursdóttir, G.M. 'Fire-raising Feminists: Embodied Experience and Activism in Academia', *European Journal of Women's Studies* 24/1 (2017): 85–99. Online. https://doi.org/10.1177/1350506815622513 (accessed 30 May 2020).

Postle, Karen and Beresford, Peter. 'Capacity Building and the Reconception of Political Participation: A Role for Social Care Workers?' *British Journal of Social Work* 37/1 (2007): 143–58. Online. https://doi.org/10.1093/bjsw/bch330 (accessed 30 May 2020).

Priestley, M., Stickings, M., Loja, E., Grammenos, S., Lawson, A., Waddington, L. and Fridriksdottir, B. 'The Political Participation of Disabled People in Europe: Rights, Accessibility and Activism', *Electoral Studies* 42 (2016): 1–9. Online. https://doi.org/10.1016/j.electstud.2016.01.009 (accessed 30 May 2020).

Shames, Shauna. 'Barriers and Solutions to Increasing Women's Political Power'. Strategy and background paper for The Women Effect Symposium. Cambridge, MA, 26 February 2015.

Sommers, Christina Hoff. *Who Stole Feminism? How Women Have Betrayed Women*. New York: Simon and Schuster, 1994.

Stone, Emma and Priestley, Mark. 'Parasites, Pawns and Partners: Disability Research and the Role of Non-Disabled Researchers', *British Journal of Sociology* 47/4 (1996): 699–716.

Young, Iris Marion. *Inclusion and Democracy*. Oxford: Oxford University Press, 2002.

12
The violence of technicism: Ableism as humiliation and degrading treatment

Fiona Kumari Campbell

2017 was a ground zero year for me. I had decided, after working in universities in various countries since 1995, to no longer accept humiliating practices that were, for all intents and purposes, ableist in origination. This decision, which had been percolating in my consciousness for some time, was brought to a head by two events that occurred in close sequence. The first concerned a guest lecture in a module that I normally do not teach on under the responsibility of another academic. The class was scheduled in a location that had to be changed because the original venue was sequestered by management for an event. The new venue, however, had a teaching platform that was elevated and hence required a portable lift to access the stage. The equipment had not been used for a while and there was an issue locating the key to turn on the device. There was uncertainty about not only finding the key, but also whether the lift was in working order. Hearing this news tapped into an accumulated memory and panic about the possibility of something going wrong: the lift on the day might not work. For the first time in my long career as an academic I had decided that I was not going to do the heavy lifting around disability access and had left the responsibility for sorting out the logistics to the module leader. As time drew closer to the scheduled lecture, things were still very uncertain about the chain of command involved in checking the equipment. A series of emails ensued between the module leader, estates and the manager of the equality and diversity unit. Although it was never verbalised, the tone of communications from some parties suggested that I should feel a sense of gratitude that action was being taken. Still, my anxiety about being humiliated in front of students if things should go wrong – bringing my disability to the foreground – persisted.

A few days later another incident occurred. The front entrance doors to our building were being repaired and would be out of order for one to two weeks. I was advised that I could access our building through a side pathway normally used as a fire door of an adjacent building. As this was a fire door there was no external access and I was told that I had to ring reception to get a staff member to come down and open the door. I had to do this every time I moved in and out of the building. News of this process induced an explosion in my head. I decided to put my foot down and inform my dean that I was working at home until the front entrance doors were fixed. Additionally, I had decided that I was not prepared to give the guest lecture given the uncertain circumstances regarding the lift to the stage. In discussing these two incidents with the dean on the telephone, I experienced a meltdown. Enough was enough – I had put up with these kinds of antics for years, but no longer would I be prepared to succumb by way of silence, to acquiesce as a party to humiliating practices and ultimately being complicit with my own experience of humiliation. Humiliation is quite an intangible experience because it involves emotions and an emotions management of daily microaggressions. Microaggressions such as these are experienced by disabled people in our private and work lives. Humiliation and ableism are intrinsically linked by technicist mentalities that govern our academic day. My lived experiences and those of others have shaped this chapter.

Ableism is everyone's business, not because of some ideological imperative but because we as living creatures, human and animal, are affected by the spectre and spectrum of the 'abled' body. Therefore, it is critical that ableism stops being thought of as just a disability issue. Ablement, the process of becoming 'abled', impacts on daily routines, interactions, speculations and, significantly, imagination. While all people are affected by ableism, we are not all impacted by ableist practices in the same way. Due to their positioning some individuals actually *benefit*: they become entitled by virtue of academic ableism.

This chapter brings together work I have done – Project Ableism – since 2001, which has explored the theorisation of ableism, the idea of internalising ableism, mitigating disability and using *Studies in Ableism* as a research methodology (Campbell 2019; 2017; 2011; 2009; 2001). Without wishing to duplicate work I have undertaken elsewhere, I first introduce the idea of ableism and then move onto a discussion about ableism's relationship to technicism, a tactic that is endemic within universities. The second part of the chapter focuses on the (un)reasonableness of equality duties and ableism as a harm in the form of humiliation in the lives of disabled academics. Finally, the chapter refocuses the idea of humiliation as an effect of *ontoviolence*, a consequence of ongoing struggles by disabled academics for accessible environments. As a strategy of resistance, it is integral to understand the processes and practices of ableism, not only to foreground the violence of ableism, but also to develop tactics of intervention that expose and disrupt pervasive ablement in settings such as universities and government.

The idea of ableism

Disabled women started speaking and writing about ableism as early as 1981. Records of this work appear in a special themed 'women with disabilities' issue of *Off Our Backs*. These disabled women activists in the US sketched their experiences of border limits and aporias, championing an analysis of ableism as the source of social exclusion (Aldrich 1981; House 1981; Rae 1981). We see the re-emergence of an attempt at definition by Rauscher and McClintock (1997), who described ableism as a system of discrimination and exclusion. What was missing from this approach were any nuances about the processes and predilections of such systems. In 2001 I tried to locate ableism as a knowledge system, 'a network of beliefs, processes and practices that produces a particular kind of self and body (the corporeal standard) that is projected as the perfect, species typical and therefore essential and fully human. Disability then is cast as a diminished state of being human (Campbell 2001, 44).

Although I have previously pointed to the conundrum of ableism's 'limited definitional or conceptual specificity' (Campbell 2009, 5) in disability research, this challenge has not been fully addressed and concept stabilisation has not been achieved. In attempting to develop conceptual clarity and work on developing Studies in Ableism as a research methodology, I revised the definition of ableism as a

> system of causal relations about the order of life that produces processes and systems of entitlement and exclusion. This causality fosters conditions of microaggression, internalized ableism and, in their jostling, notions of (un)encumbrance. A system of dividing practices, ableism institutes the reification and classification of

populations. Ableist systems involve the differentiation, ranking, negation, notification and prioritization of sentient life. (Campbell 2017, 287–8)

The above-mentioned elements – differentiation, ranking, negation, notification and prioritisation – form a template for contemporary societal interventions as well as methodological enquiry. I will return to these dividing practices later in terms of ways they acclimatise with the operation of technicism within the academy.

Since I first began writing about ableism there has been a flurry of research claiming to use ableism as an operational concept. We have witnessed a plethora of usage on Facebook and Twitter that characterises ableism as a discriminatory slight without any sense of its properties and parameters – leaving vague any sense of what kinds of practices and behaviours can be considered ableist. Our task as ablement scholars is to unveil foundational presuppositions to ferment critique for building a robust intellectual enquiry. In this paper I use 'ablement' to express a productive relation: the ongoing, dynamic processes of becoming abled. Although ablement is often used interchangeably with ableism, I prefer to use ablement when I wish to emphasise its coupling with disablement. My approach contrasts with the terminology of ability/abled or able-bodied, which are assumed to be static states. Ablement scholars, then are researchers who focus on the dynamics of being abled, or ableism as a practice, rather than primarily looking at disability per se. These states are not self-evident and require problematisation. It is necessary to unimagine and disinherit the canon of pervasive binary thinking of disability/ability, which must be thought of as a problem, and instead to think about borders and passages, placed as aporias, where 'there can be no barrier that protects itself or separates itself from something else' (Abeysekara 2011, 24). For instance, the very divisions performed as silos, deemed as 'protected characteristics' (cf. Malleson 2018) in equalities law and policy, segregate and dissipate understandings of intersectionality – as in Athena SWAN's focus on abled gender identity to the exclusion of disabled women and to a lesser extent, women of colour.

Nearly all disability studies research and recent works on ability have a predilection towards the comparative, even if this aspect is not acknowledged (Campbell 2019). The research narrative or analysis moves within a binary comparative relationship of disability and its constitutive outside, ability. The comparison is so fundamental that thinking without comparison is almost unthinkable, particularly in the field of anti-discrimination law in which the idea of the comparator is vital (see Baker and Campbell 2006 for a discussion of comparing a young school student with autism with an able-bodied 'disruptive' student). What does making comparisons involve – is it with a person with the presumed characteristics of able-bodiedness? This matter is complex and nuanced. However, the academic treatment of these hermeneutical questions is commonly uneven, as there is in many pieces of research a manifest lack of precision about the remit of the so-called 'object' or 'subject' under study – ontologically and conceptually.

The turn to the study of abledness and the idea of ableism rather than primarily focusing on disability per se provides a new intellectual playground, to map discourses of unencumbrance, academic productivity, citizenship and ethical norms, buttressed by configurations of the normative (endowed, extolled) and non-normative 'failed' bodies. The idea of 'ability' needs to be understood alongside its constitutive outside by considering those grey zones of uncertain populations that resist enumeration – the long-term ill, people with episodic/chronic illness and non-apparent disability. Deep diving is essential:

> ableism is deeply seeded at the level of epistemological systems of life, personhood, power and liveability. Ableism is not just a matter of ignorance or negative attitudes towards disabled people; it is a trajectory of perfection, a deep way of thinking about bodies, wholeness, permeability and how certain clusters of people are *en-abled* via valued entitlements. Bluntly, ableism functions to 'inaugurat[e] the norm'. (Campbell 2009, 5)

How does my approach differ in nuance from the statement below, part of an advertisement for the 'Ableism in Academia' conference held at UCL in 2018?

> However, as disabled, chronically ill, and neurodiverse academics know, ableism – discrimination in favour of able-bodied people – is endemic in academia.

At first glance, this marking of ableism seems reasonable and appears written in less academic language than my rendition. Read it again – you may notice that the formulation pivots upon a discrimination framework. A discrimination paradigm has been extremely influential, to the point, I argue, of normalisation: there is limited deep reflection on the *meaning* of discrimination and its attributes. Using a discrimination lens to study inequalities is just one of a myriad possible epistemologies. There is more going on here – this statement is making a claim that it is discrimination that is the central problem: a choice, a preference towards 'able-bodied' staff. I would want to know if this 'favouritism' is of a generalised nature or is targeted in a form of positive action towards ablement. These are questions to ponder. Any strategy adhering to this definition of ableism implies that simply identifying the discrimination would be sufficient to remove it. It is not surprising that this approach to conceiving ableism has been adopted, as a discrimination framework underpins most human rights discourse. We are seduced into believing that non-discrimination is the mechanism for remedying many social ills.

My approach, while not rejecting a discrimination paradigm outright, starts from a different premise: namely, ableism is not simply about ignorance (or even unconscious bias, a concept that is very much the flavour of the month). Rather, ableism is soma-epistemological, configuring legitimised knowledges concerning normalcy, perfection and intense ontologies of bodies; that is, what it means to be *fully* human. Ableism rewards certain classes of people for their corporeal alignment through practices such as technicism, which I will discuss later. It is important to stop and think, *think, think* – about the nature of processes and practices of academic ableism; how to drill down to ableism's subtleties and hiddenness. It is imperative that we embrace this challenge. The battle over ableism is a battle of the mind and heart. Sometimes the tactics of this battle are reduced to gaslighting – denying the humiliating experiences of disabled academics and their consequences. Humiliation is a core outcome and effect of ableist practices. For the continuation of the academy, a lot is at stake!

Integrating studies in ableism into disability- and higher education-focused research represents a significant challenge not only to research practice but also to equality and diversity operations. Ableism moves beyond the more familiar territory of disability, social inclusion, and usual indices of exclusion to the very divisions of life. Ablement and the corresponding notion of ableism are intertwined. A symptom and outcome of ableist processes, compulsory ablement compels the inauguration of a dynamic promise that suggests ablement is in reach for all – it is possible and indeed desirable to be a 'superhuman' academic. Even those who benefit from certain forms of entitlement within the academy are hoodwinked by #FetishAbleism, for the norm is indeed a cloudy shadow that one cannot catch up with. Ultimately, ableism will even catch up with these folk, as they fail to win the battle of constantly shifting grades of endowed competencies deemed average or 'normal' by the very modes of social organisation to which they owe their complicity.

As a hegemonic referential category to differentiate the 'normal' from the 'dispensable', the concept of abledness is predicated on some pre-existing notion about the normative nature of species-typical functioning that is trans-cultural and trans-historical, yet varies in its presentation and processes and hence is not necessarily universal. Ableism does not just stop at promulgating the 'species-typical', which is assumed to be demarcated, stable and self-contained. An ableist imaginary tells us what a healthy academic's body means – a 'normal' mind, the pace and tenor of thinking, energy levels and the kinds of emotions and affect that are suitable to express – all played out in student evaluations, perceptions of what an academic looks like, feedback, ideas of 'objectivity' and scores. Of course, these fictional characteristics of corporeality are promoted as an ideal, conditioned and contoured by time and place. Occasionally certain deviations are exceptionalised, such as the trope of the eccentric male, nutty professor, which in some disciplines becomes legendary rather than a handicap.

An ableist imaginary relies upon the existence of an unconscious, imagined community of able-bodied and able-minded people, who are bound together by an ableist homosocial worldview that asserts the preferability of the norms of ableism, norms often asserted by way of political codes of citizenship, including nation, corporation building and the idea of the 'productivity of the multitude' (Hardt and Negri 2005). In other words, ablement, like whiteness, is rarely acknowledged, as it is so pervasive and thus not subjected to the exceptionalising processes of differentiation as are blackness, disability or homosexuality. Ableism still preserves privileged benchmark occupational profiles, where diversity is achieved through the insertion of protected characteristics into the domain by way of selective modifications such as 'guaranteed interviews' – disabled academics enter an elusive zone within 'a matrix of declared and hidden rules' (Morley 2011, 224). Even so, the legal definition of disability as being 'substantial and long-term' negatively affects the ability of disabled academics to undertake agreed 'normal' activities, leaving this choice to narrow the purview of disability intact.

It is important to be clear here that a choice is being made in the government of disability to narrow the remit of defining disability, rather than a more expansive choice. The decision to adopt a minoritisation approach – which sees disability as discreet and insular – keeps the disabled population in its place as an insignificant minority population. This fiction masks the reality that disability could be experienced by at least 40 per cent of the population, which, if accepted, has profoundly different political and legal implications about how governments understand the diversity continuum. Indeed, there is a veiled subtext that disability is somewhat unsatisfactory, and that people should make attempts to 'ameliorate' their impairments. This ranking of assumed pre-set occupational activities, from proficient to impaired, maintains an alignment with the binary distinction between ablement and disablement. The leakiness and permeability of disability in different occupational contexts means that 'the law's conception of impairment as an *inherent feature* of an individual claimant's identity will be increasingly at odds with people's perceptions of their lived experiences' (Malleson 2018, 608). Prescribed systems of merit are not only clung to; Rosemary Deem argues that there is also a reluctance by UK universities

> to fully engage with equality policies for staff, either in rhetoric or reality, [which] may be partially explained by the extent to which many HEIs regard themselves as meritocratic institutions in which outstanding individuals are recruited on the basis of merit and where excellence in learning, research and teaching is actively fostered. (Deem 2007, 616)

Variability does not play an intrusive role in occupational remits; rather it acts as a residual ethical foreclosure. There are leakages in practices of ableism. Malleson (2018, 608) argues that 'it is quite possible that the conceptualisation of the distinction between able-bodied/disabled will follow that of sex, gender and sexual orientation towards increasing disruption of the binary categorisation'. Such ableist trajectories erase differences in the way humans express our emotions, use our thinking and bodies in different cultures and in different situations. In summary, then, able-bodiedness circulates and produces notions within a university environment of

- 'Health' – wholeness, enhancement/endowment
- Productive contributory citizens – the 'competent worker'
- 'Species-typical' functions – demarcations between human wellbeing, ill and injured workers
- Universalisms – objectivities that can be measured irrespective of university, campus and location
- Possessive individualism (ideas of autonomy, independence, being governed by reason) – the archetypical academic, although might vary by academic discipline
- Idea of human normativity (balanced, normalised functioning)

- Hegemonic proprioceptive lens (ways of sensing, experiencing university employment and relationships)

Ableism's relationship to technicism

> My dyscalculia rises like an ugly beast as I undertake the mathematical calculations for grading an assessment task. Who do I go to for help in working out the formula? I can't fulfil this part of the job description – no one in management must find out. (Campbell, diary entry, 19 January 2019)

Whether we like it or not, we must acknowledge that the acquisition of knowledge and skills also involves the acquisition of values about that knowledge and those skills (Goodnow 1990, 81). In this section I will show that ableist reasoning around the inclusion of disabled academics within universities, due to its reliance on various forms of technicism, leads to situations of *reductio ad absurdum*, rationalisations that slip into absurdity, whereby disabled academics experience forms of gaslighting through, for example, convincing them to believe that disability adjustments have been put in place, when in reality they have not, leading to feelings of confusion, frustration and a lack of recognition of the realities of lived experiences. In effect universities redirect the 'problem' of equalities compliance by way of communicating that the disabled employee is instead the problem (their attitude, flexibility, receptivity), creating a disjuncture with attributing systems failures. An obsession with *techne* or procedures can make the dynamics that happen in academic relational spaces invisible at best, or at worst erased, through the use of ableist tenors and tactics that leave in place an uncritical understanding of the productive 'academic' body, leading to doubt, despair or even self-induced death. However, I am getting ahead of myself.

Technicism, from the word *techne*, is not merely about an orientation towards technical detailing; it is a crafting of argumentation or pleading based on certain assumptions of the archetypal academic and bodyscapes. In this sense, its focus is in presenting overly instrumental views, giving primacy to scientific rationality based on a benchmark body (white, heterosexual, abled, male, Christian) that orders and structures workplace environments. A technicist mindset frames systems – and the people within them – in terms of *resources*. It is no accident that in many universities, equality and diversity units are located within human resources departments. Viewing employees as resources through turning them into objects does not feature strongly in literature about equalities debates.

Resources, like other technologies, are *characterological*, in the sense of being fit for purpose – imbuing the technology with its creator's desires, which are reflected in the technology's design and purpose (cf. Campbell 2009, chapter 4). What is that purpose, you might ask? The academic is required to be flexible and able to be shifted about in different spaces (online, scheduled classes, meetings), in various inter-/intra-campus locations and time zones – a body-for-hire that augments the delivery of education. The notion of time and temporality is filtered through these various spatial domains. Despite the rhetoric of personalisation, fitting-for-purpose means that academics need to be *moulded* to fit standardised practices such as ratio of staff, work allocation formulas for marking, and built environment specifications (based on optimum benchmark bodies to fit furniture, etc.).

Bourdieu's (1977) work notes a gulf between technicist quantifications of objective time – clocking in – and time as it is practised and subjectively understood. This chasm effectively becomes a misrecognition, whereby those in power have the capacity to legitimise or withhold disabled academics' use and experiences of time. As Morley (2011, 224) puts it, such '[m]isrecognition is also perceived as a form of symbolic violence in so far as it harms members of socially subordinated groups, but in subtle or abstract ways that are often difficult to prove'. Social exclusion by way of geographical 'lock-outs' and technicism such as those mentioned at the beginning of this chapter, has a rippling effect, with hostile and humiliating inaccessible environments communally impacting all of us, as strangers and friends observe someone else's humiliation and exclusion. Inaccessible environments make and position disabled people as problematic bystanders – we, the disabled who look in, simply imagine another possibility or, because of the degree of inaccessibility, we become alienated from organisational environments.

Warin et al.'s (2015) work on temporality and the failure of health promotion campaigns among the poor can be adapted for our analysis of disabled academic experiences. They report a spatio-temporal disjuncture between ideas of future (planning) and the tension of dealing with the present. Due to daily struggles with disability and academic ableism, a disabled academic may exhibit a short horizon in their struggle to deal with immediate challenges, resulting in 'narrowed vistas of possibility and […] improvisational practices' which are situated and limited (Warin et al. 2015, 310). In negotiating prescribed time, disabled academics may have to balance their activities with the embodied implications of fatigue, slowness and location (do they work better sitting at work or horizontally in bed at home?), to name just a few tensions.

The unencumbered, sex-neutral employee has replaced the sex rhetoric of the main (read, male) breadwinner. The able-bodied worker, inscribed as an 'unencumbered' worker, is a fictitious employee who behaves in the workplace as if he or she has a 'wife' at home full-time, performing all the unpaid care work that families require, able to be beckoned at call as a source of emotional support. 'This "gold standard" worker works full time, year round, is available to work overtime, and takes no time off for child bearing or rearing …' (Applelbaum et al. 2002, 8). Disabled academics rarely fit this mould: they may have bodily and emotional needs that cannot be mechanically routinised or normalised. Abled compensation for encumbrances is more veiled, often being absorbed by unpaid gendered care and support provided by a (female) spouse or the tactic of adaptation and morphing strategies. It then becomes challenging to deal with future goals when there is an ongoing disruption between the past, in the form of traumatic experiences, and perceptions of the present. This dynamic will be discussed in the final section of the chapter.

Professional development planning for academics embraces what Fendler (2001) refers to as 'technologies of developmentality', which promote values of choice and progressive efficiency. Here, 'technologies present as regulatory systems, the technologies of management that do not just structure the physical environment and make use of natural resources but treat people as a resource to be ordered' (Roder 2011, 65). Employers, corporations and town planners already engage in the unacknowledged process of accommodating the needs of their employees, citizens and visitors (without disability). Governments and other entities spend money and energy accommodating users 'without denominating it as such', and this is the hidden aspect of ableist models (Burgdorf 1997, 529).

An ordering of university life takes places across four domains, namely enterprise (employee opportunism, pragmatism and performance), administration (allocated roles of exchange between people, files and machines), vision (a blueprint of performativity) and vocation (capacity to be loyal and creative) (Law 1994, 75–81). These domains should not be conflated with ableism and bureaucracy; rather, the 'problem' is not restricted to a field within the uni(scape) but attends to the ableist mentality of technicism. As Manfred Stanley long ago argued, 'the true contemporary enemy of the human principle is technicism, a form of social organization that is much more pervasive in its impact and influences than bureaucracy' (Stanley 1972, 913).

Another twin domain that interconnects with academic ableism is law. Here too we find pervasive technicist ableism. Black-letter jurisprudence is obsessed with rule-making and process through the dynamic of precedent. The rule entrapment of the law works against its beneficiaries through such ideas as 'reasonableness', 'substantially limited' or even the very denotation and purview of 'legal disability'. This technicism belies the fact that objectivity or seeming neutrality is not value-free; instead, as feminist and more recently disability scholars have argued, law's body is intrinsically partial and ideological. An example of juridical technicism concerns a statement made by a university that a building used for graduation ceremonies was deemed accessible even though there was no direct access to the stage from the floor in the main auditorium. This meant that staff with a mobility disability were unable to process up to the stage, and students with a mobility disability were unable to receive their certificates on the stage. As the building satisfied the legal accessibility requirements there was no case to answer – no more to be done. The disabled academic could not participate in the ceremony alongside their peers because it was *actually* inaccessible. Yet the technicist assessment was flawed and ableist presuppositions were exposed. Functionality was minimised – the student cohort was presumed to be abled; expansive abledness negates the reality that that there are disabled staff or students. Leaving aside the questionable dissonance around the weaponisation of law, any further complaint on the part of the disabled academic was responded to in the form of gaslighting – the basis of the 'complaint' was construed as being 'unreasonable', trivial or a personal gripe. These situations are all too common. Yet still there is a pervasive endurance of a belief in law's capacity to deliver justice (Burgdorf 1997; Campbell 2001; Hunter et al. 2010; Malleson 2018; Perlin 1999; Rovner 2001; Thornton 1996).

The reasonableness of equality duties

> [i]n order to get beyond [an individual's disability], we must first take account of [that disability]. There is no other way. And in order to treat some persons equally, we must treat them differently. (J. Blackman, in *Regents of Univ. of California v. Bakke* 438 US 265 (1978))

> Out of 170 heads of institutions only five (2.4%) disclosed as disabled while 5% of staff in support roles disclosed a disability. (Martin 2017, 7)

The UN Convention on the Rights of People with Disability (2006) promotes disabled people taking up leadership positions in their communities and understands that 'disability' is a concept founded on an evolving interaction between impairment and relational contexts. Under the Convention, '"Reasonable accommodation" means necessary and appropriate modification and adjustments not imposing a disproportionate or undue burden, where needed in a particular case, to ensure to persons with disabilities the enjoyment or exercise on an equal basis with others of all human rights and fundamental freedoms' (Article 2).

Within the Convention, reasonable accommodation is not limited to employment, but covers education, accessibility, health, access to justice and legal capacity. The focus is on an individual's case and what needs to be done to ensure that the particular person can participate fully (though the adjustment may be of benefit to others). Reasonable adjustment can be denied if an undue or disproportionate burden or hardship is involved, reinstituting a conflation between disability and burden, thus making disability equality provisional. In taking into account of any characteristics related to disability that may impact on the job in order to accommodate the disabled academic's needs, employers need to de-ontologise impairment by reducing the impairment effects to 'immutable characteristics' to avoid any inferences of feigning disability or ennobling accommodations. The problem with the immutability argument is that it invokes ethically implicated divisions of 'innate' (unchangeable) and 'fluid' (how people make sense of who they are, implying 'choice' over disability). There have been moves in the United States to propose new categories in law around the idea of voluntary or elective disability, to describe individuals who 'choose' to remain disabled and resist therapeutic programs or medical interventions. This 'choice of disability' argument could be invoked by universities to justify refusals in disability accommodations (see Campbell 2009).

The current system in most universities in the United Kingdom is to corral us like wandering black sheep into a minimalist, grounds-based individualised (and hence privatised) reasonable adjustment process as determined under ss.20–1 of the Equality Act 2010 via disability support, a unit of student services (where such services exist), instead of a dedicated employee- and occupational-focused unit committed to the principles of universal design. Reasonable adjustment requires an employer to take account of the characteristics related to disability, and to accommodate them by, for example, modifying the job or the physical environment of the workplace. As Sandra Fredman (2013, 127) argues, 'instead of requiring disabled people to conform to existing norms, the aim is to develop a concept of equality which requires adaptation and change'. Instead, what actually happens produces a distortion, by resorting to a reduction to the lowest common denominator, a form of procedural violence based on tables of impairment, often bearing little resemblance to actual contextualised needs. This dissonance between the lived and the tabulated recording process is an example of a humiliating practice that can contribute to physical and psychic harm. Furthermore, in workplaces, where time often means money, assessments run the risk of being reduced to functionality scripts, resulting in the codification of need. Hence 'accommodation' or 'adjustment' has a ring of exceptionality about it, an extra gesture for which there should be gratitude. This is because typical approaches to reasonable adjustment are often predicated on the basis of equality as sameness in contrast with substantive equality, that is, treating a disabled academic differently without suggesting it is a case of 'special rights'.

Much power resides in people I have termed technicians of certification (see Figure 12.1), who aim to furnish an enumerative passport, a document of truth-telling that becomes a form of 'notification', legitimising disability. The enumerative passport is founded on diagnosis to access services and in effect enables the credibility of a disability identity. There have been huge battles over the delimitation of disability, which has resulted in restricted access not just to services but even to coverage under disability provisions in equalities legislation (Campbell 2009). The enumerative passport further entrenches suspicions and doubts on the part of the disabled academic producing distancing-relations between them and 'professionals' about the embodied realities of disability experiences within the academy. Disabled academics surveyed by Martin (2017, 7) reported that they are *told* what support they will receive rather than being *asked* what they require. It is not surprising, then, to find low rates of disability disclosure within universities by disabled staff.[1] As Martin (2017, 7) puts it, 'the term "disclosure" is in itself viewed as problematic by some disabled people. Ambivalence about disclosure, evidenced here and elsewhere, points to the impossibility of gathering reliable information about the number of disabled leaders in the sector and beyond.' (On disclosure, see also Kerschbaum et al. 2017.)

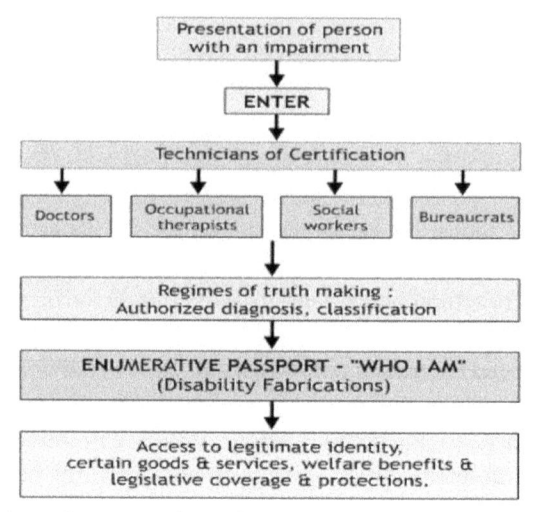

```
        Presentation of person
         with an impairment
                 ↓
              ENTER
                 ↓
        Technicians of Certification
     ↓         ↓          ↓          ↓
  Doctors  Occupational  Social   Bureaucrats
           therapists   workers
                 ↓
        Regimes of truth making :
     Authorized diagnosis, classification
                 ↓
     ENUMERATIVE PASSPORT - "WHO I AM"
          (Disability Fabrications)
                 ↓
          Access to legitimate identity,
     certain goods & services, welfare benefits &
        legislative coverage & protections.
```

Figure 12.1: Technicians of certification. Source: Campbell 2001

Liisberg (2015, 126–7) has produced a model of three concentric circles that delineate approaches to anticipatory duties: (1): the smallest circle, a weak response, with a minimalist focus on technical standards; (2) the middle circle, a medium-strength duty where compliance with accessibility standards is not necessarily sufficient to achieve the necessary level of protection; (3) the biggest circle, ensures full accessibility with practically no limitations. Instead of a focus on individualised adjustments, anticipatory duties respond to disabled people as a group, whereby the duty is to anticipate *in advance* communal accessibility needs. Liisberg suggests that UK universities fit into the middle circle, whereas I would suggest most universities operate within the smallest circle. Very few universities instrumentalise the anticipatory duties requirement of the Equality Act 2010. When it does apply, the duty is towards students, in their capacity as customers utilising services (i.e. resources of the university).

A recent European Court of Human Rights case that may have a bearing on anticipatory duties towards not only students but also disabled academics is *Enver Şahin v. Turkey* (2018). *Enver Şahin* concerns obligations for adjustments within a university setting. The case has been included here as it provides an indication of the thinking of the courts about the provision of social care as accessibility. As a recent judgement, the case has been subjected to limited analysis. The university concerned argued that economic and time restraints presented difficulties for rectifying the inaccessible environment. Reading Article 14 of the European Convention on Human Rights (ECHR) on 'prohibition of discrimination' alongside Article 2 of the UN Convention on the Rights of People with Disability ('reasonable accommodations'), the court found a violation of Article 14 as there was a failure (1) to identify Şahin's needs and (2) to explore the suitability of accessibility solutions that would provide conditions that were as equivalent as possible to his peers. Damamme (2018) argues that *Enver Şahin v. Turkey* is a move towards the assessment of the suitability of solutions proposed to [disabled people] to provide them access to classrooms in light of the principles of autonomy and safety'. How *Enver Şahin* would apply to the circumstances of disabled staff around autonomy and safety and the anticipatory duties provided for in the Equality Act 2010 is unclear.

It is equally uncertain at law as to whether this anticipatory duty applies equally to disabled staff, who, while also utilising university resources, are nonetheless contracted as employees of the university. Referring to the definition of ableism that I provided earlier, technicism is weaponised to differentiate disability adjustment requirements of staff from students, through the practices of negation – that is, arguing that disabled employees are different in *genus* from disabled students, producing two different effects. The first is to prioritise disabled students' needs over disabled staff through making available support from an administrative unit that focuses principally on students. Disabled staff become an often-unnamed afterthought, invariably zoned out of assistive flowcharts. Secondly, technicism enables the instituting of academic ableism, which formalises a hierarchy of ranking strategies that enable equality measures. Deem (2007, 615) is quite forceful about this, arguing that her research data 'suggests that equality policies for staff and students are in tension with each other, that staff policies clash with other institutional policies'.

There is strong resistance to any perceived positive actions (affirmative action) within higher education to seriously deal with asymmetrical hiring practices and pay gaps for current and prospective employees from peripheral backgrounds (Davis and Robison 2016; Deem 2007; Morley 2011). It may not be well known that the Equality Act 2010 under ss.158–9 makes provision for positive action to supplement protected characteristics specified in the Act, especially in the areas of promotion and recruitment. Davis and Robison argue that these provisions act as a public-sector duty to have regard to the need to eliminate unlawful discrimination, which 'clearly points to the need for some pre-emptive action in cases where disparate impact has been clearly evidenced' (Davis and Robison 2016, 90–1). The reality is that in most higher education institutions in the UK there is an absence of positive actions. This absence distinguishes our universities from those abroad, including low-income nations (Deem 2007, 629). Higher education institutions, as champions of the knowledge economy with real social capital, need to be brave in leading the way by promoting positive action initiatives around protected characteristics, especially disability.

Academic ableism: Humiliation as violence

> There is a need for us to separate Adele's little whims from her genuine [sic] problems. (Case notes of the agency nurse, *Price v. United Kingdom*, 2001, 34 EHRR1285, at para 16)

> Humiliation as claim does not choose its context. On the contrary, the context plays a far more determinative role in deciding the form and content of humiliation. It can be generally observed that society of the socially dead cannot provide the active context for the articulation of humiliation. Or, that a society with heaven on earth would make humiliation redundant. In fact, it is the context that decides the nature, level, and intensity of humiliation. (Guru 2011, 10)

In this final section, I turn to the sentiments expressed at the opening of this chapter and explore the humiliating effects of academic ableist practices within universities. There was something about the 2001 European Court of Human Rights case known as *Price v. United Kingdom*. Although this case had received little attention in the literature it rang bells for me. While I have never been to prison and do not have the degree of physical disability that Adele Price experienced, what I identified with were the synergies of humiliation, a process that would no doubt also be familiar to other disabled academics.

Price was brought under Article 3 of the ECHR by UK national Adele Price, a woman described as having a four-limb impairment and kidney illness due to thalidomide. As a result of refusing to answer questions in proceedings at Lincoln County Court she was committed to prison for seven days for contempt of court (with remissions, 3.5 days). The judge did not enquire where Price would be detained before committing her to immediate imprisonment in what turned out to be an inaccessible prison facility. Price was first taken to the cells at Lincoln police station overnight, then transferred to New Hall Women's Prison and placed in the prison's healthcare centre due to the general inaccessibility of the prison. During her imprisonment, Price was unable to access the bathroom, toilet and bedding facilities and was initially deprived of a battery to use her power chair. While she was provided with some personal care, this was erratic and unreliable and as a result Price contracted a kidney infection. In this sense, the experience of Adele Price was unremarkable, as disabled people in and outside universities are daily challenged to negotiate environments that are not accessible to varying degrees and have their bodily and emotional health suffer.

We do not normally think of inaccessibility as a form of inhumane and degrading treatment. The Price case was a test as to whether inaccessibility came within the remit of Article 3 of the ECHR. Article 3 states that 'No one shall be subjected to torture or to inhuman or degrading treatment or punishment'. This is an absolute right with no exemptions or limitations. The Court is required to take into account all the circumstances of the victim. In *The Greek Case* (1969) 'degrading treatment' is defined as 'deliberately causing severe suffering, mental or physical' and 'inhuman treatment' that 'grossly humiliates the [...] individual before others or drives him to act against his conscience'. In *Tyrer v. the United Kingdom* (1978), the European Court of Human Rights stated that it was enough for the victim to be humiliated in his or her eyes and not necessarily in the eyes of others. Inaccessible environments are not benign: they occur through a lack of insight, conditioned by the practices of ableism, into the situation of difference being modelled on the illusory notion of the normative (benchmark) human being. In *Price* the court concluded that inaccessibility is *ipso facto* material and ontological violence – a form of degradation and debasement, even if the parties to the action did not intend to violate the psychic and bodily integrity of Price. This is an extraordinary judgment, a radical decision swept under the carpet, through a process of restricting the decisions to only prisons and psychiatric facilities.[2] Universities are, however, on notice, as inaccessible environments constitute humiliation and debasement. The European Court of Human Rights reaffirmed the decision in *Tyrer* (1979) and found that Price's Article 3 rights had been violated despite the lack of 'any positive evidence of an intention to humiliate or debase'.

Inaccessible relations hurt and as such constitute an assault on beingness and shape our ontological character. Humiliation caused by inaccessibility can lead to low self-esteem, social phobia, anxiety and depression, pointing to a link between humiliation and ableist practices as a form of harm (Hartling and Luchetta 1999; Torres and Bergner 2010). Torres and Bergner (2010) identify four key elements of humiliation on which there is general consensus in the literature, namely

- *Calling into question* a status claim
- There is a *public failure* of the status claim
- The *degrader has status* to degrade, highlighting asymmetrical power relations
- There is a *rejection of the status to claim a status*, that is, a disabled academic is denied recognition of their claim to discrimination

There is no room in the chapter to discuss the phenomenon of microaggressions: demeaning implications and other subtle insults against minorities that may be perpetrated against individuals due to gender, race and religious difference, sexual orientation, and disability status (Solorzano 1998). Suffice to say that there is an interconnectivity between microaggressions and humiliation. Relations that read differences as forms of subordination and signs of deficiency produce suffering that humiliates and debases.

I have used the term *ontoviolence* to capture these effects that literally seep into the interior spaces of a 'cast-out' person's beingness (ontological framing), producing instant, longer-term and accumulated effects of defilements of the body and mind. As Guru (2011) reminds us, humiliation always has a context, as does the Convention's preamble, which understands the production of disability to occur within the context of interactions. Context and responses of technicism within universities towards the disabled academic often mask humiliating practices. Indeed, acts of humiliation are a direct attack on equality measures and run counter to an ethos of celebrating diversity. This is because humiliation is only possible when an individual already possesses a sense of self-determination: it is an assault on the self-respect of the victim. As Parekh (2011, 23) puts it, disabled academics 'have a certain view of themselves and the kind of minimum treatment that is due to them. When this is denied and others' treatment of them falls below their expectations, their self-respect is violated.' The very existence of a system of equality law raises reasonable expectations on the part of the disabled academic; however, it is the negation of a disabled academic's experiences – an act of *ontoviolence* that results in the caustic harm of humiliation. Ableist practices erode confidence in institutional mechanisms to resolve inequalities and are manifested by accumulated experiences of ableist defilements. Interestingly, there is a school of thought that argues that when self-respect and a sense of entitlement are lacking, individuals do not experience of sense of humiliation (Parekh

2011). I am not convinced; internalised ableism means that in order to survive some disabled staff may accept or tune out ableist interactions.

Equally, from the perspective of perpetrators, it is difficult to prove intentionality where the norms around the debasing of disability are so insidious and commonplace that they may not even arise as a conscious form of negative intentionality – that is, how institutions respond to disabled people. We may ask whether intentionality *matters* in the final instance; should we instead be focused on the effects of the 'event'? One example given by Inckle (2019), a disabled lecturer at the University of Liverpool, in response to a request for reasonable adjustment, illustrates this point: 'The university might deem it reasonable for you to go downstairs on your bottom in some situations rather than schedule you into fully wheelchair accessible rooms.' I cannot even fathom a situation whereby the above-mentioned expectation would be considered reasonable. Again, Parekh (2011, 25–6) concludes that 'humiliation is most effective when it is so deep and pervasive that it is no longer recognised for what it is, but that does not gainsay its reality'. Humiliation can involve some not-so-self-evident ironies: a sense of technicism's *reductio ad absurdum*.

At my institution there is online diversity training about disability produced by an equality consultancy business that I believe contains certain offensive assumptions and viewpoints about disability, yet in order to comply with equality training protocols, disabled employees are required to complete these packages, to further submit to humiliating practices as part of their employment contracts. Inckle (2019) points to another one of these ironies: her academic department is the School of Law and Social Justice and the vice-chancellor of the university was awarded a damehood on the basis of services to equality. Bringing about complaints means being ushered into processes within the university that further humiliate and silence, where the onus of proof is on the disabled academic to prove the validity of discrimination. This *ontoviolence* has the effect of sanitising technicist ableism and redirecting attention away from a university's equality obligations. Ultimately it diminishes the contributions of disabled academics to the intellectual life of universities. This chapter has threaded together the practices of ableism within universities in spotlighting the forms of technicism engaged and weaponised to harm and humiliate disabled academics as they go about their work. It is clear from European case law that inaccessibility is a form of *ontoviolence* and that there is a direct relationship between accessibility and discrimination.

Notes

1 Schedule 8, s.20(1) in the Equality Act 2010 states there are limitations on the requirement to provide reasonable adjustments in circumstances where there is a lack of knowledge by the university of the existence of disability. The service is not subject to the duty if they do not know about a person's disability or could not be reasonably expected to know.
2 The test used by the European Court of Human Rights in assessing Price's complaint is summarised as follows: (1) The ill treatment must attain a level of severity; (2) any assessment of this minimum level of severity is relative; and (3) depends on all the circumstances of the case, including (4) the 'duration of the treatment, its physical and mental effects, and in some cases, the sex, the age and state of health of the victim', and (5) the intention to degrade 'whether its object was to humiliate and debase the person concerned, although the absence of any such purpose cannot conclusively rule out a finding of violation of Article 3'.

References

Abeysekara, Ananda. *The Politics of Postsecular Religion: Mourning Secular Futures*. Colombo: Social Scientists Association, 2011.

Aldrich, Michelle L. 'Beginning Bibliography', *Off Our Backs* 11/5 (1981): 39.

Appelbaum, Eileen, Bailey, Thomas, Berg, Peter and Kalleberg, Arne L. *Shared Work, Valued Care: New Norms for Organizing Market Work and Unpaid Care Work*. Washington DC: Economic Policy Institute, 2002.

Baker, Bernadette and Campbell, Fiona. 'Transgressing Non-crossable Borders: Disability, Law, Schooling, And Nations'. In *Vital Questions in Disability Studies and Education*, edited by Scot Danforth and Susan Gabel, 319–46. New York: Peter Lang, 2006.

Bourdieu, Pierre. *Outline of a Theory of Practice*. Cambridge: Cambridge University Press, 1977. Online https://doi.org/10.1017/CBO9780511812507 (accessed 30 May 2020).

Burgdorf, Robert L. '"Substantially Limited": Protection from Disability Discrimination: The Special Treatment Model and Misconceptions of the Definition of Disability', *Villanova Law Review* 42 (1997): 409–585.

Campbell, Fiona Kumari. 'Inciting Legal Fictions: "Disability's" Date with Ontology and the Ableist Body of the Law', *Griffith Law Review* 10/1 (2001): 42–62.

Campbell, Fiona Kumari. *Contours of Ableism: The Production of Disability and Abledness*. Basingstoke and New York: Palgrave Macmillan, 2009.

Campbell, Fiona Kumari. 'Geodisability Knowledge Production and International Norms: A Sri Lankan Case Study', *Third World Quarterly* 32/8 (2011): 1455–74.

Campbell, Fiona Kumari. 'Queer Anti-sociality and Disability Unbecoming An Ableist Relations Project?' In *New Intimacies/Old Desires: Law, Culture and Queer Politics in Neoliberal Times*, edited by Oishik Sircar and Dipika Jain, 280–316. New Delhi: Zubaan Books, 2017.

Campbell, Fiona Kumari. 'Precision Ableism: A *Studies in Ableism* Approach to Developing Histories of Disability and Abledment', *Rethinking History* 23/2 (2019): 135–56. Online. https://doi.org/10.1080/13642529.2019.1607475 (accessed 30 May 2020).

Council of Europe. *The European Convention on Human Rights*, Rome, 4 November 1950. Online. https://www.echr.coe.int/Documents/Convention_ENG.pdf (accessed 29 June 2020).

Damamme, Joseph. 'Disability and University (Pragmatic) Activism: The Pros and Cons of Enver Şahin v Turkey', *Strasborg Observers,* 9 March 2018. Online. https://strasbourgobservers.com/category/cases/enver-sahin-v-turkey/ (accessed 30 May 2020).

Davis, Chantal M. and Robison, Muriel. 'Bridging the Gap: An Exploration of the Use and Impact of Positive Action in the United Kingdom', *International Journal of Discrimination and the Law* 16/2-3 (2016): 83–101. Online. https://doi.org/10.1177/1358229116655647 (accessed 30 May 2020).

Deem, Rosemary. 'Managing a Meritocracy or an Equitable Organisation? Senior Managers' and Employees' views about Equal Opportunities Policies in UK Universities', *Journal of Education Policy* 22/6 (2007): 615–36. Online. https://doi.org/10.1080/02680930701625247 (accessed 30 May 2020).

Enver Şahin v Turkey. App no. 23065/12. 2018. Online.

Fendler, Lynn. 'Educating Flexible Souls: The Construction of Subjectivity through Developmentality and Interaction'. In *Governing the Child in the New Millennium*, edited by Kenneth Hultqvist and Gunilla Dahlberg, 119–42. New York: Routledge Falmer, 2001.

Fredman, Sandra. 'Disability Equality: A Challenge to the Existing Anti-Discrimination Paradigm?' In *Disability and Equality Law*, edited by Michael A. Stein and Elizabeth Emens, 123–42. Abingdon and New York: Routledge, 2016, originally 2013.

Goodnow, Jacqueline. 'Using Sociology to Extend Psychological Accounts of Cognitive Development', *Human Development* 33 (1990): 81–107. Online. https://doi.org/10.1159/000276505 (accessed 30 May 2020).

Guru, Gopal. 'Introduction: Theorizing Humiliation'. In *Humiliation: Claims and Context*, edited by Gopal Guru, 1–22. New Delhi: Oxford University Press, 2011.

Hardt, Michael, and Negri, Antonio. *Multitude: War and Democracy in the Age of Empire*. New York: Penguin, 2005.

Hartling, Linda and Luchetta, Tracy. 'Humiliation: Assessing the Impact of Derision, Degradation, and Debasement', *The Journal of Primary Prevention* 19/4 (1999): 259–78. Online. https://doi.org/10.1023/A:1022622422521 (accessed 30 May 2020).

House, Seamoon. 'A Radical Feminist Model of Psychological Disability', *Off Our Backs* 11/5 (1981): 34–5.

Hunter, Rosemary, McGlynn, Clare and Rackley, Erika. *Feminist Judgements: From Theory to Practice*. Oxford: Hart, 2010.

Inckle, Kay. 'Britain: Gas-lighting, Discrimination and Humiliation: The Day-To-Day Experience of a Disabled Academic', *Brave New Europe*, 28 February 2019. Online. https://braveneweurope.com/gas-lighting-discrimination-and-humiliation-the-day-to-day-experience-of-a-disabled-academic (accessed 30 May 2020).

Kerschbaum, Stephanie, Eisenman, Laura and Jones, James, eds. *Negotiating Disability: Disclosure and Higher Education*. Ann Arbor: University of Michigan Press, 2017. Online.

Law, John. *Organising Modernity*. Oxford: Blackwell, 1994.

Liisberg, Maria. 'Accessibility of Services and Discrimination: Concentricity, Consequence, and the Concept of Anticipatory Duty', *International Journal of Discrimination and the Law* 15/1-2 (2015): 123–44. Online. https://doi.org/10.1177/1358229114558545 (accessed 30 May 2020).

Malleson, Kate. 'Equality Law and the Protected Characteristics', *Modern Law Review* 81/4 (2018): 598–621. Online. https://doi.org/10.1111/1468-2230.12353 (accessed 30 May 2020).

Martin, Nicola. 'Encouraging Disabled Leaders in Higher Education: Recognising Hidden Talents', Stimulus Paper. London: Leadership Foundation for Higher Education, 2017.

Morley, Louise. 'Misogyny Posing as Measurement: Disrupting the Feminisation Crisis Discourse', *Contemporary Social Science* 6/2 (2011): 223–35. Online. https://doi.org/10.1080/21582041.2011.580615 (accessed 30 May 2020).

Parekh, Bhikhu. 'Logic of Humiliation'. In *Humiliation: Claims and Context*, edited by Gopal Guru, 23–40. New Delhi: Oxford University Press, 2011.

Perlin, Michael. '"Half-Wracked Prejudice Leaped Forth": Sanism, Pretextuality, and Why and How Mental Disability Law Developed as it Did', *Journal of Contemporary Legal Issues* 10 (1999): 3–36.

Price v United Kingdom, App No 33394/96, 34 EHRR1285. 10 July 2001.

Rae, Arachne. 'An Open Letter to Disabled Lesbians', *Off Our Backs* 11/5 (1981): 39.

Rauscher, Laura and McClintock, Mary. 'Ableism Curriculum Design'. In *Teaching for Diversity and Social Justice: A Sourcebook*, edited by Maurianne Adams, Lee Anne Bell and Pat Griffin, 198–229. New York: Routledge, 1997.

Roder, John. 'Beyond Technicism: Towards 'Being' and 'Knowing' in an Intra-active Pedagogy', *He Kupu* 2/5 (2011): 61–72.

Rovner, Laura. 'Perpetuating Stigma: Client Identity in Disability Rights Litigation', *Utah Law Review* 2 (2001): 247–318.

Solorzano, Daniel. 'Critical Race Theory, Racial and Gender Microaggressions, and the Experiences of Chicana and Chicano Scholars', *International Journal of Qualitative Studies in Education* 11/1 (1998): 121–36. Online. https://doi.org/10.1080/095183998236926 (accessed 30 May 2020).

Stanley, Manfred. 'Technicism, Liberalism and Development: A Study in Irony as Social Theory'. In *Social Development*, edited by Manfred Stanley, 276. New York: Syracuse University Press, 1972.

The Greek Case. Council of Europe, 1969. Online. https://hudoc.echr.coe.int/app/conversion/pdf/?library=ECHR&id=001-73020&filename=001-73020.pdf (accessed 29 June 2020).

Thornton, Margaret. *Dissonance and Distrust: Women in the Legal Profession*, Melbourne: Oxford University Press, 1996.

Torres, Walter and Bergner, Raymond. 'Humiliation: Its Nature and Consequences', *Journal of American Academy of Psychiatric Law* 38 (2010): 195–204.

Tyrer v United Kingdom. App No. 5856/72, 17 Yearbook ECHR 356. 25 April 1978.

Warin, Megan, Zivkovic, Tanya, Moore, Vivienne, Ward, Paul and Jones, Michelle. 'Short Horizons and Obesity Futures: Disjunctures Between Public Health Interventions and Everyday Temporalities', *Social Science and Medicine*, 128 (2015): 309–15. Online. https://doi.org/10.1016/j.socscimed.2015.01.026 (accessed 30 May 2020).

13
A little bit extra

El Spaeth

Through poetic inquiry El Spaeth thematises reasonable adjustments. The poem represents a raw account of how chronically ill or disabled individuals are misunderstood and othered in academia.

I wear my disabilities like a cape.
These disabilities have names made by this society: lazy, naughty, difficult.
I won't stand for long
I sit cross-legged
('Do I usually do that?' my psychiatrist once asked)
I can't bear pen-clicking in meetings or when I'm teaching or foot tapping in rehearsals
or music played out loud on buses
so I ask people to stop, please, if they wouldn't mind.
Last time it just got louder.
I use a laptop in meetings to stimulate my brain because doing *just one thing* renders me incapable of engaging.
And because of this, when I write I put films on in the background.
I work from home when I can
which is hard for people to understand.
A previous manager referred to this as 'a little bit extra', and said that was how I should describe it to colleagues.
Others call me 'lucky'.
But it isn't a little bit extra. It isn't good luck.
It's what I need to cope in this place that wasn't built for me.

Concluding thoughts: Moving forward

Nicole Brown and Jennifer Leigh

Contrary to academic writing conventions, we do not start this final chapter with a synthesis of ideas from all the contributions. We will come to that; the space afforded here allows us to take a step back and reflect on the entire process of editing this collection. As outlined in the preface, this book originally came about in relation to and conjunction with the 'Ableism in Academia' conference that was held at the UCL Institute of Education in March 2018. Some contributors in this book featured in the conference, others attended but did not present and others again were not involved with the conference at all.

What we had not anticipated and therefore had not been prepared for was the reality of bringing together this edited book. While we wanted to represent a diverse and international range of contributions, the impetus from the conference means that the focus of the volume is primarily on the UK and the West. Ableism is not a construct that only occurs in these contexts, and it is easy to imagine that had we been able to include a more international focus that included perspectives from the Global South we would have encountered differing perspectives. In the West it is difficult to admit, as an academic, to being 'weak' or 'ill'. In the Global South, ableism and disability appear to be more prominent as an issue, with a need to hide perceived 'faults'. While we tried to address this deficit, through contacting people in the field who were generally positive about the need for such a book, none were able or willing to contribute directly to this volume within our short timeframe.

Most editorial teams comment on the difficulty of chasing contributions, shifting deadlines and last-minute scrambles. In the case of this book, there was the added pressure of working with contributors who identified as chronically ill, disabled and/or neurodiverse. The editorial reality was one of keeping track of emails and draft submissions that were delayed due to illness flare-ups or aggravations of symptoms resulting from individuals balancing work pressures with family commitments in addition to their ill health. Additionally, there were people who would have wanted to contribute, but then felt they could not expose themselves for personal or professional reasons. There were also colleagues who had started a chapter, but then withdrew because they felt they could not produce their chapters in the given timeframe. These changes mean that the final volume has chapters from only women authors, which has inevitably had implications for the content.

At the same time, emails are often not the most conducive way to communicate, and so misunderstandings occurred, between ourselves as editors, particularly in the last few stress-filled days, and between us and our contributors. We would like to unreservedly apologise for any words that were written too tersely or quickly. We are grateful for the support we have had from our editor at UCL Press, who was forgiving and accommodating. The reality remains, though, that fluctuating disabilities and illnesses put extra demands on contributors. In everyday experiences of dealing with symptoms of disabilities and illnesses, advocating for one's rights while continuing to manage work and family commitments, additional tasks, such as a contribution to an edited book, are often the first to be moved down in one's priority list. A huge part of the process was therefore managing expectations and navigating emotions, our own and each other's. As a consequence, as editors we worked with shorter timeframes than we would have wished for, which in turn resulted in ever-tighter turnaround times for final changes and submissions that still had to adhere to a fixed publishing timescale within the final few months of the UK Research Excellence Framework (REF) deadline. These pressures were felt by our contributors and by us as editors (for example see chapter 10 on internalised ableism). Ultimately, the practical reality of putting together this edited book is an accurate representation of what ableism in academia is and feels like. The trends towards productivity and efficiency so strongly linked with the neoliberal academy of the twenty-first century, and the tensions that this creates in all academics, but particularly those with disabilities, chronic illnesses or neurodiversity, was played out in the preparation of this manuscript.

The chapters collected here bring together a range of theoretical perspectives that include feminism, poststructuralism (such as Derridean and Foucauldian theory), crip theory and disability theory. They use technicism, leadership and theories of social justice and embodiment in order to raise awareness and increase understanding of the marginalised – that is, those academics who are not perfect. They place these theories in the context of neoliberal academia, which is far away from the privileged and romanticised versions that exist in the public and internalised imaginations of academics, and use those theories to interrogate aspects of identity and of how disability is performed, and to explore how and why, as Campbell states in her chapter, ableism is not just a disability issue.

Many of the chapters take a very personal, reflective perspective in order to translate experience into theory, as seen in the poetic contributions from Spaeth, Rode and Jindal-Snape, and chapters by Campbell, Andrews, Finesilver, Rummery and Griffiths as well as those written by us. Some authors specifically focused on autoethnographic perspectives and using this particular methodological approach to constructing and creating knowledge and sharing experience, such as Griffiths, Rummery, Finesilver, Leigh and Brown. These chapters did not tackle the same topics, and yet have been placed and paired so that they complement each other. For example, where Leigh and Brown consider aspects of the personal and political nature of internalised ableism using an embodied approach, perfectionism, pain and wellbeing, Rummery also uses autoethnography to explore how the personal journey and experiences lead to political engagement and activism, and the barriers faced therein by someone with a disability. The activism that both these chapters describe also features in Andrews' chapter on the autoimmune, and the invisible nature of disability. She draws on Derrida to demonstrate how the cycle of needing to do harder work (to prove oneself) leads to more destruction (physical ill health), which in turn results in less work. She challenges the norms of academia and uses her own lived experience with an autoimmune condition to create theory around ableism. Similarly, Campbell's chapter on technicism explores ableism in the context of the law, and shapes her theory from her own and others' lived experiences. She considers the meaning of discrimination and humiliation.

Humiliation can be considered close to paranoia, in that we become paranoid in part because we fear humiliation (among other degradations) and concern over how we are perceived by others. Aspects of paranoia occur in Rode and Snape's poems as well as Andrews' chapter and those by Leigh and Brown, Finesilver et al. and Peruzzo. Peruzzo's voice is unique in this book, as she explores being an outsider in disability research, and the validity and personal experience of someone who does not claim or disclose a disability being engaged in the discourse. She asks us to consider who should be talking about these issues, who should be involved in the conversation, and takes a poststructuralist approach to consider the power and dominance and need for necessary critique from that outside perspective. These are poignant thoughts when considered from a social justice angle privileging lived experience over theoretical knowledge. In contrast, and placed alongside, Griffiths uses autoethnography to explore the insider status of a disability researcher, the complexities of invisible disability, and considers how this impacts on disclosure in academia, reflecting on her experiences in law practice. Brown also explores the idea of disclosure in her chapter, drawing on research with academics with fibromyalgia, and her chapter, along with Martin's, are the only two that use 'research data' in the conventional sense in their work. Brown reflects on her positionality, and the impact of disclosure and language on her research participants and herself. Gillberg approaches the idea of disclosure differently, as she hones in on the ideas of the construction and gatekeeping of knowledge, social justice, activism and participation within the academy from a feminist perspective. Feminism is a motif that appears through several other chapters in this book, as it figures significantly in the development of critical theory and the validity placed on lived experiences in higher education.

The last thread woven throughout this volume is that around embodiment. While it is central to some chapters (such as Leigh and Brown, and Finesilver et al.), as might be expected given the nature of our research interests and background, embodiment also appears in many other chapters. Campbell explores the idea of 'soma-epistemology', while Andrews, Griffiths and Peruzzo also refer to various aspects and understandings of embodiment, including sociological and anthropological theories. This is important to note, as it demonstrates that scholars from diverse disciplines recognise that ableism, illness and disability are experienced with and through the body, and from these experiences we construct and understand theory. This volume as a whole fills in a gap between the lived experiences of those with chronic illness, disability and neurodiversity in academia.

What the collection shows is that, despite the emotive and sometimes bleak picture that is being painted throughout all these contributions as they discuss humiliation, pain or the personal journey towards disclosure, for example, there is still hope. In their unique ways, whether that is as a poetic expression or as a report on an empirical study, as an autoethnography or philosophical position paper, all contributors seek to educate, to raise awareness and to advocate, despite the potential detriments to their career and/or health and wellbeing. In this sense, the book is a reflective but forward-looking project that draws on the personal, experienced past in order to show the public present and to focus toward the future.

Ableism in higher education: What next?

As a sector, higher education has seen drastic changes over recent decades, with an increasing emphasis on equality and inclusion (Kerschbaum et al. 2017; Dolmage 2017; Price 2011). Initiatives such as Athena SWAN and the Race Equality Charter have led to more awareness of exclusionary practices, and there is a need to be clear on the policies for the REF and the Teaching Excellence Framework. The sector has become aware of concerns around the health and wellbeing of students and staff. Institutions are responding to these changes, and yet their responses are often fragmented and not well coordinated.

Statistics highlight serious issues in relation to disclosure rates: 16 per cent of the working age public disclose a disability, neurodivergence or chronic illness, but less than 4 per cent of academics working in higher education do so (see Brown and Leigh 2018). In many cases institutions do not know how to respond to staff needs when they are disclosed. The current reactive approach to equality, diversity and inclusion across the sector means that high-quality researchers, academics and professional staff are unable to engage to the best of their abilities and/or do not apply for open positions.

What is required instead, is an active approach to bring about change in research approaches and at policy level, which will ultimately lead to attitudinal changes. Higher education as a research field is in itself complicated. Many researchers come into the field from their specific disciplinary backgrounds, which leads to higher education research being fragmented (Harland 2012; Tight 2014) rather than unified (Brown and Leigh 2019). In addition, the emphasis of research lies on student experience, learning or developing teaching practices (Tight 2004). It is only recently that research on staff experience has gained traction, not least due to the significant changes in contractual conditions and precarious working environments of scholars in today's globalised, marketised academy (e.g. Mark and Smith 2012; Opstrup and Pihl-Thingvad 2016; Darabi et al. 2017), although initial reports relating to stress in academia were already available in the 1990s (e.g. Abouserie 1996; Blix et al. 1994). Yet within that focus on academic and professional staff within the higher education sector, particular topics still remain unexplored, of which the experience of disabilities, chronic illnesses and/or neurodiversity is one. A more strategic and systematic approach to these lived experiences within academia would be very welcome, and is much needed, as the interest in the original conference and the edited book have shown, too.

A strengthened focus on and reinforced interest in the experience of disabilities, chronic illnesses and/or neurodiversity in higher education need to take account of several considerations. In line with the disjointed higher education research field, and as this book shows, nobody – irrespective of whether or not they are disabled, chronically ill and/or neurodiverse, or which disciplinary background they are from – should be excluded from theorising their experiences, but should be encouraged to add new perspectives to the field. It is all too easy to dismiss experiences as imagined or 'in your head'; the reality remains that even if discrimination and ableist attitudes are not intentional, they are felt. For some scholars, disability studies as a field provides the much-needed theorisation of the disabled experience; but not everyone will identify with the field equally strongly and may struggle to come to terms with disability, illness and/or neurodivergence on a personal level. Again, such experiences must be taken seriously, accepted and used to inform policy and practice. This is where an attitudinal change is key. Unfortunately, change generally takes time, but attitudinal shifts often mean that resistance to change needs to be overcome (Eagly and Chaiken 2014). In relation to disabilities, attitudinal changes tend to happen through specific interventions, such as the reduction of discomfort experienced by non-disabled persons, presenting non-disabled communities with relevant information and fostering empathy (Donaldson 1980). Systematic research, autoethnographically inspired investigations, books and articles need to become more prominent (see for example Brown forthcoming), as there are many gaps that even this book has not been able to fill.

As a first step in the right direction, we would like to share the knowledge we have gained through the lightning talks and the workshop at the conference, the synchronous and asynchronous discussions related to the conference, and the formal and informal conversations we have had with colleagues as a result of the conference and our publications, as well as through the contributions on hand. We also draw on the results from three different research projects over the course of the last three years, along with ongoing work in our own and other institutions to shed light on ableism in academia. We used these to compile a practical document that shares causes for concern within academia before presenting some recommendations for practical implementations in higher education institutions. The delegates from the 'Ableism in Academia' event wanted exactly this type of practical document to take back to their own institutions, and so it is another direct result from the conference. It is more than a manifesto. It does not simply list what we want; instead it sets out in clear, business terms the risks to a university when it does not address ableism, and then gives clear, achievable recommendations to challenge the status quo, and to enact change.

Causes for concern in higher education institutions

Staff support

Student support is often well developed and easily accessible, whereas staff support is often separate, or linked to cumbersome access-to-work assessments with a smaller budget. In some universities staff register as students to be able to access adjustments, resources and support that is otherwise unavailable. This normalises the assumption that academic staff are able-bodied. The kinds of conditions that might require support include specific learning disabilities such as dyslexia, cancer, menopause, chronic illnesses, neurodiversions such as autism, ADHD, age-related impairments such as hearing loss, mental health difficulties and physical disabilities.

Conferences

Promotion frameworks often require evidence for international impact, networking with colleagues on an international level and/or conference attendance. However, many disabled, chronically ill and neurodiverse staff find conferences inaccessible (see Brown et al. 2018). Issues such as travel, fatigue and the accessibility of rooms and buildings can inhibit attendance, and remote attendance is often either discouraged, or looked on negatively as a sign of lack of commitment. In-house conferences do not always factor in accessibility considerations with a centralised checklist that each symposium or event should adhere to.

Promotions

Lack of access to support and fewer conference attendances, in addition to the extra time, effort and money required to manage a chronic condition, means staff often feel that they cannot achieve promotions or maintain a career in academia. They are either not applying for promotion, or not achieving it at the same rate as their peers. This is evidenced by the higher proportion of disabled staff nationally on zero-hours contracts or in part-time work, and the much smaller number of those in leadership roles who disclose a disability, neurodiversity or chronic illness.

Cultural and attitudinal concerns

Staff with disabilities or chronic illnesses report being stigmatised, challenged and questioned quite overtly, with some saying that they have been told they should not be trying to pursue a career in academia as they would fail anyway. Such an environment is not conducive to work, and impacts students' experiences. If staff are encouraged not to disclose, students do not have relevant role models. An institution therefore loses potentially high-quality staff and students.

Remedial work

The common approach of remedially responding to an individual's needs is not the most cost- or time-effective use of resources. In many cases the adjustments made would improve the experience of others. Ideally, universal design would be built in. A simple example is changing logos, branding and PowerPoint slides so that writing is not in a serif font in black lettering on white backgrounds. This benefits those who are dyslexic, have sensory processing issues and/or Irlen syndrome, and does not adversely affect the majority of the staff and student population – in fact, many report they find it easier to read. Such universal design can be applied to many aspects of both staff and students' experiences to support learning, teaching and conferences.

Moving forward in higher education

The changes required are not quick fixes or developments that will be implemented overnight, as ultimately the entire change of an ingrained and embedded culture of ableism is required. However, in addition to those simple changes mentioned above, there are some more steps individuals and institutions can take to move things forward.

Strategy and policy

A clear strategy with a five-to-ten-year plan and the outline of a vision for what an accessible, inclusive and diverse university looks like provides the overarching framework. This is essential for charter marks such as the Athena SWAN but also for other institutional and national initiatives and frameworks. Such a clear, detailed equality, diversity and inclusion strategy needs to be set in motion with a policy signed off from the highest levels. The policy should entail quantifiable commitments such as 'all new buildings will meet the needs of 90 per cent of all staff and students' or 'all events need to make use of the centrally available resources'. The policy could be linked to separate policies for specific conditions such as menopause (as first implemented at Leicester University; see Leicester University 2018), or be more general, given that many adjustments for specific conditions would also improve working life for others. Ideally, the implementation needs to be backed by high-quality institutional research and therefore seen as valuable by academics and professional services alike. Strategies and policies used in this way allow best practice to be showcased and disseminated across the sector.

Equality, diversity and inclusion ambassador or envoy

The role of an ambassador or envoy is to enforce the strategy and policies. All departments and professional services would be accountable and report to governance structures where needed. For example, if the policy says that all events need to be accessible, then the ambassador needs to have the right to check up on that, and follow through with sanctions. No policy or vision will be followed through or maintained in the long term if there is no enforcement.

Financial commitment

The implementation of the role of the ambassador and changes required (e.g. funds to support travel to conferences and the provision of support assistants for access-to-work paperwork) will require financial commitment and a budget. If the structures are changed to support staff disclosures, there has to be a budget to support them.

Leading by example

The validation of new modules, the implementation of new buildings, the employment of new staff etc. should all be checked against the comprehensive equality, diversity and inclusion policy. If all areas and aspects of academic life are governed by the policy, if staff are able to disclose their conditions, students will feel they have role models and opportunities to engage in education 'despite' their needs.

Ultimately, the aim of a comprehensive equality, diversity and inclusion approach would be to make a university a truly inclusive, diverse and accessible place, where gender, race, ethnicity, disabilities and chronic illnesses, neurodiversity and sexual orientation are all treated with equal respect and commitment.

References

Abouserie, Reda. 'Stress, Coping Strategies and Job Satisfaction in University Academic Staff', *Educational Psychology* 16/1 (1996): 49–56. Online. https://doi.org/10.1080/0144341960160104 (accessed 19 May 2020).

Blix, Arlene G., Cruise, Robert J., Mitchell, Bridgit M. and Blix, Glen G. 'Occupational Stress Among University Teachers', *Educational Research* 36/2 (1994): 157–69. Online. https://doi.org/10.1080/0013188940360205 (accessed 31 May 2020).

Brown, Nicole. (ed.). *Lived Experiences of Ableism in Academia: Strategies for Inclusion in Higher Education*. Bristol: Policy Press, forthcoming.

Brown, Nicole and Leigh, Jennifer. 'Ableism in Academia: Where are the Disabled and Ill Academics?' *Disability and Society* 33/6 (2018): 985–9. Online. https://doi.org/10.1080/09687599.2018.1455627 (accessed 19 May 2020).

Brown, Nicole and Leigh, Jennifer S. 'Creativity and Playfulness in Higher Education Research'. In *Theory and Method in Higher Education Research*, vol. 4, edited by Jeroen Huisman and Malcolm Tight, 49–66. Bingley: Emerald, 2019.

Brown, Nicole, Thompson, Paul and Leigh, Jennifer S. 'Making Academia More Accessible', *Journal of Perspectives in Applied Academic Practice* 6/2 (2018): 82–90. Online. https://doi.org/10.14297/jpaap.v6i2.348 (accessed 19 May 2020).

Darabi, Mitra, Macaskill, Ann and Reidy, Lisa. 'Stress Among UK Academics: Identifying Who Copes Best', *Journal of Further and Higher Education* 41/3 (2017): 393–412. Online. https://doi.org/10.1080/0309877X.2015.1117598 (accessed 31 May 2020).

Dolmage, Jay Timothy. *Academic Ableism: Disability and Higher Education*. Ann Arbor: University of Michigan Press, 2017. Online. https://doi.org/10.3998/mpub.9708722 (accessed 19 May 2020).

Donaldson, Joy. 'Changing Attitudes Toward Handicapped Persons: A Review and Analysis of Research', *Exceptional Children* 46/7 (1980): 504–14. Online. https://doi.org/10.1177/001440298004600702 (accessed 31 May 2020).

Eagly, Alice H. and Chaiken, Shelly. 'Attitude Strength, Attitude Structure, and Resistance to Change'. In *Attitude Strength: Antecedents and Consequences*, edited by Richard E. Petty and Jon A. Krosnick, 413–32. New York: Psychology Press, 2014, originally 1995.

Harland, Tony. 'Higher Education as an Open-Access Discipline', *Higher Education Research and Development* 31/5 (2012): 703–10. Online. https://doi.org/10.1080/07294360.2012.689275 (accessed 31 May 2020).

Kerschbaum, Stephanie L., Eisenman, Laura T. and Jones, James M., eds. *Negotiating Disability: Disclosure and Higher Education*. Ann Arbor: University of Michigan Press, 2017. Online. https://doi.org/10.3998/mpub.9426902 (accessed 19 May 2020).

Leicester University. 'Menopause Policy in the Workplace is Focus of National Conference', 19 January 2018. Online. https://www2.le.ac.uk/offices/press/press-releases/2018/january/menopause-policy-in-the-workplace-is-focus-of-national-conference (accessed 17 June 2019).

Mark, George and Smith, Andrew P. 'Effects of Occupational Stress, Job Characteristics, Coping, and Attributional Style on the Mental Health and Job Satisfaction of University Employees', *Anxiety, Stress and Coping* 25/1 (2012): 63–78. Online. https://doi.org/10.1080/10615806.2010.548088 (accessed 31 May 2020).

Opstrup, Niels and Pihl-Thingvad, Signe. 'Stressing Academia? Stress-As-Offence-To-Self at Danish Universities', *Journal of Higher Education Policy and Management* 38/1 (2016): 39–52. Online. https://doi.org/10.1080/1360080X.2015.1126895 (accessed 31 May 2020).

Price, Margaret. *Mad at School: Rhetorics of Mental Disability and Academic Life*. Ann Arbor, MI: University of Michigan Press, 2011. Online. https://doi.org/10.3998/mpub.1612837 (accessed 27 May 2020).

Tight, Malcolm. 'Research into Higher Education: An A-Theoretical Community of Practice?' *Higher Education Research and Development* 23/4 (2004): 395–411. Online. https://doi.org/10.1080/0729436042000276431 (accessed 31 May 2020).

Tight, Malcolm. 'Discipline and Theory in Higher Education Research', *Research Papers in Education* 29/1 (2014): 93–110. Online. https://doi.org/10.1080/02671522.2012.729080 (accessed 31 May 2020).

Afterword

Jennifer Leigh and Nicole Brown

As we finalise the last edits to this manuscript, the context of higher education has changed suddenly and unexpectedly due to Covid-19. By the end of March 2020, in the UK and across the world, people and governments are scrambling to control and contain a pandemic. Governments have mandated that the population practise social distancing, work remotely and stay home wherever possible to reduce the spread of this novel coronavirus, and to protect the vulnerable – that is, those who are elderly or who have underlying health conditions. Higher education institutions move to provide teaching and assessment online, with academics and students having to quickly learn how to use new technology and introduce different pedagogical and research approaches.

In many ways this can be interpreted positively. It shows that it is possible to work remotely, and that it can be effective and efficient. Physical presence may no longer be seen as a requirement for teaching, learning, research and the dissemination of research. The barriers around lack of accessibility that those with chronic illness, disability and neurodiversity have encountered may be tumbling down. Inability to attend physically may no longer be seen as a barrier to promotion and progression. Institutions are rolling out technology and guidance to ease access, and it is hard to see that these will be taken away once we have ridden out this current crisis. Those of us who live with measures of social distancing already are used to isolation and practised at engaging online, and we are happy to share our experiences so others may learn and adjust to these new ways of working and living. The able-bodied academy has much to learn from those in our position as we suddenly become the experts.

And yet. On Twitter and other social media, while there is much appreciation for the sudden increase in access and accessibility, there are undercurrents of anger and fear as well. Many of us who are chronically ill, who are disabled, who are neurodiverse have been asking and fighting for access and accommodations for remote working, remote presentation and remote learning for a long time, and all too often these demands remained unanswered. There is a frustration that it has taken a pandemic and the threat to the able-bodied for these working practices to become accepted as mainstream. The feelings of vulnerability, anxiety and fear that many people are experiencing as we write are present for those of us with chronic illness, disability and neurodiversity all the time, but now we have a new fear. If we have an underlying health condition, and live every day knowing the cost to us if we fall ill, then this is magnified with the increased pressure on ICU beds and ventilators. As disabled or chronically ill people, are our lives seen as less important? If medical professionals have to choose who has access to life-saving resources, will those of us with underlying health conditions or disabilities be seen as expendable? What happens once countries are starting to reopen after lockdown and reboot their economies? What are the implications of post-lockdown strategies for disabled staff (Brown et al., forthcoming)?

Things are changing day by day. Some countries are showing signs of recovery while others have the worst yet to come. At some point, hopefully soon, we will be in a position to look back and reflect on how this crisis has changed conversations around accessibility, disability equality and ableism in academia.

Reference

Brown, Nicole, Nicholson, Jacqueline, Campbell, Fiona Kumari, Patel, Mona, Knight, Richard and Moore, Stuart (forthcoming). 'COVID-19 Post-Lockdown: Perspectives, Implications and Strategies for Disabled Staff'. *ALTER: European Journal of Disability Research/Revue Européenne de Recherche sur le Handicap*.

Index

ability: in academia   38, 40, 45–7, 153;   to best of   16;   of bodies 37, 167;   creating subjects of   33;   disability   104–6, 115, 125, 205–8;   as efficiency   41;   to forget 63;   hyper-ability   112–14, 117;   impairment   77, 158;   to manage time   172;   to network   199;   to perform   xv, 112, 116, 128, 145, 156;   to reflect   67
able: *see* ability; abled
able-bodied: *see* discrimination, in favour of able-bodied
abled: abledness   206, 208, 213;   being   156, 205;   not being   176;   compensation   212;   and gender 206, 210;   norms   151;   students 213;   *see also* ablement
abled-normative   146–7
ableism: and activisim   188 199;   autoimmunity and   106;   challenging   18–20;   combatting 97, 135, 230;   critique of   31;   discourse of   38, 41–4, 46, 226–8;   experiences of   5, 6, 87, 94, 119, 150, 154, 156, 194–7, 211, 227, 229;   history of   19, 23, 25, 204–7;   internalised   176–7, 227–8;   and leadership   76;   position in   32, 42, 176;   medical model of   85;   and sexism   195;   social construction of   86;   structural 80, 197–200;   studies of   3–8, 77, 96, 115–17, 157–8, 203–9;   *see also* technicism; humiliation
ableism in academia: discourse and theories of   5, 46, 203, 207, 231, 238;   practices of   xiv, 207, 211, 217, 218;   *see also* ableism

Ableism in Academia Event   xiv–vi, 32, 42, 130, 206, 226, 232
ableist attitudes   xv, 86, 89, 92, 94, 231
ablement   203–5, 207–9
abnormal   41, 109, 146
academia: *see* universities; academy; academic identity; higher education institutions
academic identity   52, 58, 63, 130, 164
academic work   8, 53, 118, 144, 161, 174–7
academy: and activism   182–4, 198–200, 229;   activities in   112, 116, 118;   and autoimmunity 104–6;   casualisation in   167;   diversity in   158;   inclusion in   8;   isolation of   46;   neoliberal   7, 114, 169, 227, 230;   resentment of 167;   resistance   191;   values of 144, 164, 207;   *see also* universities, higher education institutions
acceptance   17, 68, 131, 147, 172–6, 184
access to work   89, 90, 92, 102, 232, 234;   *see also* adjustments; universities
accessibility: arrangements or accommodations   145–9, 156–7;   attention to   96, 118;   barriers to   237;   calculating accessibility 150–1;   at conferences   xvi, 232;   discrimination   222;   increase in   238;   legal accessibility   8, 213, 216–17;   of research approach 82;   speaking up about accessibility 176;   in the workplace   19, 90;   *see also* adjustments

239

accommodations *see* adjustments
activism, social   8, 17, 24, 26;   in academia   15, 186, 189, 198–200, 229;   definition of   16;   disability   13, 111, 133, 185;   role of   14;   political   177, 182, 188, 198, 200, 228
Addams, Jane   15–18, 23, 24
additional labour   13, 156;   *see also* emotions, emotional work
adjustments: to illness or disability   65, 131–2, 145, 148–9, 238;   reasonable in law   77, 82, 117, 128–9, 221, 225;   reasonable personal   13, 61, 89–94, 131–3, 196;   reasonable policy   8, 88,–94, 214–17;   workplace   62, 109–12, 126, 210, 232–4
advocate, advocating for   7, 58, 65, 111, 133, 229;   self-advocacy   87, 2277, 58, 65, 87, 111, 133, 227, 229
affirmative model   86, 108
age, ageism   4, 78, 96;   ageing   96, 153;   and identity   140;   and illness   60, 70, 232;   of leaders   80;   and precarity   112, 117;   as protected characteristic   128
anxiety, disorder   87, 104, 219;   internalised   110, 174;   personal experiences of   130–1, 203, 238
autism   58, 84, 87, 183, 206, 232
autobiography: *see* autoethnography
autoethnography: narrative   139;   as research   124–5, 150–5, 165, 174, 189–90, 228–9, 231
autoimmune   7, 103–120, 127–8;   *see also* hyperimmune
autonomy,   2, 40, 85, 164, 189, 204, 217;   autonomous   104, 185
awareness, of disability   1, 51, 69, 188;   embodied   109, 143–4, 172;   of living   70;   raising   6, 145, 228–30

barriers: *see* obstacles
binary: ability/disability   45, 107, 146, 205, 209;   disability/illness   8;   impairment/disability   35, 38, 107;   science/art   125
biomedical   103
body: academic   31, 34, 38, 39–41;   defilements of   220;   discourses of   5, 36–7, 115, 117 143–6, 171–4;   different   8, 161;   failing   14, 52, 134, 152–7, 166–8;   at fault   4;   disabled   20, 67–8, 110, 190, 229;   hyperimmune   103–4;   normative, healthy or abled   7, 203, 208, 210–11;   *see also* knowledge, bodies of

bodyminds   105, 107–8, 110–11, 115–16
Bourdieu, Pierre   211
brain fog   52–6, 67–9, 103, 153, 166, 194
Brown, Nicole   7–8, 19, 131, 136, 228–9
Butler, Judith   33, 36–7, 41–2

Campbell, Fiona Kumari: on ableism   8, 41–2, 115, 228–9;   on leadership   76–7;   as keynote   xvi;   on microaggressions   195;   on normalcy   133
cancer, perceptions of   64, 68;   after treatment   85, 89, 93, 152, 155, 232
chronic illness, as other   4;   academics with   5, 125–7, 134–6, 145, 150, 229–35;   accepting   61, 130–1, 137, 139, 176;   covid-19   237–8;   diagnosis   65;   disability   128, 132–3, 147, 149, 155–6, 206;   fluctuating   67, 106, 151;   students with   12;   and wellbeing   172–3
coming out: *see* disclosure
conferences,   130–1, 150, 156, 166, 232–4;   *see also* Ableism in Academia Event
consciousness: consciousness raising   114, 185, 189, 202;   disability   125, 129;   public   1, 146;   stream of   8, 161
contested, condition   7, 52, 62, 66, 68–9, 74, 147;   discourses   33, 78, 132, 143, 189
cost, cost–benefit   2, 63, 152;   ethical   43, 175;   personal   149–52, 156, 168, 176, 238
creativity   78, 86, 144, 153, 166, 168
crip theory   7, 19, 23–4, 105, 146, 227;   cripistemologies   109, 119;   resistances   111
critical race theory   109
critique: of ableism   31–4, 205;   of academia   38–9, 41–5, 47, 109;   of power   21;   of self   46;   of research   18, 229;   of women's studies   184
culture: of academia   67–8, 93, 152–8, 176;   change   97, 127, 187;   group or society   19, 33, 117, 173, 209;   university contribution to   18;   *see also* perfectionism; ableism; overwork

deficit   133, 194, 226
degrading treatment   219
democracy   12, 18, 22, 45, 117, 184

240   INDEX

Derrida, Jacques   7, 103–4, 106, 120, 228
deviant   62, 64, 85, 116, 147, 208
diagnosis: *see* medical, diagnosis; chronic illness, diagnosis
dichotomy   35, 47, 68, 145, 147, 149
difference: admitting   104, 108, 150; as disability   85, 110, 118, 136, 146, 149; embracing   5, 68, 117, 129–30, 134, 140; as expression   32; unwelcoming to   156, 219–20; *see also* knowledge, difference in
Disability Discrimination Act   77, 92, 154, 158
disability identity   106, 108, 110, 215
disability rights: movement   107, 111, 124, 186, 188; scholarship   7, 19, 184; in society   95, 120
disablism   46; *see also* ableism
disadvantage   xv, 92, 128
disclosure: *see* lived experience, disclosure of; negotiation, disclosure; higher education institutions, disclosure
discrimination: in favour of able-bodied   32, 157, 204–7; against disabled community   3, 145, 228, 231; in institutions   91, 129, 156, 165, 177; intersectional   188, 195; against invisible conditions   62, 68; law   81, 87, 128, 217, 220–22; fear of   83, 126, 176; *see also* Disability Discrimination Act
disruptions   125, 174, 204, 206, 209, 212; *see also* interruptions
distributed leadership   78, 88, 98
diversity: of bodies   135, 220; in disability   136, 145, 209; equality diversity units   207, 210; in leadership   76, 88, 93–8; strategy   157, 230, 234–5; training   221; in the university   34, 39, 93, 156–8, 202–8, 230

embodiment: of disability and illness   37–8, 115, 131, 166, 212, 215; embodied experiences   33, 35, 109–11, 143–4, 166, 190; theorising   5, 119, 136, 143, 171–4, 227–9
emotions: acceptable   208–9; emotional labour   52–3, 69–70; emotional needs   212, 219; emotional response   60, 65, 150, 165, 192–3, 227; emotional work   1, 5, 66–7, 156, 171–7, 203; engage with   133–6, 143–5, 184; *see also* autoethnography

empathetic   14, 69, 147, 157
empathy   6, 70, 138, 155, 231
employee: concerns   61; control   171; with a disability   81, 86, 90, 210–11, 217, 221; perfect   212; being present   11
employers   126, 172, 212, 214; *see also* universities
empowerment   23, 33, 35, 185
entitlement   31, 113, 170, 203–4, 206–7, 221
Equality Act 2010, definition of   77, 82, 90, 128, 133, 214; duties of   129, 156, 216–17; limitations of   85, 222; protection by   81, 91–2, 97, 111, 154
ethics: clearance   82; dilemma   138; as philosophy   17, 22–4, 32–46, 206, 214
ethnography,   182, 185, 189–91
European Court of Human Rights   216–19, 222
exclusion   32, 34, 42, 230; from activities   151; from careers   116, 175; from higher education   186; practices that exclude   31, 34–5, 37, 43, 47 105–10; from society   117, 132–3, 145
expression   5, 7, 74, 173, 229

Facebook   177, 205
fatigue: in fibromyalgia   52, 55, 67–8, 72, 74; cost of academia   156, 169, 174, 212, 232; as impairment   81, 85, 103, 133; as symptom   107–9, 127, 130, 153
feminism: feminist activism   17, 177, 196; feminist perspective   1, 17, 227, 229; feminist philosophy   5, 15; feminist pragmatism   17, 22–6; feminist research   18, 21, 31, 183–9; feminist scholars   14, 19, 33–5, 136, 182, 213
fibromyalgia   52–69, 74, 183, 194, 198, 229; *see also* adjustments; brain fog; chronic illness, fluctuating; fatigue, fibromyalgia
fictionalised narrative   150, 153
fluctuating: invisible symptoms   8, 132; health   12, 54, 128; work commitments   66, 147–50, 156, 158, 176, 227; *see also* chronic illness
fluid   33, 67–8, 105, 147, 170, 214
Foucault, Michel   7, 31, 33–4, 36–47
framework: institutional   3, 25, 195, 232; legal   128; normative   18, 112–13, 117–18, 206–7; participatory   20; theoretical   1

freedom: in the academy   2, 65; fundamental   214;   and power   32, 34, 38, 43–5, 47

gatecrashing   14, 16–17, 26
gender, gendered knowledge   11;   in academia   80–1, 101, 118, 212, 235;   critique of   33, 109–13, 220;   intersection with disability   87, 108, 188, 198, 205, 209
Goffman, Erving   5, 133, 139
Goodley, Dan   14, 116, 118, 125, 140

HESA (Higher Education Statistics Agency)   32, 78–81
hidden: conditions   60, 68–9, 81, 127, 132, 139;   cost   156;   labour   144;   rules   208;   see also invisible illness
high achieving/ performing   31, 41, 169–71, 175
Higher Education Funding Council   xv
higher education institutions: causes for concern   232–3;   disclosure   130;   elite   186;   funding systems   2;   and law   77;   moving forward   8, 135, 233–5;   positive action   218;   teaching in   171, 237;   see also universities
higher education see academy; universities; higher education institutions
human rights   31, 34, 190, 207, 214
humiliation   8, 117–18, 202–4, 207–11, 215–21, 228–9
hyperimmune   103–4

identitarian   34
identity: see academic identity; disability identity; identity work
identity work   5, 62
illness: see chronic illness; invisible illness; fluctuating
impairment: see ability; adjustments; binary; fatigue; fluctutating; individual model of disability; intellectual; lived experience; legislation; medical model of disability; social model of disability
imposter   8, 161, 170
inaccessible: see accessibility
inclusion: see promotion, of inclusion
inclusive: practices   7, 88, 90, 157, 169, 234;   research   125, 136, 172;   society   26, 135, 177;   see also language; terminology
individual model of disability   145

injustice   19–20, 24, 26, 105, 116–17, 178;   see also justice
Insider/Outsider   32, 124, 137–9, 229
intellectual: curiosity   11, 184, 205–6;   impairment   84, 96, 194;   practices   21, 34, 46, 144, 149, 199, 221;   virtue   19
interactional model: see Shakespeare, Tom
internalisation   110, 164, 174;   see also ableism, internalised; anxiety, internalised;
International Classification of Diseases and Related Health Problems (ICD)   35
interruptions   53, 55, 57, 106, 194
intersectionality   26, 81–7, 91–4, 108, 196, 205;   see also discrimination
invisible disabilities: see hidden; invisible illness; unseen
invisible illness   32, 74, 149, 166;   see also chronic illness; hidden; unseen

justice   13, 119, 213–14;   see also social justice

Kafer, Alison   13, 17, 23–4, 105, 114
knowledge: academic   11, 115, 117, 170, 184, 210;   bodies of   12, 15, 25, 204, 207;   collective   109;   difference in   7;   established   12, 14–17, 144, 197;   exchange   118, 125, 135;   gaps in   63;   privileged   38;   production   5–7, 14–18, 119, 156–7, 175, 185;   sharing   2, 218, 228–31;   use of   16;   see also crip, knowledge; gender, knowledge

labour market   137
language   36, 87, 107–8, 146, 183, 229;   see also sensitivity
lawyer   13, 126–9, 138–9
leadership: ableism in   76, 78, 81–98 101–2, 214, 227;   charismatic   199;   who disclose   156, 233;   as male   186
Leder, Drew   143–4
legal profession: see lawyer
legislation   86, 102, 112, 116, 130, 156, 215;   see also Disability Discrimination Act; Equality Act
Leigh, Jennifer   8, 19, 131, 136, 171–2, 228
LFHE (Leadership Foundation for Higher Education)   76, 85
liminal   67, 136
limitations   69, 107, 117, 147, 216

lived experience: in academia   145;
    of disability   7–8, 12, 33; 67, 133,
    173, 183;   disclosure of   64,
    177;   ontology of   26, 228–9;
    perspectives of   17;   research into
    51, 127

marginalised: identities   108, 167;
    groups   21, 23, 118;   voices   6,
    228
marketization: of bodies   41–2, 47;   of
    higher education   2, 15, 40, 67, 230
McRuer, Robert   105, 114
media, social   15; 51, 130, 162,
    177, 190, 238;   abuse on   196;
    appearances   197;   coverage
    196;   *see also* Facebook; Twitter
medical: diagnosis   52, 62, 85, 103,
    109, 150;   doctor   14, 145, 238;
    patients   59, 214;   research   21,
    26;   understanding   33, 35, 110,
    136, 173
medical model of disability   4, 85, 107,
    129, 132–4
medically unexplained   15, 68, 69, 147
medicine,   13–15, 107
mental health: hidden disability   84,
    198, 232;   stigma   81, 193, 196;
    worsening   70, 110, 126, 154–5,
    171
Merleau-Ponty, Maurice   143
methodologies   17–18, 21–2, 24,
    113, 182, 205, 228;   *see also*
    methodology
methodology   22, 26, 82, 105, 203–4
microaggressions: personal impact
    of   115, 195, 203, 220;   theory of
    150, 156, 198, 203–4
mind: in academia   144, 157,
    207–8;   difference   8, 135, 161,
    225;   incoherence of   103, 167;
    perceptions of   172, 190, 195, 220;
    state of   70
modernism   34

National Association of Disabled Staff
    Networks (NADSN)   82, 96
narrative: *see* fictionalised narrative,
    autoethnography
National Association of Disability
    Practitioners (NADP)   82, 96
negotiation: ableism   20;   accessibility
    19, 90, 118, 148, 211, 219;
    disclosure   13;   illness   69, 106
neurodiversity: in academia   1, 5–6, 32,
    51, 136, 206, 227–31;   accepting
    61;   discrimination of   175–6,
    206;   strengths   86;   support for
    230–35;   in wider society   58, 107,
    237–8

neurotypical   157, 176
non-disabled: academics   7, 31–4,
    37–8, 42–7, 185, 190;   colleagues
    67;   leaders   76, 80–1, 95;
    people   86, 106; 145, 147, 231
non-normal   58;   *see also* norms
non-visible   124–6, 129–35, 138–9;
    see also hidden; unseen; invisible
    illness
normalcy   110, 130, 133, 135, 207;
    see also norms
normalisation: attainment   112;
    bodies   37, 232;   challenging
    118;   discrimination   133, 206;
    society   62, 209;   ways of working
    5, 7, 114, 116, 125
'nothing about us without us'   35, 77,
    124, 176

Oakley, Ann   11, 15, 17, 19, 24
objectivity   26, 57, 184, 208, 213
obstacles   14, 200
Oliver, Mike   76, 86, 132–6, 145, 183,
    190–5
ontoviolence   204, 220–22
othered   xv, 2–3, 133–4, 225
overwork   67, 112, 154, 167–70, 172,
    174–6

pain: *see* chronic illness
paranoia   228;   *see also* humiliation
Parliament   182, 185, 190, 193
participatory: *see* frameworks;
    methodology
passing as non-disabled   7, 81, 106;
    choosing to pass   60–1, 69, 134,
    137, 139, 178
patient   14, 21, 57–9, 111
peer support   91, 95–6
perfection: able-bodied   32, 110,
    116–17, 204, 206–7;   perfect
    academic   4, 41, 168–9, 174–6,
    228;   perfectionism   4, 135, 137,
    153, 170–1
performance: *see* performativity
performativity   4, 36, 40–1, 45, 174,
    212
personal experiences: *see* lived
    experience; reflexivity
personal narrative: *see* autoethnography
person-first language   58, 146
phenomenology   125, 127, 137, 139,
    143, 220
physical disability   67, 133, 148, 218,
    232
poetic inquiry   5–6, 74, 161, 225,
    228–9

policy: accessible travel 51;
  employment EDI 135, 157, 177;
  influence 11; makers 32, 187,
  197, 230; policy/practice 91, 94,
  102, 182–4, 231, 234–5
political engagement 8, 23, 177,
  183–4, 187; *see also* activism,
  political
politically correct 59
positionality 130, 184, 190, 229
postmodernism 34, 36,
poststructural 5, 33, 36, 227, 229
power: *see* Foucault
precarious work 64, 156, 175, 230;
  skills gained in 112, 117–18
private: connecting to public 6–8, 11,
  26, 62, 165, 174; life 65, 68–9,
  138, 187, 203
privilege: challenging 21, 228; 171;
  position 64–5, 92, 117, 198;
  universities xv, 1, 46, 164, 184,
  208; *see also* knowledge, privilege
problem-solving 85–6, 98
productivity: demand for 119,
  137, 171, 174, 206–8, 227; and
  disability 161–2, 168; in work
  3–4, 40, 64–9, 108
professional identity 164
professions 11, 13–14, 21, 23, 52, 187
promotion of inclusion 39, 77, 95–6,
  157, 214, 217; criteria 232–3;
  passed over for 198, 237–39, 77,
  84–5, 89–90, 92, 95–6, 97, 140, 157,
  162, 198, 214, 217, 232–3, 237; at
  work 84–5, 89–90, 92, 97, 140, 162
protected characteristics 81, 128–9,
  205, 208, 217–18
psychosomatic 64, 74
public spaces 46

queer 24, 69, 108, 111

racism 4, 87, 105, 108, 115–17, 197;
  see also discrimination
rape 182, 192–3, 198; *see also* sexual
  harassment
rationality 104, 115, 174, 177, 184,
  210
reciprocal learning 16–18
recommendations 7–8, 85, 90–1, 95,
  97, 231–2
reconciliation 38, 42, 164
reflection: critical 44–7, 67, 135, 146,
  206; difference 7; fictionalised
  150–5; personal 4, 78, 124–5,
  130, 165–9, 196–9, 228–30; on
  research 22–3, 34, 137–8, 182–4,
  189–90; of society 5; spaces
  118–19, 226

reflexivity 124, 144, 190
relational model 13, 17, 23–4, 134
Research Excellence Framework (REF)
  40, 91, 112–13, 227, 230
resistance 21, 111, 182, 191, 204,
  217, 231

self: *see* autoethnography; reflexivity
self-doubt 7–8, 74, 161
self-fulfilling prophecy 63
sensibility 51, 53, 57
sensitivity 7, 51–3, 57, 60, 69–70
sexism 4, 78, 115–17, 185–9,
  194–200; *see also* discrimination
sexual harassment 1, 188, 189, 191
Shakespeare, Tom 76, 86, 134–5
shame 107, 113–16, 119; *see also*
  shameful, stigma
skills: academic 12, 199;
  development 108, 112, 210;
  employability 2; leadership 77,
  86, 88, 97–8
social activism: *see* activism
social citizenship 15–16
social exclusion 8, 187, 204, 211
social justice 6–7, 12–19, 32, 76,
  105–7, 221–9
social media *see* media, social; Twitter;
  Facebook
social model of disability: activism
  111, 132, 134; critique of 136,
  145–6, 186; language of 58, 134;
  understanding disability 16, 34–5,
  51, 86, 107, 132
social oppression 134–5, 189
society: *see* disability rights, in
  society; exclusion, from society;
  neurodiversity, in wider society;
  normalisation, society
soma-epistemology 207, 229
stigmatisation 14, 19, 81, 131, 133;
  in academia 62, 126, 153, 233;
  of disability 35, 64, 68–9, 108,
  139; of identity 133; symbol
  69; *see also* mental health, stigma;
  Goffman, Erving
strategic planning 82, 88, 90–1, 95,
  98, 235
strike 118–19
structural inequalities 176; *see also*
  ableism, structural
subjectivity 44–5
survive 68, 104–5, 113, 117–19,
  153–4, 199, 221
survivor 193

Teaching Excellence Framework (TEF)
  3, 40, 113, 230

technicism   203–5, 210–13, 215, 216–17, 220–1, 227–8
terminology   21, 36, 58–60, 205;   *also see* language
Tremain, Shelley   14–15, 31, 33, 36
truth: *see* knowledge
Twitter   xiv–xvi, 15, 32, 59, 136, 205, 238;   *see also* media, social

UN Convention on the Rights of People with Disability   92, 214, 217
Universal Design for Learning UDL   82, 88–90, 92–6, 97, 157
universities: ableist practices   155, 218–19, 221;   access to work   92–3;   as businesses   2–3, 232;   change in   18, 97;   competition   113;   disability services   94, 149, 214, 232;   and disabled people   186;   disclosing to   62, 64, 136, 215;   law   216–17;   neoliberal   31–4, 47, 67, 105–6, 113–14;   Open University   12;   peer support   95–6;   policies   234;   rankings   18, 25;   systems   108, 111, 176, 183, 209, 212;   work in   39, 119 171–2, 174, 202, 210;   *see also* academy; accessibility; technicism
unseen   5, 84, 114, 124, 132;   *see also* hidden; invisible illness
UPIAS, Union of the Physically Impaired Against Segregation   107, 132

validation,   18, 23, 62–5, 170, 173, 235
values: cultural or societal   51, 113, 144, 174, 212;   personal   82, 101, 164, 174, 210
vignettes: *see* fictionalised narrative

weakness   7, 19, 63–7, 146, 152, 195
wellbeing: and medicine   14;   research on   126, 171;   for self   140, 160, 171–4, 199, 228–9;   and services   111, 209, 230
Wendell, Susan   14, 107–8
wheelchair, types   xv; 67–9, 87–9, 96, 146–51, 221
workplace *see* academy; higher education institutions; universities

INDEX   245

Ingram Content Group UK Ltd.
Milton Keynes UK
UKHW011423130323
418489UK00001B/1